OTHER TITLES OF INTEREST FROM ST. LUCIE PRESS

Reengineering Performance Management: Breakthroughs in Achieving Strategy Through People

Total Productivity Management: A Systemic and Quantitative Approach to Compete in Quality, Price, and Time

The Costs of Bad Hiring Decisions and How to Avoid Them

Attribution Theory: An Organizational Perspective

Total Quality and Organization Development

Total Quality in Managing Human Resources

Reengineering the Training Function: How to Align Training with the New Corporate Agenda

Creating Productive Organizations

The Motivating Team Leader

Team Building: A Structured Learning Approach

Organization Teams: Building Continuous Quality Improvement

Leadership by Encouragement

Skills of Encouragement: Bringing Out the Best in Yourself and Others

The New Leader: Bringing Creativity and Innovation to the Workplace

Mastering the Diversity Challenge: Easy On-the-Job Applications for Measurable Results

For more information about these titles call, fax or write:

St. Lucie Press
2000 Corporate Blvd., N.W.
Boca Raton, FL 33431-9868

TEL (561) 994-0555 • (800) 272-7737
FAX (800) 374-3401
E-MAIL information@slpress.com
WEB SITE http://www.slpress.com

S_L^t

The
High Cost
of Low Morale
...and what to do about it

Carol A. Hacker

St. Lucie Press
Boca Raton, Florida

Phone: (561) 994-0555
E-mail: information@slpress.com
Web site: http://www.slpress.com

S_L^t

Published by
St. Lucie Press
2000 Corporate Blvd., N.W.
Boca Raton, FL 33431-9868

DEDICATION

This book is dedicated to the men and women who graciously contributed their time and ideas to this project and to all managers who face the challenge of building and maintaining morale in their organizations.

CONTENTS

Preface xiii
About the Author xix

1 Pin the Tail on the Donkey (Making Good Hiring Decisions) 1
   Plan for Retention 2
   Forecast Staffing Needs 3
   Develop Recruitment Sources 4
   Know What You're Looking For 5
   Become a Skilled Interviewer 6
   Measure Against Job Requirements 7
   Look for Versatility 8
   Be Sure They're Willing, as Well as Able 9
   Test Them 10
   Hold Auditions 10
   Make Commitment Possible 11
   Start with Quality Employees 12
   Be Selective 13
   Seek People-Oriented Leaders 14
   Hire People Who Are Better Than You 15
   Try Team Interviewing 16
   Troubleshoot Recruitment Problems 17
   Avoid "The Mirror Test" 19
   Consider Internal Candidates 20
   Hire for Today's Generation 21
   Check References 22
   Make Sound Hiring Decisions 24

2   Up Your Attitude (A Good Attitude = High Morale) 31
    Enjoy What You Do 33
    Don't Waste Time on Negative Thoughts 34
    Find Ways to Learn New Things 35
    Demonstrate the Work Ethic You Expect 35
    Start Each Day with a Positive Thought 36
    Helping Others Helps Yourself 37
    Set Your Mental Barometer 38
    Even When You Don't Feel Like It 38
    Find a Release 40
    Don't Air Your Dirty Laundry 40
    Find Your Creative Attitude 41
    Make It Easy on Yourself 42
    Live By a Personal Mission Statement 43
    Stay Physically and Mentally Fit 46
    Don't Take Life Too Seriously 47
    Set Goals 48
    Associate with Positive People 49
    Talk to Yourself 50
    Why Not You? 51
    Kick the Habit 51
    Once Upon a Time 52
    Reward Yourself 53
3   Pygmalion's Fair Lady (The Power of Expectation) 59
    Remember Clementine 61
    Start with Number One 62
    Give Me No Choice 62
    There's More Than One Way... 64
    Recognize the Family 64
    Structure Positive Situations 65
    It's All in Your Mind 66
    Do What Failures Are Afraid to Do 67
    Dream Impossible Dreams 68
    Make Them Feel Special 69
    Recognize Assets 70
    Keep Them on Your Radar Screen 71
    Offer Approval and Acceptance 72
    Lift Self-Imposed Limitations 73
    Take the Bull By the Horns 74
    Have a Game Plan 75

On My Honor... 76
Nothing Happens 'Til Somebody Sells 77
Get Out of the Way 78
And They Wiped Their Minds Clear 78

4   Ma Bell Did It (Communicate) **83**
Mission Possible 85
Think It Over... 86
Give Criticism in the Helping Spirit............................. 88
Make Learning Easy 89
Stay "Checked-In" 90
Share the Vision.. 91
Try Toastmasters 92
Be Accessible.. 93
Give Everyone a Say 93
Speak From the Heart.. 94
Make Them Decision Makers 95
Clarify Expectations 96
Keep Them Informed.. 96
Encourage Feedback 97
Explain the "Why" 98
Build the Listening Habit.. 99
Use Humor To Get Your Message Across 100
Consider a Survey 102
Use Performance Appraisals as Communication Tools 102
Take Inventory 104
Try "Rolestorming" 104
Why Do You *See* It That Way? 105
Hear What Employees Are *Not* Saying........................ 106
Don't Discourage Small Talk 107

5   -Ch-Ch-Ch-Change (Take Charge of Change) **113**
Offer "Inplacement" 115
Ask for Advice 116
Take Care of the "Me" Issues.. 117
Get Resistance to Change Out in the Open 118
Little Things Make a Difference 119
Validate the Positive Results of Change 120
Delegate, Especially During Change 121
Get Buy-In 122
Plan for the Change Reaction 122

Think Like "One" Company 123
Beat the Downside of Downsizing... 124
Anticipate Highs and Lows.. 126
Acceptance Is a Four-Stage Process 127
Give Them Time 129
Reinvest in Employees 130
Diversify 131
Change Comes in Familiar Packages 133

6   Get 'Em Psyched (Build Fun into Your Organization) 139
Consider an R&R Fund 141
Learn to Have Fun 142
Show Appreciation 143
Give Us This Day 143
Provide Education as an Incentive 144
Reward Them When They Least Expect It 145
Get Casual 145
Make Safety Count 146
Host a Gag Nite 146
Offer Them "Hidden Paychecks" 147
Name Your Customer... 148
Count on Retirees 149
Modify the Nature of the Work 150
Be There to Greet Them 150
The 1212 Club 151
Do Something Extra to Reward Dedication 152
Consider Sabbatical Leave 152
1 Million Dollars for Your Thoughts 153
It's in the Cards 154
Create Olympic Performance Events 155
The Leader of the Band 156
Help Them Regain the Spirit.. 157
Give Them Ownership 158

7   Who's on First? (Is It Leadership Or Is It Management?) 163
Offer Small Rewards 165
Be a Coach, Not a Cop 165
Be Flexible 166
Learn from the Past 167
Reward Risk-Taking 168
Don't Be a Pretender 169

Light Their Fires 170
Encourage Talking Back 170
Catch Them Doing Something Right 171
View Problems as "Golden Eggs" 172
Exhibit "Friendly Bravery" 173
Blend Strategy with Culture 173
Eliminate the Obstacles to Innovation 175
Balance Skills 175
Link Pay to Performance 176
Share Compliments 177
Don't Cut Corners 178
Make Them Business Partners 178
Reduce Fear 180
Use Your Muscles 181
Get Them Involved 181
Laugh in the Face of Stress 182

8   Close Encounters of the Worst Kind (Managing Difficult
    People) 187
Don't Dwell on Past Mistakes 189
Don't Wait Too Long 190
Trade Complaints for Solutions 190
Think Before You Act 191
Grease the Squeaky Wheels But... 193
Beware of "Buckaneers" 194
Don't Let Them Play Dead 195
Get the Facts 196
Personal Problems of the Worst Kind 197
Turn Conflict into Cooperation 198
Disarm the Argumentative 200
Learn How to Negotiate 201
Care Enough to Confront 202
When the Boss Is Difficult 203
Employee Health Problems and ADA 204
Accept the Help of Others 205
Reduce the Risk of Workplace Violence 206
Focus on the Issues 207
Trying But Failing 208
Fire Without Creating a Mess 209
Conduct Exit Interviews 210
When Turnover Is Good 213

9   All Aboard (Orientation and Training) **219**
    Use Training as a Motivator 221
    View Employees as Investments 222
    Rechart Career Paths 223
    Teach Them the Business 223
    No Matter How Good the Product... 224
    Don't Leave Them Behind 225
    Develop Tomorrow's Leaders 226
    Be Sure They Get What They Need 227
    Have 20/20 Vision 228
    Make It Informal But Meaningful 229
    Link Training to Corporate Initiatives 231
    If You Were Expecting a Package... 232
    Consider a Mentor Program 233
    Show Them How 234
    Value Employees from Day One 235
    Leadership 2000 237
    Environment Makes the Difference 238
    Don't View Training as an Expense 239
    Consider Apprenticeships 239
Appendix **247**
Glossary **251**
Index **253**

PREFACE

At age three, I was blessed with a second-hand phonograph. One of my first records was Rudolph the Red-Nosed Reindeer. Excited until I heard the words, I cried when the song got to the part about the other reindeer ostracizing poor Rudolph. I knew that they hurt his feelings, and I worried that he might never get better. As I look back to that time in my life, I realize that I already understood how the hurtful actions of others impact morale. I didn't know then that someday I would have the opportunity to influence how employees feel about their managers, but now I know.

Morale is an elusive quality. It's a feeling that's created within every employee. When morale is high, it's worth its weight in gold. When morale is low, the cost is tremendous. The factors that help create high morale in the workplace are the same as those found in every healthy family environment—many businesses think of themselves as a family. A sense of belonging and lots of positive feedback help promote high morale.

Motivation and morale have a lot in common. Morale, whether positive or negative, determines motivation. There's no such thing as an employee who's not motivated. The individual's just not motivated to meet the manager's expectations. Consequently, motivational energy may be directed into acceptable or unacceptable channels. Motivating and building morale in an organization takes time and commitment, but the payoffs are enormous.

I wrote this book because I believe it can help leaders learn to reduce the high cost of low morale and turnover. Interviews with successful supervisors, managers, vice-presidents, CEOs, and business owners offer insight into ways to keep top performers motivated. These proven strategies work, regardless of the industry, employees' positions or levels of sophistication, pay status, or seniority. I hope that you will read this book with an awareness of the morale level in your business.

The problems associated with low morale among employees—particularly high turnover—plague employers in every industry. It affects employee performance and willingness to work, which, in turn, affects individual and organizational objectives.

Although there are many definitions of morale, a common one is that it is a state of mind and emotions. It's about attitudes of individuals and groups toward their work, their environment, their managers, and the business. Morale is not a single feeling but a composite of feelings, sentiments, and attitudes.

Why fuss about morale, which management often views as elusive? Because it's tied to profits, efficiency, quality, cooperation, productivity, and financial competitiveness.

Others factors also impact morale. These include:

❖ Employee and employer attitudes toward change.

❖ Consensus on organizational goals.

❖ Standards and values.

❖ Concern for people.

❖ Reward and punishment.

❖ Communication.

❖ Market and customer orientation.

❖ Team pride.

These variables affect morale and the future success of every organization. High morale is often seen as unpredictable or even unattainable. That's unfortunate, because without a positive attitude, nothing constructive is likely to occur. Like it or not, much of what happens is determined by the manager. Most managers want productive employees who will stick with them for the long haul. However, there has to be a chemistry and willingness by both parties to join together and do what it takes to tackle morale problems.

Getting good employees to stick with you can be a challenge. I call this phenomenon "The Elmer's Glue™ Principle." When you're gluing two things together, the glue has to make good contact and dry to effectively hold the items together. Some items bond together immediately. Others, depending upon the type of material used, take longer. It's no different with people. For many managers and employees it comes easy, but for some the bonding never occurs.

Charles L. Hughes, Ph.D., and Vincent S. Flowers, Ph.D., co-founders of Center for Values Research, identify employees as one of four types:

1. **Turnovers** are not happy with their jobs, have few external reasons to stay, and will leave at the first opportunity.

2. **Turn-offs** have negative attitudes about their jobs and stay because of "golden handcuffs" (financial security, benefits, or fear of not finding anything better).

3. **Turn-ons** have positive attitudes and stick with an organization because they enjoy the work. They're greatly affected by their environment and will leave if they don't get continual job satisfaction.

4. **Turn-ons-plus** are the most likely to stay for the long run because they like their work *and* the environment. Even if occasionally dissatisfied, it's not enough to lead to resignation unless dissatisfaction continues over an extended period of time.

Employees are unhappy for any number of reasons. Their unhappiness shows in their behavior and performance. Poor attendance and attitude reflect negative feelings. Some employees turn to drugs or alcohol to escape a bad situation. Some express dissatisfaction through theft and ignoring safety rules. Although no manager can offer employees everything they want, appreciation and understanding go a long way. Good management gets the job done through people. Failure to reach personal and/or company goals can lead to dissention or loss of morale, which is often contagious. It's not hard to spot low morale. It saps the energy and desire for working, and sometimes living. It reveals itself in less effort and poorer results, both of which impact profitability. When productivity doesn't soar as expected, everyone's disappointed and morale drops.

There are three main reasons why turnover caused by low morale occurs:

❖ Inadequate compensation.

❖ The wrong fit.

❖ Weak managers who hurt employee morale.

Estimated costs to replace an employee who leaves range from 30% of an employee's annual salary for entry level and unskilled workers to five times the annual salary for executives.

Costs fall into the major categories of:

❖ **Separation** (severance pay, unemployment compensation, extended medical benefits under COBRA).

❖ **Replacement** (advertising, travel expenses for interviews, time it takes to interview).

❖ **Training** (may be minimal on-the-job training or extensive classroom education).

❖ **Lost productivity** (unhappy employees often slack off).

Organizations have a lot to gain by reducing turnover, the single most important indicator of low morale. Although sometimes viewed as inevitable, turnover is a controllable expense. Unfortunately, companies frequently overlook the potentially devastating impact on their finances until it's too late. Turnover is a cost that's not easy to measure. For that reason, it's often not identified until after profits are directly affected.

Getting employees to commit to long-term employment begins with understanding why employees leave. Is it really for better pay or career advancement as they often claim? Some employees believe that quitting provides the only solution to an unhappy situation. Lack of commitment to the employee or personality conflicts may also be involved.

Psychologist Abraham Maslow developed a theory called the Hierarchy of Needs. He suggests that individuals have certain physical and psychological needs which they attempt to satisfy in every area of life—even employment. Maslow's approach to employee satisfaction is still recognized as good reason to find out what motivates people to excel.

Employees want to be satisfied with their work and themselves. They're more likely to stay if they get what they want and need.

A survey of 5,000 highly productive employees provided six key reasons people quit their jobs:

- ❖ Insufficient opportunity for advancement.
- ❖ Feel uninformed.
- ❖ Hesitant to express their feelings.
- ❖ Believe management isn't interested in their ideas.
- ❖ Managers fail to praise good work.
- ❖ Managers use unfair promotion practices.

Turnover is highest among employees in their first year of employment. The turnover problem is compounded by a predicted labor shortage in the United States. The birth rate has fallen significantly during the past 30 years. That means a shortage of young workers to fill entry-level jobs. Therefore, it's especially important that newly hired people go through some type of orientation to the job and the business.

Don't accept turnover as a fact of life—it's expensive. If you can't measure it, you can't fix it. Develop a retention attitude but be careful not to keep poor performers or you may find yourself with an organization full of marginal workers and low morale.

Acknowledging management's responsibility for morale and turnover opens the door to creative solutions. This book offers many practical ways to increase the percentage of retention and decrease the high cost of low morale.

I hope you enjoy reading this book as much as I enjoyed writing it. It's been a learning experience for me. I've met either in person and/or by telephone many wonderful people who generously shared their ideas.

Take some of the suggestions and creative solutions and put them to good use in your own business. Some of the ideas in the book may appear to require a touch of risk-taking—but that's up to you; others may seem a bit far-out. Whether you use them is your choice—it's your decision as to whether you want to make a change and try something new. I believe that unless we're open to giving new ideas a chance, we cheat ourselves out of opportunities and even some adventures.

Most of all, however, I hope that this book will truly make a difference for you and your organization in the future.

Acknowledgments

Help from several very special people made writing this book easier. Many thanks to Judy Rogers, a wonderful editor and friend, and her husband John, whose cheery greeting always made my day. Kathie Stebick did a great job of typing the manuscript. The editorial group of which I am a member adopted me and offered lots of encouragement and constructive criticism—thanks to Cecil Murphey, Woodrow McKay, Richard Stanford, and Judy Rogers.

The hundreds of leaders with whom I interacted while conducting research and interviews provided the greatest resource for this book. They shared ideas, feelings, and experiences. They openly and honestly discussed the issues and challenges covered in this book. I am grateful for their assistance and hope what we have learned together will give the readers of this book a new perspective on the high cost of low morale and what to do about it.

Special thanks to Dennis Buda, Drew Gierman, and Dennis McClellan of St. Lucie Press, who believed in me enough to offer me another contract. Thanks also to Sandy Pearlman, Sandy Koskoff, Julie McManus and the rest of the team at St. Lucie for their able assistance. I couldn't have done it without them.

Finally, special thanks to my family—John, Maggie, and Nick, who allowed me time away from them to write my second book in two years—no easy task. Somehow, "thank you" doesn't seem like enough.

ABOUT THE AUTHOR

Carol A. Hacker is president of Carol A. Hacker & Associates, a leading training and consulting company headquartered in Alpharetta, GA. For more than two decades Carol has been a significant voice in front-line and corporate human resource management to Fortune 100 companies as well as small businesses. She's also the author of numerous published articles, as well as the highly acclaimed books *The Costs of Bad Hiring Decisions & How to Avoid Them* and *Hiring Top Performers—350 Great Interview Questions for People Who Need People*. Ms. Hacker earned her B.S. and M.S. with honors from the University of Wisconsin.

Carol is available to speak to companies, at association meetings or conferences, or to consult with organizations on the topics of selecting and keeping winning employees.

For more information contact her at:

209 Cutty Sark Way
Alpharetta, Georgia 30202
770-410-0517

DISCLAIMER

This publication is designed to provide accurate and authoritative information with regard to the subject matter covered. It is sold with the understanding that the publisher and the author are not engaged in rendering legal, accounting, or other professional services. If legal advice or other expert assistance is required, the services of a qualified professional person should be sought. (From a Declaration of Principles jointly adopted by a Committee of the American Bar Association and a Committee of Publishers and Associations.)

$

PIN THE TAIL ON THE DONKEY

1

(Making Good Hiring Decisions)

"Your reputation as a manager is on the line with each hiring decision you make. You are 'playing God' when you hire, and people will suffer if you use your influence unwisely. So, you owe it to yourself, your employer, the person hired, and the nation to be as thorough, professional, sensitive, fair, and objective as you can be."

—Bradford D. Smart
from *The Smart Interviewer—
Tools and Techniques for
Hiring the Best*

• •

At children's birthday parties in earlier years, guests played Pin the Tail on the Donkey. It was one of my personal favorites, even though I wasn't especially accurate at finding the right spot. An outbreak of laughter always awaited blindfolded victims who pinned the tail on the donkey's face, or worse yet, the wall. This delightful game entertained

1

party-goers for decades before the introduction of other more exciting activities to stimulate young minds.

That game reminds me of how some managers select new people. Their hiring process is almost as random as the efforts of the blindfolded player. Some don't know how to get started. Others jump in and hire without a strategy. Many hire in haste and hope the new employee will stick. Hiring the wrong people is like pinning the tail on the wrong end of the donkey—it doesn't work. The results, unfortunately, are not a laughing matter.

Poor hiring decisions are often at the root of existing as well as future morale problems. Bad choices create endless confrontations, disappointments, hurt feelings, and significant costs. When first choices are bad choices, no matter how talented your people, morale declines, and so does performance.

As a consultant to the management teams of several major league ball clubs, I've worked with and had the opportunity to compare player recruiting strategies to screening and hiring strategies for many types of businesses. The teams are just as eager to avoid making bad choices among ball players as you are to avoid hiring a misfit for your organization.

So, as you prepare to hire, first consider the needs and wants of people. Everyone you bring into your organization is unique. Employees want an understanding of a company's vision and how management's decisions will affect them and their families. Each individual you employ has a variety of concerns, and money isn't the only motivating factor. Many low-paid, unskilled workers are happy and motivated to do a good job. Top wages offer no guarantee that your new personnel will not become a morale problem. What are you doing to prepare for the first step in avoiding the high cost of low morale?

PLAN FOR RETENTION

Why employees stay is more important than why they leave. For many, self-esteem is more important than money. A pleasant physical environment can be a motivator, as can social interaction and an emotionally supportive manager. Job security is one of the biggest factors in why people stay. In addition, everyone wants respect and managers who will recognize and reward their best efforts. Many employees hang on until something or someone causes them to leave. Factors outside the organization, which include wanting to remain in the community they live in despite job dissatisfaction, also make people want to stick with you.

One of the most serious and persistent problems confronting managers is selecting employees who will work in the business for a long time. Turnover represents considerable costs in the continual recruitment and training of new employees. Even the best people are of little value to you if they leave the position after a short period of service.

As you prepare to hire new people, do so with an eye toward the future. Find out what motivates them *before* you offer the job. Look for individuals who are willing to make a long-term contribution to your business.

Organizations can manage turnover or be managed by it. How well it's managed has a lot to do with the manager's commitment to the task. No matter what the size of your business, the answer to turnover is simple. So, if you have an excessive employee turnover problem and can't find the cause, you might try looking in the closest mirror.

FORECAST STAFFING NEEDS

What has your business done to anticipate changes in staffing needs? The more prepared you are to fill a vacancy, the smoother the transition for everyone, especially new employees. Many companies don't spend enough time planning for future personnel demands. When an opening occurs in a large organization, managers often simply ask the human resources department to find a replacement. In smaller businesses, however, it's the manager's responsibility. A basic plan for when and how to hire and promote definitely impacts morale.

A formal development program can also help manage tragedy. On April 3, 1996, Secretary of Commerce Ron Brown's plane slammed into a hillside. The accident killed him and 32 other business leaders. The following week, President Clinton named Brown's successor. Some corporations who lost a management team member on that flight had no one in mind to fill the void. Forecasting can save time, eliminate hasty decisions, and create smooth transitions when the unexpected occurs.

DEVELOP RECRUITMENT SOURCES

Identify reliable sources for finding good candidates in advance of your need. It will reduce the pressure when you suddenly have to fill a vacancy or find the right person for a newly created position.

Many managers use newspaper advertisements because it takes the least amount of effort. They place an ad and wait for applicants to send in resumes. It's easy, but not always the best method for finding top performers.

Most people like to be asked for suggestions, so boost morale by giving your employees an opportunity to help. Employees who enjoy what they do and respect the organizations they work for will be eager to refer people to you. However, be sure they understand you reserve the right to accept or reject referrals without further explanation. Having a pool of people from which to choose is ideal. That's why keeping a resume/application file is valuable.

There are many other sources that work well but are often overlooked, such as:

- alumni associations
- branches of the military
- celebrity-hosted events
- cinema billboards
- direct mail
- door hangers
- ex-offender programs
- former employees
- internet
- job fairs
- job hotlines
- job lead organizations
- layoffs/closings
- magnetic signs
- on-campus interviews
- open houses
- posters
- presentations at community event
- professional associations
- radio advertisements
- referral cards
- resume databases
- scholarships
- senior organizations
- telemarketing
- television advertisement
- trade magazines
- unsolicited resumes

You may have other ideas on which you can develop your own strategies for finding and keeping winning employees. There's more than one way to ease the burden of securing new people in record time.

KNOW WHAT YOU'RE LOOKING FOR

Hiring is one of the most critical tasks you can assume. The process may become especially burdensome if you neglect to define what you're looking for in advance of the interview.

Start by deciding the least you'd be willing to accept in terms of:

❖ Specific skills.

❖ Specific work experience.

❖ Specific education or certification needed to do the job.

Identify what you're looking for in a candidate—then proceed with advertising, interviewing, and checking references.

Mike Cooney, compensation and human resources manager for President Baking Company, Inc., has a benchmark-type strategy that works. When department managers need people, he asks them to identify their top performers and decide what makes them the best. Then he matches candidates against the criteria for success as defined by the hiring manager. For example, "In our customer service department, we need people who are dynamic, have a strong work ethic, are tenacious, and willing to go the extra mile for the customers," said Cooney.

He starts the interview with questions about a candidate's skills, work experience, and abilities. He then moves to behavior-based questions. Or he might ask, "What is your ideal job?" If the answer is out of sync with what he has to offer, Cooney knows the candidate is not compatible to the position.

"Personality has a lot to do with success, whether employees stand alone or work together as a team. Some will have to deal with difficult people more often than not. I strongly consider attitude, motivation, and personality," said Cooney. It's important to him that everyone understands that choosing the person who best fits in with the rest of the people and manager will have a significant impact on morale and productivity.

He believes it's critical to know what you're looking for before getting started. He works closely with managers and supervisors to be sure they know too.

BECOME A SKILLED INTERVIEWER

The most important part of the hiring process is the face-to-face interview. Nothing takes the place of well-organized and thorough questioning. You can't learn enough about a candidate through written information to make a decision based solely on a resume or application. References are sometimes unreliable. Pen and pencil tests aren't always accurate. The best way to determine if a candidate is the right fit is to use a list of prepared questions and probe for more information. Gut feelings or intuition can be misleading, particularly when relied upon exclusively.

As you begin the interview, help the candidate feel relaxed and comfortable. Think of the interview as more than an exchange of dialogue. You're building a relationship so that you can get to know the candidate. Then you can decide whether he or she has the skills, work experience, educational background, and personal qualities you need.

The interview process is critical in today's labor market. Stiff competition gives added importance to hiring the right person the first time. Employee selection should never be a roll of the dice.

The following tips can help you become a skilled interviewer:

- ❖ **Don't give too many clues**. If you describe the qualities you're looking for and then ask candidates if they have them, you know what their answers will be.

- ❖ **Spend 80% of the interview time listening**. The #1 mistake interviewers make is talking too much.

- ❖ **Don't depend on candidates' self-evaluations**. If you ask them how they rate their problem-solving skills, they probably will answer, "Great." It's better to ask, "Give me an example of a difficult problem you had to solve in your last job." Then decide for yourself.

❖ **Don't always trust your first impressions**. Good candidates may initially turn you off and bad candidates may unjustly WOW you. Don't make hasty judgments.

❖ **Know exactly what the job requires**. Then you can compare candidates' qualifications to what you need.

❖ **Understand state and federal laws**. Asking questions that are not job-related can land you in legal hot water. The burden of proof is on the employer.

❖ **Probe for clarification**. If you are afraid to ask follow-up questions, you miss the opportunity to learn more about the candidates, especially if what they've said is unclear.

❖ **Don't make hiring decisions on gut feelings alone**. A good interview is still the best way to determine qualifications and fit.

MEASURE AGAINST JOB REQUIREMENTS

Comparing candidates with your requirements helps you determine the best fit. Candidates may dazzle you in many areas, but if they can't add a column of numbers or write a complete sentence, they won't be a good choice if that's what the job requires. Stay focused on finding a candidate to match your requirements—not on trying to find reasons to hire a candidate you like. "Hire the best and avoid the rest," says Michael Mercer, Ph.D., in his book of the same name. But will you recognize the best when you see them?

Suppose you have a candidate who looks great. She's a Phi Beta Kappa, eligible to sit for the CPA exam, and has held leadership roles since elementary school. She wrote her master's thesis on global finance and the Asian marketplace. She was a teaching assistant in graduate school, is an accomplished pianist, and has run the Boston Marathon five times. She speaks, reads, and writes three languages. She looks like a winner, but is she really what you want? Despite her qualifications, she isn't if she doesn't meet your specific job requirements.

LOOK FOR VERSATILITY

In addition to quality, look for versatility. This desirable trait is sometimes difficult to spot in an interview. Whether hiring for entry, senior level, skilled, or unskilled positions, look for people who are open to challenge and to learning new things and who can grow with the business.

The best way to determine versatility is to ask behavior-based questions. Such questions require candidates to reveal specific information about how they handled particular situations in the past. The past can reliably predict the future. The more recent the past, the more reliable the information.

Several examples of behavior-based questions are:

❖ Tell me about a time when your last supervisor asked you to do a job that wasn't part of your job description.

❖ Give me an example of when you felt apprehensive about accepting change, making adjustments, and moving forward on an assignment.

❖ What did you do in your last job that showed versatility?

❖ Tell me about a past effort to sell a new idea to a team member.

❖ Describe a project you were responsible for that required a high amount of energy over a long period of time.

These questions, and others like them, will help you find out more about candidates and whether they're the right fit for your business. Keep all questions job-related and stay away from anything a candidate might view as discriminatory.

Even though some people are content to remain in the same job for a lifetime, it doesn't mean they lack a versatile outlook. Find them. Interview them. Hire them. Challenge them. Reward them. And they'll be a positive influence on morale.

BE SURE THEY'RE WILLING, AS WELL AS ABLE

For employers, avoiding morale problems starts with identifying candidates who are willing to make a commitment to the job. Determining whether candidates have a strong level of commitment isn't easy. The interview helps you find out or at least get closer to the answer.

"Candidates have to like what they're doing. There's no sense in fooling prospective employers or themselves; it's a lose-lose situation when that happens," said Tom Schlinkert, senior vice president with Drake Beam Morin, Inc., one of the largest outplacement firms in the world. In his one-on-one executive counseling sessions, he emphasizes the importance of being willing, as well as being capable of performing the job duties.

Many candidates are desperate to find work. Some have been unemployed for months, even years. A few are open to accepting anything that comes along. Some will take the offer while they continue to look for a better position. When that happens commitment is lost along with the motivation it takes to do a good job.

LeRoy Lashley, president and owner of three Auto Service and Tire Super Marts and authorized Firestone care service centers, echoes those sentiments: "I hire people who I feel have a good work ethic, enjoy people, and like what they do. They must also have an appreciation for the position customers are in when needing car repairs. Many customers have an 'uneasy feeling' when having to deal with automotive service," said Lashley.

In the car care industry, there's a tremendous shortage of people who want to do automotive service work. Lashley says that if 100 qualified and motivated candidates came into town in the morning, "they'd all have a job by nightfall."

Lashley's been in the business for over 35 years. He feels he's a good judge of character and has been successful in hiring good people. "If you start with people who are highly skilled but lack motivation, you've made a bad choice. Technical qualifications are important, but not as critical as having their heart in what they'll be doing for you," added Lashley.

TEST THEM

Retention has a lot to do with having the right people. Misfits create miserable situations for both the manager and themselves.

BellSouth Advertising and Publishing has a rigid screening process. New sales trainers come from within the organization, work as trainers for two years, and go back into the field. The company screens internal prospects using a written questionnaire and simulation activity. Each candidate must also present a short training module.

Terry Ingwersen, director of training, explains, "We only hire people who are good facilitators—those who understand and use the principles of facilitative learning. Anyone who subscribes to the 'yell and tell' technique would not be a good choice."

In questioning her further, Ingwersen said that not everyone who wants to be a trainer passes.

At the end of the evaluation, each person finds out whether his or her probability of success in BellSouth's sales training environment is high, medium, or low. Most do pass, but some don't and are very disappointed. However, only the best facilitators are accepted.

Ingwersen believes in surrounding herself with good people. Once she finds them, they stick with her, and she lets them shine.

HOLD AUDITIONS

Asking candidates to demonstrate what they claim they can do is in vogue, especially for middle- and upper-middle management positions.

Microtraining Plus conducts Macintosh computer training. Candidates for trainer and sales positions are asked to make an hour-long presentation to an 8-member team on anything but computers. Topics they've heard about include instruments in an orchestra, the solar system, and in-line skating.

The best candidates are well organized and have a take-charge attitude. They're good at handling disruptive participants and focus on the CEO during the presentation. While the audition method may not be something every company will want to use when hiring new employees, written evaluations from customers reflect the positive results of this method for Microtraining Plus.

MAKE COMMITMENT POSSIBLE

Use honest recruiting efforts. They're important to the success of any new employee. If your organization practices less- than-truthful tactics in an attempt to sway candidates' decisions, you're taking a risk. Candidates who become employees and then find out they've been misled are likely to cause problems. To avoid this recruiting error, be sure everything you communicate in the interview is accurate. False promises can also lead to lawsuits.

For example, Candus Ruiz had an interview that led to a job offer as a medical secretary in a hospital on the West Coast. She accepted. It wasn't long before she discovered the truth. The actual job differed greatly from what she had been told in the interview. She felt cheated by her new employer.

Ms. Ruiz, for financial reasons, felt she had no choice but to stay with the job until she found another. But in the meantime, her morale was less than desirable from the employer's perspective. She became disruptive. In addition, the word was soon out that the hospital which hired her had been dishonest during the interview.

Although Ms. Ruiz eventually chose to seek other employment, it was an expensive lesson for the hospital when she resigned in disgust.

This mistake didn't have to happen.

The topic of honest recruiting brings to mind Kelly Moran, branch manager, and Steve Widmer, major accounts manager for Gordon Flesch, the largest privately owned Canon dealership in the nation. They share the same successful philosophy when it comes to hiring and keeping winning employees.

"We're very honest in the interview about the job responsibilities and what candidates can expect once they become employees," said Moran. They even show the finalist actual W-2's with names deleted so there's no misconception about earning potential. Questions are encouraged because they want to make sure that what candidates learn about the company is, in actuality, what they can expect.

Their turnover is low, with 60% of the sales force having tenure of more than four years. Widmer said that sales quotas are high, but when people know what to expect before they start, there are no surprises. That means reduced turnover, high morale, and team spirit.

START WITH QUALITY EMPLOYEES

I often hear managers complain about the incompetent or troublesome employees they hired or inherited. The latter is a more difficult problem because they had no choice, but hiring mistakes are preventable.

"Start with quality employees" is the motto of Storehouse, Inc., an upscale furniture retailer, and its president and COO, Clyde Mynatt. They hire only the best and promote from within. "Sound recruiting practices are a must. Referrals from our employees are a great resource—good people associate with people like themselves," said Mynatt. He believes that their formula for success is a combination of things. "Once we hire quality people, we provide them with an environment that allows future stars to rise to the top. Almost 85% of all promotions are internal. We offer a level playing field. We work as a team," added Mynatt.

Those sentiments are shared by Randy Wood, vice president of sales and director of stores for Storehouse. He explained, "We've found that ambitious people don't feel that their employer owes them something. They're full of energy and drive. It's that desire to be successful that we look for in the people we hire. Education and work experience are secondary." The result is minimal turnover among their more than 120 store and assistant managers. Hiring quality people has helped them outpace their competition. Promoting quality employees from within is the second step in their success. Wood himself has been promoted several times, and those who report to him know he understands the challenges they face. He said, "It helps to have lived it, at least in our business."

Storehouse starts with the best and sees to it that everyone gets the training needed for success. Also, the company believes that money spent to educate managers in how to supervise, as well as sell, is an investment they can't afford *not* to make. They offer a high quality product and have only high quality people representing them.

B E SELECTIVE

Have you ever been in a situation where you needed someone to fill a job and you needed them yesterday? Did you feel desperate and willing to take the first marginally qualified person who came along? If you've ever found yourself in this situation, you probably have made your share of hiring mistakes, which, of course, impacted morale in your organization.

At Goody Products, Inc., they pride themselves in hiring selectively. They never hire on a hunch and offer jobs to only the very few who meet their qualifications. They would rather leave a position unfilled than hire a bad fit. According to Fred Fratto, vice president of human resources, they do their best to anticipate in advance the kinds of openings they'll have to fill, especially in the exempt category. Although, that's not always possible, they never make hasty hiring decisions even if it means waiting 3–4 months to fill a vacancy.

President William Berry said, "We hire people who can think on their feet, can handle a fast-paced environment, and are highly competitive. They have to be aggressive about their careers and be motivated to make money." The company has found that people who fit this profile make the most successful employees.

When asked how they identify such people, Fratto said, "First, we never restrict our search to a particular part of the country or the local community. We're always willing to relocate the best people. Comprehensive interviews involve meeting with several people in the company. They use an outside psychologist who administers a test and conducts a 2-hour interview. Testing includes evaluation of numerical, verbal, and spatial perception, and reasoning abilities.

The company believes in hiring people who can maintain a balance between their work and personal lives. They're not easy to find, however. "We reject people who other companies may be very happy to have. They're just not what we're looking for," explained Fratto.

They view the hiring process as a two-way street. "When we don't offer a job to someone, I tell them that it's for their good, too—that they would not be happy and successful at our company based on our predictions," said Fratto. Goody pays for performance, and there's no place for people who don't meet expectations.

The company knows that by hiring selectively, they can reduce, if not eliminate, the high cost of low morale. They've found that people work well with people who have the same work ethic and outlook on life.

SEEK PEOPLE-ORIENTED LEADERS

The kind of management personnel you employ helps determine the success of your organization. If your team is led by people who value the contributions of others and are able to set a good example, you're off to a good start.

Such a team is in evidence at South Baldwin Hospital in Foley, AL. I witnessed firsthand a group of people-oriented leaders in action when I was admitted to the emergency room on July 3, 1996. I interfaced with eight medical staff members, all of whom were empowered to handle the many problems confronting them. Cases ranged from a swimmer who dove to the bottom of a pool to multi-car accident victims. The second shift maintained, and helped patients keep, a sense of humor throughout the 2- to 3-hour wait for less serious cases. They were an incredible team of medical professionals facing life and death situations in a tense and crowded work environment. I never doubted their abilities to care for me.

As I wondered how good could possibly come from the bad, I realized that I was watching a group of people-oriented leaders save lives. That was good enough for me.

HIRE PEOPLE WHO ARE BETTER THAN YOU

Many managers feel threatened by people who know more than they do. If the threat involves candidates with superior talents, they won't hire them. I've worked for both types of managers— those who are eager to hire people more skilled than themselves, and those who won't hire anyone they suspect might know more than they do. The first group sees talented employees as assets. The second group is afraid that skilled people will take their jobs. What kind of leader would you rather work for? What kind of leader would your employees rather work for?

No one person can possibly have all of the qualities needed by a superstar. Therefore, organizations are best served by a leader with a good reputation and track record for hiring people who:

❖ Are able to challenge the process.

❖ Inspire a shared vision.

❖ Enable others to act.

❖ Are self-confident and assertive.

❖ Are organized, energetic, and persistent.

❖ Are creative.

❖ Are good listeners.

❖ Are analytical in their thinking.

❖ Are sensitive to the concerns of others.

❖ Are not afraid to challenge conventional ways of doing things.

"Most of what we call management consists of making it difficult for people to get their work done," offers business consultant, Peter Drucker. He suggests that once a year, all managers should stop and ask the frontline troops what they, the managers, are doing that keeps the troops from serving the customers—then stop doing it. If the answer is, "we're not hiring the kind of people needed to get the job done," then you may need to examine your motives and selection methods when choosing which candidate(s) to hire.

TRY TEAM INTERVIEWING

Interviews in which several people meet the candidate at the same time are growing in popularity. However, some people equate team interviews with stress interviews. Others believe they take too much time.

In the case of Sea World, a marine life theme park in California, Marianne Flowers, director of sales, finds team interviewing a valuable and reliable use of time. "We have three phases to our interview process. First, we start with a telephone interview. Second, we conduct a one-and-one-half-hour, face-to-face team interview where the candidates meet with three sales managers. Third, the final candidates meet with me. I give them an overview of the company and tell them what they can expect."

In the company's team interview, each manager uses a list of prepared behavior-based questions. Some of the questions they find helpful, based on the competencies they identify prior to interviewing, are:

❖ Tell us about a time when you had to get your point across to a co-worker.

❖ Give an example of when an initial "no" from a potential customer changed to "yes." What did you do to modify the decision?

❖ Give me an example of a time when you had to put forth your best effort.

Flowers finds many advantages to team interviews. Usually three people take turns asking the questions. The advantage is that the person asking a question can maintain good eye contact with the candidate and really listen to the answer while the other employees take notes. You also have more people observing whether the candidate has understood key questions. To help put candidates at ease, the interviewers explain to candidates that the benefit of the team interview is that there's less chance of missing a word here or there that might cause misinterpretation of answers.

The steps for team interviews include the following:

❖ Select interviewers.

❖ Provide orientation and training for interviewers.

❖ Determine the dimensions or skills to be evaluated.

❖ Write questions and decide who will ask what.

❖ Design or find an interview form and decide on a ranking system.

❖ Schedule the interviews.

❖ Conduct interviews and rate candidates.

❖ Reach a post-interview consensus on ratings and rankings.

❖ Follow up, including meeting with the decision maker(s), to discuss recommendations if the team is not the final decision maker.

❖ Provide feedback to internal candidates and notify external candidates eliminated from consideration.

Sea World has found many advantages to structured team interviews and believes they are far more valid predictors of job success than traditional one-on-one interviews. "We hire many entry-level people with 2–3 years of sales experience. We don't have five months to train them. They're expected to promote the park and distribute complimentary information shortly after joining us," said Flowers.

She also feels that the team approach in interviewing is no different than what candidates can expect to experience after they're hired. Everything they do is a team effort, including their sales goals, which are team-related.

TROUBLESHOOT RECRUITMENT PROBLEMS

Recruitment is often a common source of conflict between an organization's line management and the human resources department. Line managers sometimes maintain that they don't get the support they need, charging that the human resources staff sends too few qualified candidates or doesn't pay enough for good people. On the other hand, human resources people complain about line management's lack of cooperation. They point out that most managers are seldom available for interviews, frequently keep candidates waiting, and are slow in making decisions.

Whether you're a manager or a human resource professional, fault-finding is a sign of trouble. No one wins when arguments occur over who's doing what. In-house bickering leads to low morale and often a poor choice in candidates.

For example, a plant manager liked to do his own screening and leave human resources out of the process. He felt that he knew better what he needed and wanted. He not only violated the principles of interview etiquette, but he also asked questions that violated state and federal laws. One day he announced that he had invited a candidate to fly across the country for a face-to-face interview. When he quickly determined that the candidate was not a good fit, the plant manager then asked the human resources manager to "get rid of him." This resulted in a heated discussion between the two managers.

Recruiting is marketing. Just as your business image affects the sale of your product or service, it also affects your ability to attract the type of candidates you want at a price you can afford. Hiring is a difficult job at best, and when managers don't share the same philosophy about how to recruit and treat candidates, it becomes even more difficult.

There are several things you can do to facilitate better communication among those responsible for hiring:

- ❖ Compile a list of questions to ask each candidate. Make sure developing questions are part of the standard operating procedure.

- ❖ Be sure everyone knows what they can and cannot ask the candidate.

- ❖ Discuss the skills and background needed by the ideal candidate before you begin the interview process.

- ❖ Decide what parts of the job, if any, are unattractive and how you will discuss this with candidates.

- ❖ Have a plan to gather and share feedback among managers if more than one manager is involved in the hiring decision.

There is no magic formula for successful recruiting. Continually improving the recruiting process, however, can provide dividends that enable the organization to hire top-notch people. A regular audit of your business's recruiting program, along with a plan for troubleshooting, may be an important first step in ensuring maximum effectiveness.

AVOID "THE MIRROR TEST"

If you're bragging about how quickly you can hire people, chances are you're not hiring people who will make an impact. Some companies jokingly talk about giving candidates "the mirror test"—if candidates can fog a mirror, they're hired. But hiring decisions are no joke. Once you extend an offer of employment, you've entered a "for better or for worse" relationship. When new employees turn out to be "for worse," it's a lot more difficult to get rid of them than it was to hire them. Misguided hiring can take a toll in "soft" costs—customer confidence and internal morale.

Many organizations, including Saturn (the General Motors subsidiary) and K-Mart, have joined the ranks of businesses who use pre-employment exercises as part of the hiring process. For example, K-Mart uses a pre-employment questionnaire. They ask all prospective hourly workers to complete a questionnaire, designed to help the company predict which candidates will stick with the job, perform well, and give superior customer service.

Saturn's stringent selection process, although it ultimately affects dozens of employees in dealerships, is really about choosing individuals. Any dealer interested in selling Saturns must fill out a comprehensive application form that measures not only the retailer's financial strength and market penetration, but its recent customer satisfaction index scores. Prospective dealers who survive the initial application review process then receive a field visit. Two Saturn officials spend an entire day at the facility. They talk to managers, service technicians, sales representatives, and as many other employees as they can. They also issue a survey to every employee at the facility. It's during these hands-on, frontline visits that Saturn demands evidence that the dealership takes good care of its customers and employees.

In an opposite example, a company who traditionally uses "the mirror test," has found themselves in difficult situations on numerous occasions due to bad choices. Sievers Electrical has never considered hiring to be a major concern—until now. Sam Sievers said, "I let my managers make their own decisions. Sometimes I'm disappointed in the choice, but feel I can't be too hands-on as the boss. I admit it has cost me money but when we need help, a person who's barely breathing may have to do."

Sievers isn't particularly happy with the results of his company's hiring practices. So, he's made a commitment to learn how he and his managers can exceed the "warm body" philosophy. He also recognizes that sound hiring decisions are based on formal, disciplined processes rather than mirrors, gut reactions, or managers willing to hire anyone who walks through the door.

CONSIDER INTERNAL CANDIDATES

Internal candidates—the most cost-effective way to fill vacancies—are an excellent resource that is often overlooked. They are a known entity—you know them or of them, and they know you and the organization. The best part about promoting from within is the fact that it sends the message that people can learn, move up, and grow with the business.

I'm often asked how to handle internal recruiting. My best advice is to start with an action plan—follow your recruitment policy. Include these steps:

- ❖ Post the job requirements. This will eliminate rumors and misunderstandings concerning what you're looking for.

- ❖ Decide how long job postings will be up.

- ❖ Make sure everyone knows how to apply.

- ❖ If you're considering someone in another department, notify his or her supervisor before you speak with the employee. You don't want to get a reputation for "stealing" employees.

- ❖ Be open-minded when evaluating candidates.

❖ Use a list of prepared questions. Ask the same questions of each candidate.

❖ Notify those who were not selected. You may also want to indicate what areas they need to develop further to improve their chances for advancement in the future.

Here's an example of an internal recruiting success story. Joe Lincoln, a college graduate, worked as a maintenance mechanic for a manufacturer. He applied for an internal position as a maintenance supervisor. Initially, the company would not consider him—once a mechanic, always a mechanic. The soft-spoken Lincoln was disappointed. He talked to the human resources manager, who took his side and fought for an interview for him. Lincoln prevailed; he's been a maintenance supervisor for over ten years—the best they've ever had. Morale didn't surge after Lincoln won his fight for consideration, but the event did send a clear message that internal candidates had a chance.

Be sure that all employees know what you're looking for and what it takes to qualify. Encourage people to try. Reward those who do. Let them know that you value existing talent—that you're willing to give everyone an opportunity to move up. Remember, your most reliable employees frequently come from inside the operation.

HIRE FOR TODAY'S GENERATION

Saun Chang, CEO of Geodesy, Inc., has very definite ideas about hiring only those people who fit the corporate culture. "I'm looking for people who are not mentally stuck in the last generation. In order for us as a company and a nation to survive, we need people to realize what they do has to contribute to the bottom line. Everyone needs to share responsibility for making decisions," said Chang.

For example, when a delivery man dropped off a package, Chang noticed a bald tire on the man's truck. He mentioned it, and the driver said it wasn't his problem. Chang was concerned about safety, to which the man replied, "It's the company's problem. If I get hurt they'll pay for it."

Chang focuses on bottom-line results and knows that if you hire someone who isn't willing to meet today's business challenges but is content merely to get by, the business can't survive. "Employees make their own long-term job security. I want to make sure before I hire someone that they understand that what they do makes a difference."

He and his business partner, Tom Demetriou, president of Geodesy, Inc., want to develop leaders for today's generation from the people they hire. Today's generation has nothing to do with biological age. Mentality is the prime consideration, along with whether or not the candidate would be happy in the company. Demetriou mentioned a quote from *Selling the Dream* by Guy Kawasaki that sums up his feelings about leadership. "Managers say 'go.' Leaders say 'let's go.' Our hiring philosophy is in line with the quote. We want people who are proactive—who have a vision of where they and the company are headed," said Demetriou.

Chang and Demetriou both agree that they look beyond the immediate and hire only those who share their dreams.

CHECK REFERENCES

One of the final steps in the hiring process is checking references. It's often neglected. Yet, it's your last chance to avoid hiring a misfit and suffering the subsequent impact on morale. In order to maintain the quality of a company's work force and avoid claims of negligent hiring, employers should conduct a thorough investigation of all candidates.

Resume fraud can range from slight exaggerations to outright lies. The Society for Human Resource Management reports that 25– 75% of all resumes are embellished. An informal survey of more than 1,200 potential job candidates conducted by Smith James Group found at least one misrepresentation on 21% of the resumes sampled—all the more reason to thoroughly check references.

Louis B. Meyer, partner with the law firm of Poyner & Spruill, L.L.P. in Raleigh, NC, shares some DO's and DONT's for an employer when conducting reference checks.

❖ DO ask a candidate to sign a release that will permit reference checks and prior employers to provide information without fear of legal action. Otherwise, a prior employer may refuse to give any information about a former employee other than dates of employment and job duties.

❖ DO obtain as much information as possible from a reference or prior employer. In addition to verifying information provided by the candidate, due diligence calls for a prospective employer to ask questions such as, "What are the candidate's strengths and weaknesses?" "Was he a hard worker?" "How did he respond to criticism?" "How would you compare her performance with others who held a similar position?" "How did he get along with co-workers and supervisors?"

❖ DO ask a prior employer questions such as, "Will you be replacing her?" "Was he fired or did he resign?" "Would your company rehire her?" "Is there anything you know about him that we should consider in deciding whether to hire him?" An employer must make all reasonable efforts to determine whether a candidate is suitable for employment.

❖ DO listen carefully to all comments made by a reference or prior employer. You may have to "read between the lines" if a person is trying to be cooperative but is obviously being careful not to comment on controversial matters.

❖ DO ask to speak with a candidate's former supervisor. Firsthand information about the candidate's abilities is most helpful.

❖ DON'T ask questions about a candidate's age, citizenship, national origin, ethnic background, religion, or marital status. To avoid claims of discrimination, an employer should not ask questions that tend to identify a candidate as a member of a protected class or which might be interpreted as indicating a preference for candidates that are not in a protected class.

❖ DON'T ask questions about a candidate's health or physical characteristics, or drug or alcohol problems. The Americans With Disabilities Act (ADA) prohibits employers from asking questions likely to elicit information about a disability. You can, however, ask a previous employer about a candidate's prior work attendance record and whether he or she can perform essential job functions.

❖ DO document all your efforts to contact references and prior employers and all of the information you obtain from them. If a reference or prior employer refuses to provide certain information or answer certain questions, document this as well.

❖ DON'T make a final decision based on a negative reference without considering the need for further investigation. The person who provided the reference may have had a personality conflict with the candidate, or they may not want to see the candidate gain employment with a competitor. If the candidate can adequately explain the negative comments, or the criticism is not material to your hiring qualifications, a job offer may still be in order.

❖ DO ask a candidate to provide additional references if you are not satisfied with the responses from the ones initially identified by the candidate.

MAKE SOUND HIRING DECISIONS

When it's time to make the final hiring decision, it's often done arbitrarily or by gut feeling. Although intuition has a place in the process, it should not substitute for a thorough interview and careful consideration of each finalist.

In an interview with Sherrí Harper, human resources manager for MTS Systems Corporation-Sensors Division, she offered the following, "We have several people involved in making each hiring decision. The interview starts in the human resources department, and, in addition to being interviewed by the hiring manager, the candidate is interviewed by several peers."

They use an interview evaluation form that has ten general factors against which they evaluate candidates. Each interviewer provides a score and supportive details or comments on each interviewee. "I like the form because it gives employees something to talk from. It's a guide, and it works well for us. They look for specific information on each candidate. They must justify each decision rather than make a decision off the cuff," added Harper.

In one particular situation, they were not quite happy with the candidate's qualifications. The scores on the evaluation forms reflected their dissatisfaction. They discussed it among themselves and decided they had two options; they could back down on what they wanted or continue to search for someone who more closely met their needs. They decided to keep looking.

When you've invested time and money in a search for the best candidate, don't blow it at the end of the process. It happens too often. Find a system and stick to it so that when you make the final decision, you have no doubts about your choice.

The sample evaluation form (pages 27–28) that MTS Systems uses is reprinted with written permission of G. Neil Companies (1-800-999-9111).

S UMMARY

Most companies with high turnover have a weak selection process. A growing business with an employee attrition rate of less than 5% annually indicates it is hiring and retaining the right people. If your rate is between 6% and 10%, it may be a sign of emerging problems. An attrition rate above 10% could mean serious morale problems.

As you embark on one of the most important decision-making processes you undertake as a manager, don't lose sight of the fact that hiring the wrong people may lead to disciplinary problems, conflicts, and low morale. It can also mean dissatisfied customers, low productivity, quality problems, and damage to the organization's image. On average, when you hire and terminate a misfit, the position remains vacant for 13 weeks. It's estimated that about 50% of the position's efficiency is sacrificed during the vacancy period.

Help prevent bad hiring decisions and eliminate unnecessary turnover by learning how to protect yourself from the professional interviewee who shines in the interview but tarnishes quickly once employed. Learn to identify those who are dependable, stable, honest, loyal, versatile, and responsible. Ask the right questions and avoid selecting individuals based on the subjective rather than objective—vibes rather than facts—all of which are more susceptible to bias and prejudice.

The hiring decisions you make today will directly impact your work force in the year 2000. If projections hold true as predicted in the publication *Workforce 2000* by the U.S. Department of Labor, nearly 85% of new employees will be African-Americans, native-born women, Hispanics, Asians, and other nonwhite immigrants. The publication also reports that the average number of workers between 16 and 24 years of age will decrease by 8%. The average age of the American worker will be 39 years old; it is currently 34. And the report predicts that more than 60% of women over the age of 16 will be working outside the home. These trends will directly impact the American work force in general, as well as your organization.

Successful businesses recognize that the bottom-line impact is predicated on sound and defensible hiring decisions. What are you doing to ensure you make the right decisions for your organization? Answers to the following questions will guide you in screening and selecting employees who will stick with you and contribute to positive morale.

Name of Applicant_____Date_____
❑General Interview   ❑Position Interview   Job Title_____
This is   ❑1st Interview   ❑2nd Interview   ❑3rd Interview

Interviewer_____Title_____

Department Manager/Supervisor (if applicable)_____Title_____

Instructions: Carefully evaluate applicant's interview performance in relation to the essential functions of the job. Check rating box to indicate the applicant's performance. Indicate N/A in the points box if the rating category is not applicable. Assign points for each rating using the scale provided and write this number in the points box. Points will be totaled and averaged for an overall interview performance score.

O – Outstanding – Applicant is exceptional. Is recognized as being far superior to others.
V – Very Good – Applicant clearly exceeds position requirements.
G – Good – Applicant is competent and dependable. Meets standards of the job.
I – Improvement Needed – Applicant is deficient or below the standards required of the job.
U – Unsatisfactory – Applicant is generally unacceptable.
N /A – Not Applicable.

GENERAL FACTORS	RATING SCALE	SCORE	SUPPORTIVE DETAILS OR COMMENTS
1. **Experience** – The extent to which the applicant's background and experience are consistent with the essential functions of the job.	O V G I U	❑ 100-90 Points ❑ 89-80 ❑ 79-70 ❑ 69-60 ❑ Below 60	
2. **Education** – The extent to which the applicant's schooling is relevant and sufficient for the essential functions of the job.	O V G I U	❑ 100-90 Points ❑ 89-80 ❑ 79-70 ❑ 69-60 ❑ Below 60	
3. **Job knowledge** – The extent to which the applicant possesses the practical/technical knowledge required to perform essential functions of the job.	O V G I U	❑ 100-90 Points ❑ 89-80 ❑ 79-70 ❑ 69-60 ❑ Below 60	
4. **Information about general work field** – The extent to which the applicant has thorough knowledge or is familiar with the field.	O V G I U	❑ 100-90 Points ❑ 89-80 ❑ 79-70 ❑ 69-60 ❑ Below 60	
5. **Communication Skills** – The extent to which the applicant effectively expressed and conveyed ideas.	O V G I U	❑ 100-90 Points ❑ 89-80 ❑ 79-70 ❑ 69-60 ❑ Below 60	
6. **Motivation** – The extent to which the applicant appears to have a true desire to work and has an interest in the position.	O V G I U	❑ 100-90 Points ❑ 89-80 ❑ 79-70 ❑ 69-60 ❑ Below 60	

GENERAL FACTORS	RATING SCALE	SCORE	SUPPORTIVE DETAILS OR COMMENTS
7. **Creativity** – The extent to which the applicant appears to be innovative and inventive.	O V G I U	❑ 100-90 Points ❑ 89-80 ❑ 79-70 ❑ 69-60 ❑ Below 60	
8. **Initiative** – The extent to which the applicant appears to be willing to seek out new assignments and would readily assume additional duties when necessary.	O V G I U	❑ 100-90 Points ❑ 89-80 ❑ 79-70 ❑ 69-60 ❑ Below 60	
9. **Composure** – The extent to which the applicant appears to be in control. The applicant's ability to handle stress.	O V G I U	❑ 100-90 Points ❑ 89-80 ❑ 79-70 ❑ 69-60 ❑ Below 60	
10. **Overall impression** – The extent to which the applicant's overall appearance, manner, and responsiveness are consistent with the requirements of the job.	O V G I U	❑ 100-90 Points ❑ 89-80 ❑ 79-70 ❑ 69-60 ❑ Below 60	

OVERALL INTERVIEW PERFORMANCE SCORE

Calculate applicant's overall interview performance score by adding the ratings for each interview category rated above and dividing this sum by the number of categories rated. Check the appropriate score range below.

Total Points _____ ÷ Number of Categories Rated = _____ Overall Rating

Outstanding	100 - 90
❑ Very Good	89 - 80
❑ Good	79 - 70
❑ Improvement Needed	69 - 60
❑ Unsatisfactory	Below 60

This applicant is:
   ❑ A strong candidate.
   ❑ A possible candidate.
   ❑ A possible candidate for another position (explain below).
   ❑ Of no further interest.
   ❑ Other _____

Alternate position(s) for which applicant seems better qualified:_____
_____

Additional Comments:_____
_____
_____

CHECKLIST FOR

MAKING THE RIGHT HIRING DECISIONS

√ Do I really need to fill this vacancy now or ever?

√ What's the quickest, most reliable source for finding good candidates?

√ What am I looking for in talent and personal qualities?

√ How will I judge if they're willing as well as able?

√ Am I willing to be honest in the interview about the job responsibilities?

√ Do I feel comfortable hiring someone better than me? If not, why not?

√ If I'm not involving other members of my team in the interview, how could I benefit from doing so?

√ How will I handle recruitment problems if they arise?

√ Am I willing to consider internal candidates? If not, why not?

√ How much time and effort can I commit to checking references?

√ Could I improve the process for making final hiring decisions? What am I doing now that doesn't work?

√ Could I benefit from using an interview evaluation form?

Additional Reading

Allison, Loren K., Esq. *Employee Selection—A Legal Perspective.* Alexandria, VA: SHRM Foundation, 1996.

Beatty, Richard H. *Interviewing High-Performers—Every Manager's Guide to Effective Interviewing Techniques.* Somerset, NJ: John Wiley & Sons, Inc., 1994.

Bell, Arthur H. *Extraviewing—Innovative Ways to Hire the Best*. New York, NY: Irwin Professional Publishing, 1992.

Byham, William. *The Selection Solution: Solving the Mystery of Personnel Selection*. Canonsburg, PA: DDI Press, 1996.

Cook, Mary F. *The Human Resources Yearbook*. Englewood Cliffs, NJ: Prentice Hall, 1995.

Fyock, Catherine D. *Get the Best—How to Recruit the People You Want*. Homewood, IL: Business One Irwin, 1993.

Hacker, Carol A. *Hiring Top Performers—350 Great Interview Questions For People Who Need People*. Alpharetta, GA:, 1994.

Hacker, Carol A. *The Costs of Bad Hiring Decisions & How to Avoid Them*. Delray Beach, FL: St. Lucie Press, 1996.

Lauer, Steve and B. Jack Gebhardt. *Now Hiring! Finding and Keeping Good Help for Your Entry-Wage Jobs*. New York, NY: American Management Association, 1996.

McGill, Ann M. *Hiring the Best*. Homewood, IL: Business One Irwin/Mirror Press, 1994.

Mercer, Michael, W. *Hire the Best...and Avoid the Rest*. New York, NY: American Management Association, 1993.

Morgan, Ronald B. and Jack E. Smith. *Staffing the New Workplace—Selecting and Promoting for Quality Improvement*. Milwaukee, WI: ASQC Quality Press, 1996.

Morrison, Don A. *Employee Recruitment and Selection in a Post-ADA Environment*. Amherst, MA: HRD Press, Inc., 1995.

Risser, Rita. *Stay Out of Court: The Manager's Guide to Preventing Employee Lawsuits*. Englewood Cliffs, NJ: Prentice Hall, 1995.

Rothwell, William J. *Effective Succession Planning—Ensuring Leadership Continuity and Building Talent from Within*. New York, NY: AMACOM, 1994.

Sack, Steven Mitchell. *From Hiring to Firing—The Legal Survival Guide for Employers in the 1990s*. Merrick, NY: Legal Strategies Publications, 1995.

Shackelford, William G. *Minority Recruiting—Building the Strategies and Relationships for Effective Diversity Recruiting*. Dubuque, IA: Kendall/Hunt Publishing Company, 1996.

Weiss, Donald H. *Fair, Square & Legal—Safe Hiring, Managing & Firing Practices to Keep Your Company Out of Court*. New York, NY: AMACOM, 1996.

Wendover, Robert W. *Smart Hiring for Your Business*. Naperville, IL: Sourcebooks Trade, 1993.

Worthington, E. R. and Anita E. Worthington. *People Investment—How to Make Your Hiring Decisions Pay Off for Everyone*. Grants Pass, OR: Oasis Press, 1993.

<table>
<tr><td>$</td><td># UP YOUR ATTITUDE</td><td>2</td></tr>
</table>

$ UP YOUR ATTITUDE 2

(A Good Attitude = High Morale)

"The greatest discovery in our generation is that human beings, by changing the inner attitudes of their minds, can change the outer aspects of their lives."

—William James

● ●

"Good guys finish last." "Good things come to those who wait." "Everything that can go wrong, will." "If at first you don't succeed, try, try again." In the words of Ann Gerhart, writer for the *Raleigh News and Observer*:

> "If you live by platitudes one and three, you're a pessimist, doomed to wandering this earth depressed, of weakened spirit and poorer health, less likely to succeed. If you live by platitudes two and four, you're an optimist, accustomed to floating down the sunny side of the street, of resilient body

and mind, higher-achieving at work, school and sports. When you meet defeat, you pick yourself up, dust yourself off, and start all over again."

When I think of attitude, I also think of Keith Harrell, a motivational speaker whose motto is "Attitude is Everything." His unique and charismatic style of delivery compels his audiences to take a "fix it or kick it" approach toward desired changes in attitude.

A good attitude is an ingredient employees *must have* in order to be productive. Success is determined to a great degree by attitude. It's one of the few things that each of us controls about ourself. Through your attitude, you can help create an environment in which employees want to do their best. Managers should learn to enjoy their work and, in turn, make sure employees enjoy theirs. It's not about cheerleading because cheers have only a short-term effect. The goal is to provide a positive work setting that challenges employees to be creative and take calculated risks.

People respond best when they are treated as valued members of a team. They work better in a place where they are thought of as co-workers, not just employees. Some companies call their employees "associates" or even "co-owners" to help promote a positive atmosphere. These organizations understand that people work best when mutual respect and trust are the rule, not the exception.

There's a big difference between a manager who's demanding and one who is simply disliked. Often managers who expect a lot may actually motivate employees more than managers who are laissez-faire. The results stem from the manager's attitude and the way they manage. Employees who set their sights high want to work for successful managers even though they demand a lot and set tough standards. Everyone wants to work for a winner, and employees may respect a demanding manager whether they like him or not.

For example, my fifth grade teacher was Mrs. Dries. We felt she made us work too hard, much harder than the teachers of the other two fifth grade classes. However, we also realized that by expecting a lot from us, she did the most to prepare us for sixth grade. She had a wonderful outlook and encouraged even the most timid of the 50 students in her class to do their best. Also, she was fair, and we knew it. Mrs. Dries inspired more than one student to follow in her footsteps and become teachers, including myself.

Several ways to let your employees know through your attitude that you care are:

* ❖ Be sure they know how important their particular jobs are to the organization's success.

* ❖ Let them participate in setting attainable and specific goals.

* ❖ When possible, assign employees to teams in which they are most compatible.

* ❖ Ask for their opinions.

On the surface, attitude is the way you communicate your moods. It's a mindset. You're born with the ability to manage what goes on inside your head. How you handle your thoughts impacts how you manage people. Employees know when you care. They notice when you value their efforts and are willing to listen to their ideas.

Managing with a good attitude is about establishing a healthy business climate, as well as setting a good example. You don't have to be a Pollyanna, but you have to carry your weight. Employees will know when you're shirking responsibility. They'll resent you for asking them to do what you aren't willing to do yourself.

Most employees produce good results if they are both challenged and supported by a manager with a positive attitude.

A great attitude brings about great results.
A good attitude brings about good results.
A fair attitude brings about fair results.
A bad attitude brings about bad results.
—Earl Nightengale

ENJOY WHAT YOU DO

Blair Boyer, director of career services at DeVry Institute of Technology-Atlanta, loves her job. "If you don't like it, you can't fake it." Boyer has worked for the college for nine years, and she admits she's hit some low points in her career. She feels fortunate, however, to have worked for people who found ways to challenge her until her next promotion.

She also believes it's important to recognize when you need a change. "Read your own barometer; it's the best way to get along with yourself. It will help you make it easier on your employees when you're having a rough day." When she's doing the work she loves but feels especially stressed, she's honest about it with her staff, and they give her space.

Boyer enjoys the many different people with whom she interacts. She encourages others to discover what they like to do and supports decisions that lead to new opportunities.

DON'T WASTE TIME ON NEGATIVE THOUGHTS

Difficult situations, tough decisions, and just plain bad days can interfere with your success. Some believe it doesn't have to happen, that it's all in the way we look at life. One of those people is Hal Platt, business consultant at American Software. For over a decade, he's worked in a rapidly changing, high tech environment. While some people have fought the coming of the computer revolution, Platt has welcomed change.

> "I look for ways to stay current by reading and learning on the job. Because I train customers how to use our products and software, I need to keep up with new trends in the industry. I learn from participants in my classes. I encourage questions to my way of thinking—I recognize my thoughts influence how they learn. I try not to let a problem or how I feel personally interfere with my job as an instructor and representative of the company."

Negative thoughts are also seen as destructive by Ellen Bernstein. "As a supervisor in charge of 150 women in a sewing room, I know that if I'm having a bad day, it will impact my workers immediately. I can't afford to have them against me—I'm outnumbered. I consciously keep my attitude in check and if I don't, they let me know."

FIND WAYS TO LEARN NEW THINGS

Professional associations provide stimulation for learning. However, sometimes you think you're too busy to attend a dinner meeting or seminar. You may be tired or bored with the idea of networking with people.

There's another perspective, however, which is shared by Jean Rode, product manager for Global Payment Systems. She joined her local Chamber of Commerce and became a member of a subgroup that focuses on quality. Each month they meet and discuss quality practices in the areas of customer service, training, hiring, performance appraisal, and anything else that falls within the main topic.

"Being able to participate is a perk that's comparable to a pay increase," said Rode. Her employer allows her one-half day each month to attend meetings. In addition, she's permitted another five hours of company time to participate on another committee. She finds that her energy level is recharged after she interacts with different people with new ideas. "It helps me stay focused and fresh as a manager."

Why not make a commitment to yourself to get involved in a professional association or community activity? You may be surprised at the impact on your attitude.

DEMONSTRATE THE WORK ETHIC YOU EXPECT

Everyone has a need for attitude renewal from time to time. Being a manager is a tough job, right up there with being a parent. If you're not in a good frame of mind, everyone around you suffers.

For example, a friend of mine who's a partner in a prestigious law firm had a reputation for being hard-nosed and unforgiving. His direct reports had lost respect for him when one day they noticed a subtle change in his attitude. They waited for the other shoe to drop; it didn't. He gradually changed and evolved into one of the most well-liked and highly thought of employees in the firm. One year later, he was a different man.

He didn't have a major life change or a near-death experience. He learned the importance of demonstrating the work ethic he expects after another partner took him aside and shared information about how others felt about his behavior. It was a difficult criticism to swallow, especially from a peer, but he now walks the talk. Turnover has dropped significantly in his department. His employees no longer avoid him. He's a decent guy to be around.

START EACH DAY WITH A POSITIVE THOUGHT

How you begin your day is up to you. A positive thought or goal will impact everyone you come in contact with.

In an article entitled "Off The Cuff" by Jennifer Laabs, which was published in *Personnel Journal*, readers were asked at random the following question:[1]

> "Is there one thought, goal, or assumption that you always begin your day with?"

> Al Doran, director, HRMS York University in Ontario, Canada, responded, "As for the major thought each day—it's one of pride to be working with a first-class team of professionals on a great project. As for an assumption—because I'm dealing with all new technology, the day will be full of surprises. As for a goal—it's to make some progress toward the major milestone in a project: extending the HRMS system to a wider user community is just around the corner, bringing an opportunity to apply technology to a number of human resources issues.

> "Although I'm not a religious person," says Don Grimme, manager, human resources programs for Motorola in Fort Lauderdale, FL, "the *Serenity Prayer* is often in my thoughts at the beginning of (and during) my day: 'God grant me the *Serenity* to accept the things I cannot change, the *Courage* to change the things I can and the *Wisdom* to know the difference.'"

> Kurt Greene, lead training specialist for GE Power Systems in Schenectady, NY, answered, "I always start each day with a

little planning and solitude. Stephen Covey has his seven habits, and since there are seven days of the week, I spend a few minutes pondering 'today's habit.' Then, I wrap up this session thinking about 'the four F's': be *Focused*, be *Fast*, be *Flexible*, be *Friendly*."

Janet Garber, employment/employee relations manager for Cornell University Medical College in New York, NY, says, "I try to start each day with a commitment to a philosophy/ motto I adopted a year ago: 'Happiness is a choice.' This way of looking at things—essentially totaling up my blessings and not dwelling on my failures—works for me, and I try to impart this viewpoint to others whom I counsel. As someone who grew up in New York City, cynical and negative, I've found that I've become increasingly positive as the years go on (I'm 48). I've learned: Life is what you make it."

HELPING OTHERS HELPS YOURSELF

Rod Kennedy, Ph.D., a psychologist with the U.S. Department of Labor, keeps a positive outlook, not only for himself, but for the dozens of people on his yearly caseload. "I enjoy my work and recognize that my attitude has a profound affect on my clients," said Kennedy.

A vocational counselor for over 25 years, he works with individuals who are making career changes, choices, and adjustments. Some have been downsized and have been looking for work for 12 months or more. "It's hard for them not to lose hope when they can't find a job and have a family to support," added Kennedy. He encourages, teaches, and in many cases, locates resources for additional education or retraining.

"As a counselor I have to remain emotionally free from their problems. I stay away from irrational thinking. Many of the people I see have experienced an injustice—there's a lot of that in the workplace. Some have been abused by their employers. I can't help them if I get upset about their problems."

He keeps a positive attitude because he knows that he is of most value to his clients if he teaches them to help themselves. And, in return, the gratification he gets from his work helps him keep a positive attitude.

SET YOUR MENTAL BAROMETER

Managers are responsible for their attitudes. If they can't manage their own thoughts, it's difficult to positively influence others. Stephen Covey, in *The 7 Habits of Highly Effective People*, writes about vision, leadership, and the idea that the way we see the problem is the problem.

Michael Schneider, regional vice president for Omni Hotels, also has a similar strategy for maintaining a positive attitude—he works at it every day.

> "I look at the physical, spiritual and mental sides of my life. I do something daily to fulfill each aspect. For example, I work out at least one hour each day. I get up every morning at 5:30 and read from my favorite trilogy of Dr. Norman Vincent Peale books. I believe, as he did, that whatever you feel, you experience. If it's negative, you've got a lot to overcome."

Schneider's employed in the fast-paced hospitality industry. He works hard at polishing his management skills in a high-turnover environment. He sets the tone for the day by making an extra effort to say "good morning" to each team member. He improves his communication skills by concentrating on listening and reflecting back what he hears. He recognizes the positive impact of a manager's good attitude on the work force and is always striving to improve.

"Picture yourself succeeding, and your subconscious will respond accordingly," added Schneider. He has faith in himself and his ability to be a good manager—but he works at it.

EVEN WHEN YOU DON'T FEEL LIKE IT

My paternal grandmother passed away in 1930 at the age of 58. I never knew her—my father barely did. She had 11 children who grew to adulthood, and she left a legacy for 12 grandchildren. Four feet and eight inches tall, she carried a weight on her shoulders that only an immigrant could appreciate. It was a hard life.

I've been told she had a positive attitude even when she didn't feel like it. Some would view her as trapped—she saw herself living a dream. She accepted responsibility for her situation. She learned to manage her environment and get what she needed for her family.

Attitude is critical to the success or failure of grandmothers as well as leaders in businesses. Research shows that people are hired and promoted because of their attitude as much as anything else. Yet, how often do you think to yourself, "I don't like my job," or "I hate my boss," or "I have to find another place to work—I can't stand it here?" You may not always feel like doing what you're supposed to be doing, but you may not have a choice.

Here are some ideas you might want to try "when you don't feel like it":

❖ Accept the idea that you alone are responsible for your happiness.

❖ Picture yourself in control of your environment.

❖ Look for the best in people and life.

❖ Don't talk about your problems.

❖ Fantasize about your ideal job—then make plans to get it, step by step.

❖ Separate work from pleasure—plan for relaxation.

❖ Take on an attitude of self-confidence.

❖ Treat everyone like a VIP.

Life is a smorgasbord of opportunity; yet many people eat hot dogs and beans by choice and complain about it. One person who fit this profile at one time is Steve Zorn. He saw himself as a leader in his organization, but he grumbled a lot when "he didn't feel like it." His attitude created problems for himself and his employees. He made himself miserable but didn't recognize the problem. It took a team of sensitive employees to help him adjust his attitude. He now carries the torch and helps others, as Earl Nightingale said, "Turn on the lights and bring up the music."

Remember the "rotten apple principle"—one bad apple can spoil the whole barrel. Don't let it be you.

FIND A RELEASE

The pressures of professional and personal lives can interrupt the positive energy of even the most enthusiastic managers. When it happens, it also affects the people around us.

Seeing the best in people and situations is how Patricia Forsyth, director of marketing and public relations for Planned Parenthood of Atlanta, lives her life. When she's facing a negative situation, like the downsizing she was part of several years ago, she looks for a release and a way to turn a negative into a plus.

Dancing provides the physical and emotional release she needs. She started ballet classes almost three years ago. "I began late in life something I thought I would enjoy. Dancing helps me remove myself from what's bothering me, as well as from stress in general," said Forsyth. Other members of her class range from professional ballerinas to aspiring children. "I spoil myself in this way, sometimes five to six classes each week. I love dancing. It helps keep my attitude where it always needs to be—up."

DON'T AIR YOUR DIRTY LAUNDRY

No one wants to listen to your problems. Complainers are shunned almost everywhere. It's no one's business except your own and that of your manager if you have a complaint. Jane Duggan, M.D., chief of anesthesiology at Wesley Woods Geriatric Hospital, an affiliate of Emory University System of Health Care, feels very strongly about this subject. "A leader with a negative attitude is like a malignancy that spreads negativism everywhere," said Duggan.

She believes that one of the ways to control bad attitudes is by discouraging employees from complaining to each other over and over instead of seeking a resolution. She added, "Anything less than a positive attitude allows people to feed on each other's unhappiness. If you have a problem, you need to speak with your supervisor or someone else who can do something about it."

It's easier to stay in shape mentally than to get back into shape once you've lost a positive attitude. She believes that it's okay to have an 80/20 split in attitude as long as the 80 is the positive side.

FIND YOUR CREATIVE ATTITUDE

Padi Selwyn is a speaker specializing in creativity and innovation for business. She's also president of Selwyn Associates and the co-author of *Living Your Life Out Loud: How To Unlock Your Creativity and Unleash Your Joy.*

Known as "The Entrepreneurial Energizer," she believes that by adopting a creative attitude, you can enhance your creative powers and help those around you do the same. All you need is:

1. **A Yes *And* Attitude**—Rather than a yes, *but* attitude. Try being an angel's advocate rather than a devil's advocate. Rather than focusing on what won't work, try thinking about how to take an idea and elevate it to its next step.

    Watch out for the tendency to kill ideas. Statements such as "It's never been done before," "It's too complicated," "Our attorneys will never let us do it," or "We've tried that two years ago, and it bombed" inhibit creativity. During meetings, don't allow any negative comments until all ideas are out on the table. Encourage crazy ideas too—questions such as "What are some ideas that could get us fired?" are terrific idea stimulators and often lead to usable ideas with some variations.

2. **Have a Beginner's Mind**—Looking at old problems with new, fresh insight isn't easy, but it can be done. When a child asked Edward Land why he couldn't have his photo right after Land took it (back in the 1940s), Land took on the child's challenge and went on to develop the Polaroid camera.

Inviting input from people who know little or nothing about the problem can often lead to breakthrough ideas. One East Coast company in the creative consulting business brings 10-year-olds to clients' meetings for just this reason. Ignorant and uninformed people often ask the obvious questions we don't see, leading to exciting new innovations.

3. **No Need to Be Right**—Keeping an open mind and letting go of our need to be right helps keep us receptive to new ideas. Avoid hardening of the attitudes by being open-minded. Notice how often you need to be right and lighten up. It will loosen your creative strings by doing so!

4. **Willingness to Suspend Judgement**—New ideas are very fragile—stomp them out as they come up and soon they'll stop coming altogether. Ideas are like red wine, they need time to breathe. Learn to be an encourager of ideas, and withhold judgement as long as possible. This goes for your own ideas and your colleagues ideas as well. Silence the inner censor and watch creativity in your organization soar.

5. **Recognize and Let Go of Assumptions**—When we look at our assumptions, we often find opportunities hidden inside them. By learning to let go of our assumptions, we can bring marvelous new innovations to light. Keep asking why, why, why and you'll be surprised at the answers. Watch new possibilities blossom.[2]

MAKE IT EASY ON YOURSELF

Some people unknowingly clutter their lives with negative factors that make it difficult to be positive. They surround themselves with unnecessary problem-producing possessions, people, or commitments. Then they complain about the complexities of their lives.

It's easy to get overcommitted. When someone asks for your help, it's a lot more difficult to say "no" than "yes."

For example, when a friend joined the Newcomers organization upon relocating for her husband's new job, she found herself caught up in several volunteer activities. She took on the roles of leader for community involvement and co-chair for travel and tours, and agreed to serve a one-year term as vice president of membership. Newcomers was looking for new faces and new leadership—she fit the profile. Don't get me wrong. They're a wonderful organization. She just didn't know when enough was too much.

Aside from being a full-time homemaker with three children under the age of ten, she sang in the church choir, was a Cub Scout leader and coached girls' soccer. Her husband traveled extensively, so it wasn't uncommon for her to be alone with the kids for two weeks at a time. A once bright attitude began to fade. She considered the possibility of dropping out of some of her activities. She felt they needed her but so did her family. She compromised. Her outlook on life improved, and no one thought any less of her.

An uncluttered focus allows us to accept and enjoy life's pleasures. The next time you're feeling overwhelmed with responsibility take a look at the "clutter" you're hanging onto. Are there unused, unnecessary, and unwanted possessions? Are there too many commitments? Is your career-home relationship out of balance? Do you find yourself putting off the important things? Are you holding on to a worn-out relationship? If your answer to any of these questions is "yes" and your attitude is not where you think it should be, it may be time for a change.

LIVE BY A PERSONAL MISSION STATEMENT

In June of 1996, while attending the Society for Human Resource Management conference in Chicago, I met many people and interviewed several of them for this book. One individual particularly stands out in my mind because of his personal philosophy for life and leading people. I'm speaking of Jim Jose, Ph.D. and senior advisor for human resources for Alyeska Pipeline Service Company in Anchorage. This incredibly positive human being graciously shared his personal mission statement with me. It's his way of staying on top of his attitude.

Personal Mission of James R. Jose

PREAMBLE

There are three things that matter most to me:

- ❖ faith in God, the source of all natural laws and goodness;

- ❖ love of family and friends, faith's fullest expression;

- ❖ making a difference in the lives of others, love's ultimate gift.

MISSION

Accordingly, my mission is:

- ❖ to lead a principle-centered life, and, through this commitment, to help others to become more effective and successful in their work and their life;

- ❖ to help organizations develop and maintain healthy cultures;

- ❖ to make a positive difference in the life of at least one individual every day and to have meaning to everyone with whom I interact for any length of time.

LEGACY

In pursuing this mission, I want to create a legacy that will be articulated by those who understand me as follows:

- ❖ We were **compassionate** when he understood and believed in a vision and felt he could make it happen, because sometimes he succeeded and sometimes he did not, but always with some measure of elegance;

- ❖ We were **trusting** when he told us that we each were blessed with opportunities for growth and change, including himself, because we knew he would be there to help us realize these opportunities and that he would ask that we do the same for him;

- ❖ We were **hopeful** when he assured us that something good would come from well-intentioned efforts that were grounded in principles, enriched with values, and nurtured with feelings;

❖ We **understood** his passion was in his giving, because then is when he did his best and could learn to do better;

❖ We **embraced** his greatest opportunity for growth to first understand, then to be understood, because he knew that in understanding what another was communicating was the key to finding value;

❖ We **valued** his desire to influence the development of organizations and to make them healthy through the development of people, because we knew that he was committed to the principle that people were the purest and most robust resource of any organization;

❖ We were **moved** by his love of coaching and teaching others—particularly team leaders—to love, and work, and laugh, to learn and to grow beyond their current ranges, for he believed that deep within each of us was a need to go beyond our comfort zones, if only for one step, one day at a time, for the rest of our lives;

❖ We were **impressed** that he could have random thoughts on any topic, and yet was disciplined by his understanding that he had to make choices before acting on those thoughts;

❖ We **appreciated** his belief that he did not control the consequences of his actions or the actions of others;

❖ And, we **accepted** that the true meaning of responsibility to him was the ability to respond, because in responding, he could exercise the freedom to choose;

❖ We **respected** his conviction that the ultimate human freedom for him was the power to choose his response to any human condition—the power to choose his attitude in any situation—even those over which he had no control; he understood that he could pattern his actions accordingly;

❖ We were **inspired** that he did not let the things he could do nothing about interfere with the things he could do a great deal about;

❖ We were **at peace** when we knew his principles and values were clear, because we knew that, then, his decisions were easy, and we could embrace them;

> ❖ We were **motivated** by his unending pursuit of personal mastery and the core values of proactivity, balance, humility, genuineness, courage and growth, because he convinced us they were worthy pursuits and that we, too, should pay attention to them;
>
> ❖ And although we were sad when he faltered, our tears of sadness were blended with tears of understanding, even joy, because we knew he would try to learn from those times, and we knew above all that deep within himself, he truly believed that he was a winner at life and living;
>
> ❖ And, finally we were **enthused** by his devotion to the teachings of his favorite prayer and his favorite hymn: the *Serenity Prayer* and *Amazing Grace.*

Jim Jose is not only an interesting man but, I suspect, a wonderful leader. His closing thoughts include an inspiring quote from an unknown author:

"When we reach the edge of all the light we have and take the step into the darkness of the unknown, we must believe one of two things will happen: There will be something solid to stand on, or we will be taught to fly."

STAY PHYSICALLY AND MENTALLY FIT

I met Lynn Bates, human resources director for Zadall Systems Group, Inc., in Dallas and knew immediately that I was about to spend the day with a very positive woman. I have no doubt that she impacts the people she interfaces with in many ways. When I asked her what was behind her energy and enthusiasm for life, Bates had two things to say: "I believe in being physically fit. Vitamins, good nutrition, and enough sleep all play a big part in how I feel about myself. I lift weights, take aerobics classes, bike, run, use the stairclimber and generally do whatever it takes to stay in shape. But that's only half of what it takes to keep a good attitude."

Second to physical health for Bates is mental health.

"I have to be very organized to be happy with myself. I guess I was born with a personality that requires staying on top of things in order to feel comfortable. If I have 100 items on my "to-do" list, that's fine as long as I know it's there and what I need to do to keep it under control. But if I have 10 items on the list and am not organized, it's a problem for me," explained Bates.

A single mom, she works and goes to school. She knows that if she doesn't balance personal and professional, physical and mental, her attitude may not be at an acceptable level for herself.

When she took the position as human resources director at Zadall, she had no predecessor. Therefore, she had no policies, procedures, new hire orientation program, etc., in place to help her get started. The company who purchased Zadall was very supportive. Together with corporate human resources, Bates built a department from scratch. Once again, she relied on a combination of staying physically active and mentally fit.

DON'T TAKE LIFE TOO SERIOUSLY

Jennifer Black, operations manager for Procter & Gamble, has a good sense of humor, laughs a lot, and says she never takes life too seriously. She also looks for ways to motivate her staff to follow her example.

Black enjoys sending cartoons and funny stories to her employees. It helps everyone lighten up. She doesn't hesitate to make fun of herself either. On a sales call to a major grocery chain, she said she "dramatically failed." In sharing the story with her employees, she joked about it and then told them how she turned that adventure into a successful sale. "I went back to the store, used my sense of humor and said, 'Let's pretend I was never here and start over.'" It worked, and she got the order.

There's a lot of laughter at quarterly sales meetings. Black awards "Kudo" bars for a good job and mylar balloons for small accomplishments. Once she even awarded herself the "sweet tart award," a silly recognition for something she goofed up. In addition, they always have fun and do something new and special. Sometimes they bowl or attend a baseball game.

She's also a problem-solver and very supportive of her team. She encourages them to try. She backs her people 100%. She trusts them and if they fail, it's OK—together they look at ways to correct the problem and maybe even have a good chuckle. Of course, they all learn from every experience—good or bad.

In talking about her philosophy and why she never takes life too seriously, Black shared this, "Life is short, and you better enjoy it while you're here. Don't be afraid of new things; you may never get the chance again."

Black continues to live life by her philosophy of laughter, and imparts her energy, enthusiasm, and positive attitude to all who know her.

S ET GOALS

Have you ever heard the expression, "Be careful what you wish; chances are you'll get it?" Translated into business terms, it means—before staking goal posts and racing down some field with the ball, it's important to take a close, careful look at your goals. It's essential to take the time to define what success means to you.

Researchers have found that most peak performers are obsessive goal setters motivated by compelling, burning, internal goals. Goal-setting has a critical impact on your attitude.

It takes time to set goals, but it's worth the effort. Your goals should be:

❖ **Clearly defined, specific, and measurable**. You waste a lot of time when you have only vague goals or no ideas of what you want to accomplish.

❖ **Realistic**. They need to be attainable to prevent frustration.

❖ **Your own**. They need to be your own, not imposed by someone else unless you agree.

❖ **Stated positively.** Psychologists say that if you could tape record your conversations on any given day, 95% of what you say could be classified as negative. State your goals in a positive way.

❖ **Flexible.** Your goals should change as you do.

❖ **Continually updated.** By the time you reach a goal, you should already have a new goal in mind.

❖ **Set with a deadline in mind.** Deadlines help you avoid procrastinating.

❖ **Visualized.** Every chance you get, play a picture in your mind of what you plan to accomplish.

❖ **Written.** Then carry them with you wherever you go. Take them out when you're stuck in traffic. Tape your goals to your bathroom mirror so that you see them at least once each day. Do whatever it takes.

The most effective people don't waste time on trivia; they focus their efforts on worthwhile, important, strategic matters. They ignore or delegate the less important things. They know that goal setting definitely impacts their attitude.

ASSOCIATE WITH POSITIVE PEOPLE

Nothing does more to boost a sagging attitude than association with positive people. In the words of Earl Nightengale: "A great attitude...seems to magically connect us to all sorts of opportunities that were somehow absent before the change."

For example, Moses Brand, an independent consultant, is a happy-go-lucky guy, and the kind of person everyone wants to be around. He says he can't take full credit for his attitude and outlook on life because he gets lots of help from his friends. "I associate with positive people—those who like to have fun, enjoy a good laugh, and leave their mark on others."

Becky Hastings has the same wonderful outlook. She always seems to find some good in the bad that inevitably creeps into everyone's life.

Hastings is also someone who draws a crowd at a party because of her energy and enthusiasm. She said, "I learned long ago that negative people could emotionally bring me down. I know that's something I want to avoid at all costs, so I seek out positive people. I don't have time for the morale busters."

Many years ago my husband and I decided to have a party and invite 50 of the most fun-loving and positive people we knew. It was an experiment of sorts to see what would happen when so many people with similar personalities gathered together. Most didn't know each other; but by the end of the evening, which was really the early morning hours, we thought the roof would blow off from the energy within the house. It was incredible!

A positive attitude brings personal satisfaction, better relationships, and success in a meaningful career. Positive people will help you come closer to reaching your life goals. You win any way you look at it.

TALK TO YOURSELF

We all know that the thoughts which enter our minds aren't always upbeat. It's easy to fall into the trap of scolding ourselves with negative self-talk. It's a bad habit, and it's contagious but changeable.

For John Ginty, a classified advertising account executive for *The Boston Globe* newspaper, self-talk works well. He said, "I consciously think positive thoughts. It helps me stay on an even keel, especially when facing production deadlines."

Ginty networks with other executives in similar positions and has discerned that many other account executives also find positive self-talk valuable in maintaining a good attitude.

Even his student intern has caught on. Together they use self-talk and humor when they're under pressure and a bit discouraged. They laugh as they remind each other that "This is not a normal day," said Ginty. Self-talk has helped him maintain a positive attitude and contributed to his successful career of nearly 30 years with the same employer.

WHY NOT YOU?

At the funeral for a friend's father, her grieving mother was overcome with sadness. When she spoke aloud "Why me?", an insensitive mourner responded, "Why not you?"

I've always remembered that story. However, I use the "Why not you?" to my advantage. Whenever I have a doubt about being able to accomplish something, I say to myself, "Why not me?" Why shouldn't I be the person who's awarded the contract, who writes the book, who gets the speaking engagement? Why should it be someone else? Of course I don't always get what I want, but more often than not I do. I believe it's because of the "I can do it attitude" which I've always had, but like most people, sometimes forget to use.

KICK THE HABIT

A bad attitude is like a bad habit—usually difficult to kick. But not for Don Frenner, who recently retired after 33 years as a U.S. Postal Service carrier. "I was the person who delivered your mail on time. I walked through rain, sleet, and snow as well as 100-degree temperatures. I've also had my share of dog bites. I'm not complaining but there was a time when I wasn't very pleasant to be around—until I 'kicked the habit.'" Frenner refers to a negative attitude that he believes earned him a reputation as a grouch. He also thinks it kept him from a promotion. However, he blames only himself. "I didn't know when to keep my mouth shut," said Frenner.

He changed his attitude by insulating himself against things that bothered him. Elwood N. Chapman in his book *Attitude—Your Most Priceless Possession*, calls it isolating or detaching negative thoughts so they can't impact attitude too strongly. Chapman encourages people to "find methods to push bad thoughts to the outer perimeter of your focus in order to reduce them in size and keep them at bay."

For example, when Frenner's attitude started to deteriorate, he thought about his three children and how they depended on him—what would happen if he lost his job? Sometimes he worked faster and harder to get the work done. The speed and intensity helped him shift his focus away from the negative thoughts in his head. He devoted ten minutes in his mind each day to dealing with problems, then forced himself to push his bad feelings out of his mind as quickly as they occurred. He reserved time after dinner for negative thinking. "It was the best way for me to rid myself of negative thoughts, like how inconsiderate people are by not shoveling their walks in winter. One of my pet peeves, it drove me crazy. I'd harbor those feelings and when I got back to the post office, I'd explode," explained Frenner.

Lastly, he made a commitment to himself to change his attitude toward customers. "Sometimes I saw them as the enemy. Dirty kids, untamed pets, rude reactions when asked to sign for a delivery—I forgot about all the good people on my route. I focused only on the few I didn't like," said Frenner.

Fortunately, he kicked the habit before it destroyed his relationship with his boss and co-workers. His supervisor's image of him improved as his attitude did, almost like magic.

Today, Don Frenner is busy enjoying retirement and his seven grand-children. He makes an extra-special effort to set a good example for them. He realizes that changing his attitude changed how people feel about him.

ONCE UPON A TIME

John LaCroix, manager of planning and information on the governmental affairs staff at Ford Motor Company, uses writing to keep his attitude where he wants it. He started writing books for children and young adults as an escape from some of the job pressures. He's always done a lot of writing in his work at Ford, but the idea of writing novels came about when he helped his son start a business after college. "He's very creative, and, together, we built a 1800s Christmas village to scale that was 16 feet high. It filled an ice arena. In the end, we were cheated out of $30,000, my money, and I was more than furious!"

To channel his anger into positive energy, he started to write. This Christmas show, where a friend displayed a castle that was 8 feet long, 8 feet high, and 4 feet deep, was the turning point for LaCroix. He wrote a short story about the castle. Children could read the story written on parchment as they viewed the castle. It grew to a 4,200-word short story that is now a 175-page novel for young adults—and there will be a sequel.

His newest book, based on personal tragedy and recovery is titled *Why Do I Have to Die?* With a background in philosophy and theology, he's capturing the hearts and minds of a diverse population of readers through his work. He also writes poetry.

Being a manager and working for someone else may not always be a wonderful experience, but there are many ways to continue to grow, learn, and keep up the attitude needed to be a successful leader inside or outside your organization. For LaCroix, "once upon a time" was the beginning of a dream come true.

REWARD YOURSELF

Most of us, consciously or not, reward ourselves when we reach a goal or are happy with an achievement. Rewards range from purchasing an item we've been wanting to treating ourselves to a special lunch or dinner—and everything in between. When Barbara Daniel, a police officer for 22 years, rewards herself, she does so for a reason. "I feel when I've worked hard on a special project or have a great day, I've earned some extra time for me. I reward myself with reading strictly for pleasure. I love to browse through cookbooks and magazines."

On days when she's not as happy with her attitude or accomplishments, she reminds herself that she's not perfect and that there are times when she won't be as successful as she would like. "I remind myself of my past successes and practice focusing on the blessings in my life. I often think about the things I'm grateful for first thing in the morning and again at the end of the day," said Daniel. She finds positive self-talk valuable and a reward in its own way.

In addition to her work in law enforcement, specifically crime prevention and community relations, Daniel is a motivational speaker. She is well-known for her presentations on women's safety, which she's been doing for 30 years.

SUMMARY

We all have times in our lives when we need to renew our attitudes. An attitudinal rut is no fun. According to Jeffrey J. Hallett, author of *Worklife Visions: Redefining Work for the Information Economy*, in any work force, there are three attitudes guaranteed to generate low morale, low productivity, and inability to compete effectively. They are:

1. To believe we work strictly for someone else.

2. To believe there is a result that's good enough.

3. To believe there is some needed effort that's not our job.

He points out that you can't force people to work smarter, more creatively, or more passionately. That effort comes from inside. Those who make the biggest contributions to an organization do so because they are self-motivated. Positive attitudes transmit friendly vibrations. A good attitude attracts like a magnet.

Your attitude is tied to your survival in the business world. Shifting work values, technological change, organizational downsizing, and a host of unforeseeable challenges—many of which are beyond your control—impact your attitude and morale. Successful living is the direct result of being in charge of your attitude and not allowing your sense of self-worth to be dependent on your successes or failures.

Arlene V. Keen, former director of senior adults for Dorchester-Waylyn Baptist Church in Charleston Heights, SC, wrote an article which reminds me of the importance of a good attitude. I've had it tacked on a bulletin board in my office since May, 1980, when I first read it. It's called *My Mountain—It Takes a Lifetime to Climb*.

> I remember one particular vacation in the mountains with friends several years ago. It seemed that everyone had an insatiable desire to climb to the top of that one mountain. We, too, started out to do so. We had not gone far before two of us decided we would just rest and let the others go on— we felt that there was not that much excitement and interest to give us the desire to go on. Then, a sprightly old gentleman coming down saw us sitting there, and stopped and said, "What's the matter, can't make it?" He turned and pointed

toward the top of the mountain and continued, "You don't know what you're missing; it shore is purty up there. I'm 85 today, and I made it all the way to the top. Too bad you can't make it." With that, we practically ran to get to the top.

Looking back, that mountain experience somehow parallels my life. For more than 65 years, I have been climbing a mountain called "life." Now, I have entered a new phase of my "life mountain," nearing the top—retirement.

I am not finding a wealth of material things but a storehouse of spiritual wealth. I want to guide the footsteps of younger climbers who seemingly cannot find their way. I want to encourage them by telling them what a wonderful climb they can have.

Life is a journey, not a destination. The business of life is not about being busy—it's about living. Some say the ingredients of happiness are so simple that they can be counted on one hand. People are not happy with life unless they are reasonably satisfied with themselves. The quest for tranquility begins with attitude.

CHECKLIST FOR

GETTING IN TOUCH WITH YOUR ATTITUDE

√ Do you enjoy your work? If not, maybe it's time for a change.

√ How do you rid yourself of negative thoughts?

√ How do you demonstrate the work ethic you expect?

√ What do you do to relieve stress?

√ When you have a problem, are you tempted to complain to others? How else could you handle it?

√ What do you do for fun?

√ Do you set goals for yourself? If not, what's holding you back?

√ What kinds of people do you enjoy associating with the most? If they're not positive people, why are you wasting your time?

√ What do you do to prevent negative self-talk?

√ What do you do to reward yourself?

√ How has your attitude impacted those around you in the last 30 days?

√ If you're not happy with yourself, what can you do to change that?

Endnotes

1. Reprinted with permission of *Personnel Journal*, ACC Communications, Inc., Costa Mesa, CA, all rights reserved. "Off The Cuff" by Jennifer J. Laabs, © February 1996.

2. Reprinted with written permission of Padi Selwyn.

Additional Reading

Alston, Harvey. *"Be the Best"—A Focus on Individual Responsibility for Achieving.* Dubuque, IA: Kendall/Hunt Publishing Company, 1994.

Araoz, Dr. Daniel L. and Dr. William Sutton. *Reengineering Yourself—A Blueprint for Personal Success in The New Corporate Culture.* Holbrook, MA: Bob Adams, Inc., 1994.

Beatty, Maura. *Bootstrap Words (Pulling Yourself Up!)* Dubuque, IA: Kendall/Hunt Publishing Company, 1994.

DeAngelis, Barbara. *Confidence—Finding It and Living It.* Carson, CA: Hay House, Inc., 1995.

Deep, Sam and Lyle Sussman. *Yes, You Can!—1,200 Inspiring Ideas for Work, Home and Happiness.* Reading, MA: Addison-Wesley Publishing Company, 1996.

Dyer, Wayne W. *Staying on the Path.* Carson, CA: Hay House, Inc., 1995.

Dyer, Wayne W. *Your Sacred Self—Making the Decision to Be Free.* New York, NY: Harper Collins Publishers, 1995.

Ford, Henry. *Success Is You.* Dubuque, IA: Kendall/Hunt Publishing Company, 1994.

Gower, Stephen M. *What Do They See When They See You Coming?* Toccoa, GA: Lectern Publishing, 1994.

Harrell, Keith D. *Attitude Is Everything—A Tune-Up to Enhance Your Life.* Dubuque, IA: Kendall/Hunt Publishing Company, 1995.

Jaffe, Dennis T., Cynthia D. Scott and Glenn R. Tobe. *Rekindling Commitment—How to Revitalize Yourself, Your Work, and Your Organization.* San Francisco, CA: Jossey-Bass, 1993.

Jolley, Willie. *It Only Takes a Minute to Change Your Life!* Dubuque, IA: Kendall/Hunt Publishing Company, 1994.

Mannering, Dennis E. *Attitudes Are Contagious...Are Yours Worth Catching?* Green Bay, WI: Options Unlimited, Inc., 1992.

Minchinton, Jerry. *Maximum Self-Esteem—The Handbook for Reclaiming Your Sense of Self-Worth.* Vanzant, MO: Arnford House Publishers, 1993.

Patent, Arnold M. *You Can Have It All.* Hillsboro, OR: Beyond Words Publishers, 1995.

Rasberry, Salli and Padi Selwyn. *Living Your Life Out Loud: How To Unlock Your Creativity and Unleash Your Joy.* New York, NY: Pocket Books, 1995.

Ribeird, Lair, Dr. *Attitude Is No Success.* New York, NY: St. Martin's Press, 1996.

Rich, David A. *How To Stay Motivated on a Daily Basis*. Dubuque, IA: Kendall/Hunt Publishing Company, 1994.

Shechtman, Morris R. *Working Without a Net—How to Survive & Thrive in Today's High Risk Business World*. Englewood Cliffs, NJ: Prentice Hall, 1994.

Tibbs, Gloria. *The Goldfinger Attitude*. Dubuque, IA: Kendall/Hunt Publishing Company, 1994.

PYGMALION'S FAIR LADY

(The Power of Expectation)

"If you take a couple of drops of human dignity and respect—just a couple of drops—and put them on an employee, and if they believe you, they'll swell up just like a sponge."

—Tom Melohn

● ●

In George Bernard Shaw's *Pygmalion*, Eliza Doolittle explains,

"You see, really and truly, apart from the things anyone can pick up (appearance and manner of speaking), the difference between a lady and a flower girl is not how she behaves, but how she's treated. I shall always be a flower girl to Professor Higgins because he always treats me as a flower girl and always will; but I know I can be a lady to you because you always treat me as a lady and always will."

In Greek mythology, Pygmalion was a sculptor who carved a statue of a beautiful woman who came to life. The goddess Venus endowed the statue with life in response to Pygmalion's prayers.

Pygmalion, the basis for the musical *My Fair Lady*, has a similar theme—one person, by his or her effort, can transform another. Managers often play Pygmalion-like roles in developing employees who go on to surpass even their own expectations.

The idea of a self-fulfilling prophecy was conceptualized by Robert Merton, a professor of sociology at Columbia University. In his 1957 work, *Social Theory and Social Structure*, Merton said this phenomenon occurs when "a false definition of the situation evokes a new behavior which makes the original false conception come true." That is, once an expectation is set up, even if it isn't accurate, we tend to act in ways consistent with that expectation.

A dramatic illustration of the "Pygmalion effect" achieved notoriety in the 1960s when reported in *Look* magazine as "Sweeney's Miracle." Jim Sweeney taught at Tulane University and supervised for the biomedical computer center. He insisted that he could teach the janitor to operate a computer. Sweeney threatened to quit unless the administration allowed him to give the man a chance. Not only did the janitor become an operator, but he wound up overseeing the main computer room and training new employees. Sweeney's story illustrates an important point. The "Pygmalion effect" really begins with a belief in your own ability to manage yourself and others. The best managers share this belief.

In a 1969 *Harvard Business Review* article called "Pygmalion in Management," J. Sterling Livingston, a professor of business administration at Harvard University and president of the Sterling Institute, wrote this about managers:

> "If he has confidence in his ability to develop and stimulate them to high levels of performance, he will expect much of them and will treat them with the confidence that his expectations will be met. But if he has doubts about his ability to stimulate them, he will expect less of them and will treat them with less confidence."

In 1971, Robert Rosenthal, a professor of social psychology at Harvard, conducted an experiment. He told a group of students that he had developed a strain of superintelligent rats who could run mazes quickly. He then passed out normal rats at random, telling half of the students that they had the "maze bright" rats and the other half that they had the "maze-dull" rats. The "bright" rats improved daily in running the maze. They ran faster and more accurately. The "dull" rats refused to even budge from the starting point 29% of the time, while the "bright" rats refused only 11% of the time.

Managers with high expectations for their employees have a powerful tool for influencing the performance of others. Forming expectations of others, including employees, is natural and unavoidable. It all ties in with productivity, which is the key to success, but it doesn't happen automatically. It's the result of hard work by motivated, satisfied employees.

The first step to becoming a positive Pygmalion is to understand how you consciously and unconsciously manage people. Learn how to create high expectations, and the "Pygmalion effect" will work in helping you become a better manager.

REMEMBER CLEMENTINE

Many years ago a woman named Clementine worked for me. Her co-workers in the factory frequently serenaded her with *My Darling Clementine*. She had worked in the tobacco fields as a young woman and was proud to work in a factory at what she called a "respectable job."

One day I posted an opening for a Uniform Coordinator—someone to order, inventory, and distribute uniforms to new employees, as well as see to it that current workers had clean attire. Clementine applied along with a dozen other people.

After I interviewed all of the qualified applicants, I selected Clementine for the newly created position. I chose her because she knew everyone, was well-liked, and had what I perceived as the ability to learn the job. Her co-workers gave her a big "stepping up" party. I didn't know that Clementine had a lot of self-doubt about her capabilities that would prevent her from learning. Within a few days, however, I saw the problem. I discovered that she couldn't sleep for a week before she started her new job. I told her that she had been selected above all the others because I knew she was qualified and that she could learn everything she needed to know. I convinced her that she could master her responsibilities in the new environment, and she did.

Later, she taught herself to type and use a computer and was promoted to the position of office assistant. She excelled beyond everyone's expectations, but most of all her own. Today, she continues to encourage others—she's become a Pygmalion too.

START WITH NUMBER ONE

Increase productivity, improve employee relations, influence performance—it's "do-able" if the leaders at the top of the organization believe in the power of expectation and in themselves. No one knows the importance of managers who have faith in their people better than Bob Alton, chairman, president and CEO of Hickory Tech Corporation.

Not too long ago Alton found himself in a tough situation. Subsidiaries were losing money, and he knew a change in leadership was inevitable. The new players stepped in and made a dramatic difference. "We needed people who could inspire the work force through sincere belief in achieving what no one thought possible. Morale suffered until the right managers took over. They shook hands, walked around, rolled up their sleeves, and got involved. It sent a positive message," said Alton.

Encouragement and empowerment have helped the subsidiaries become profitable again. Employees feel good about themselves, their jobs, and the company. The power of expectation played a major role in the turnaround, according to Alton. But it started at the top.

GIVE ME NO CHOICE

Robb Jenkins, president of Excel Temporary Services, a subsidiary of AccuStaff, identifies his pet peeve as turnover. The company, which he started in 1990 after working for similar organizations, boasts very low turnover. In my interview with Jenkins, he shared the following: "Part of my job is to tell people they're doing a good job everyday. I see myself as a cheerleader who empowers the staff to maximize their potential."

He believes that the key to low turnover is to provide people with growth opportunity. Most people want some degree of autonomy and also want to learn new things. Although some of the positions offer more opportunity for advancement than others, there's something for everyone, according to Jenkins.

Part of the thinking here concerning power of expectation is that everyone is on equal footing. The operations staff who fill orders and have customer contact, members of the sales team, and corporate employees are given incentives to grow the business. "Everyone has a stake in the growth of the company. I want employees to feel like entrepreneurs—the ups and downs and be rewarded accordingly," said Jenkins. He says that's not the case in many other temporary agencies.

Contests to grow business involve all employees. They want to see each other succeed because it impacts everyone's pocketbook. He says they're all "rooting" for one another.

Lead Dog Group is the name of their company newsletter. Their mascot is a dog, and their motto is: "If you're not the lead dog, the view never changes." They even have postcards shaped like a dog looking over his shoulder. Employees send these to each other for a job well-done. "The postcards are very popular. Employees write a note of congratulations or thanks. I see them proudly displayed everywhere. It's a simple idea, but people love it," said Jenkins.

He's even coined the phrase "Give me no choice" in reference to sales people who want to have their own branch office. He lets them know that if they have the customer base to justify an office, they've got it. They have a lot of freedom to make decisions. "We call our branch offices 'branchises' as opposed to 'franchises,' which we are not. Managers can run the business as if it were their own without taking the financial risk of owning a franchise."

Excel Temporary Services has more than 20 locations and over 100 employees. With turnover running well below the industry average,

Jenkins insists that empowering leads to employees going above and beyond expectations. Bonuses, parties, and other goodies are all important, but believing in and supporting his people is what works best for his company.

THERE'S MORE THAN ONE WAY...

There are many ways to communicate the power of expectation—to be a Pygmalion to someone who needs your help. You can gently push as you encourage, or you can take a slightly different approach to express your confidence. That's exactly what Kathleen Tank, graphics manager for WITI-TV in Milwaukee, WI, did.

Tank had an employee who moved from on-air to print graphics. "I wanted her to believe in herself. I made suggestions to help her add depth to her designs. I pushed her into trying new things," explained Tank.

However, it wasn't until Tank hired a summer intern and put the employee in charge of teaching the intern the ropes that the employee began to blossom. "It always helps when you teach someone else—it solidifies it for yourself. It also helps build self-confidence," said Tank. That's how she helped the employee grow beyond her own expectations.

The employee eventually left the company and took a job with another organization where she had the opportunity to start a graphics operation from scratch. Tank believes that some of the employee's belief in herself came from having the chance to be a teacher—to share her expertise and, in turn, boost her own self-confidence.

RECOGNIZE THE FAMILY

Successful employees are backed by the faith their managers have in them. They work for leaders who provide support in good times as well as bad. One of those leaders is Nancy Peoplis, national accounts manager for Pharmacia & Upjohn Company. She believes the sky's the limit, and there's nothing her people can't do.

When congratulations are in order, employees receive her personal note of thanks. It says, "I told you someday all of this would be yours, and it is!" However, she doesn't stop there. Peoplis also sends a separate note to the employees' children: "Your mom/dad couldn't have done it without you." She personally expresses appreciation to family members when she meets them with a simple, "Your husband/wife does a great job for us."

Another way Peoplis involves family members is by taking the children of employees to lunch. It's her way of showing appreciation for their understanding of their parents' need to travel. She often includes employees' children in the special things she does. She wants the kids to feel part of their parents' careers.

When employees or their spouses have a baby, Peoplis sends a gift for the baby, mother, father, and siblings. She believes that small gestures of recognition for *all* family members are a nice way to show appreciation and earn employee loyalty.

In addition, Peoplis and her husband have prepared dinners in their home for her staff and their spouses. Everyone receives a gift with a handwritten note. She mentioned one dinner party that was especially meaningful. They had all had a disappointing year. They couldn't change the past, so they celebrated the future. They talked about what they had learned and what they planned to do differently in the next year. Spouses felt they had the opportunity to share in the company's future too.

STRUCTURE POSITIVE SITUATIONS

Leaders are often in a position to assure success for their employees by assigning tasks that make them winners. It's done by providing information about what you expect, offering incentives, making sure you support them and helping them achieve. Success breeds success.

Greg Adams, vice president of finance for a small family-owned research marketing firm, is known for his concern for people.

"I make positive results possible for my employees. For example, when my cost analyst had trouble on a project, we strategized and came up with a solution. He told me he needed more lead time. I knew that wasn't always possible, but we compromised. He does a great job if he feels comfortable with the amount of time he has in which to get the work done. I can control scheduling to a degree, and this helps him and the company meet set goals. It's a good situation for everyone," said Adams.

Anything a manager does to foster positive results will bring a certain mount of healthy self-respect to the workplace. And that leads to heightened morale and reduced turnover.

I T'S ALL IN YOUR MIND

Some Pygmalions are naturals. Others have to work at it. One who is definitely in the first group is Anne Kaiser, Southeast director of business development and sales support for KPMG Peat Marwick. When I spoke with Kaiser, she talked about her approach to managing people. "I have a mindset. I see one of my roles as helping individuals meet personal goals which, in turn, helps the firm meet business goals."

Kaiser accomplishes this by doing many different things to support and enjoy her employees. For example, she has working lunches once each month. "Breaking bread and the good that comes from the fellowship promotes positive energy," said Kaiser. She's always looking for ways to encourage people to dream and think about what they're doing, where they're going, and where they want to be. Sometimes she asks, "What's holding you back?"

Kaiser sees herself as a coach as well as a Pygmalion. She's mentored others and offered encouragement but, most of all, she's told them they could do whatever they set their minds to. For instance, she challenged one of her people to stretch and work on improving self-confidence, which ultimately resulted in a promotion for the employee. In Kaiser's words, "I gave the employee a chance to fly."

In questioning this ten-year veteran further about her dedication to the growing of others, she went back to the mindset. "If you're going to be successful in the firm, you have to like who you are. That goes for the manager as well," explained Kaiser.

In addition to her M&M candy dish, spirited messages on voice mail, and funny notes, Kaiser recognizes her staff with books—Pygmalion-type books that add to what she tries to offer them herself. Two of her favorite gifts are *The Sacred Journey* and *Too Good For Her Own Good*.

DO WHAT FAILURES ARE AFRAID TO DO

Even if you're not a sports fan, you probably know that Babe Ruth was a famous baseball player who hit more home runs (714) than any other major leaguer—until Henry Aaron broke his record. If you equate hitting a baseball in terms of success and failure, the biggest success would be a home run and the biggest failure, a strike-out. Theoretically, Babe could be considered one of the biggest successes— and, at the same time, one of the biggest failures—in baseball history. Even though the immortal Babe struck out nearly twice as many times as he homered, nobody remembers him for the strike-outs.

What's my point?

People who fulfill their potential, who achieve the most out of life, who are most successful, are those who are willing to take a risk—to take the chance of failing. Managers need to recognize that what causes most people to fail is that after one failure, they just stop trying.

Here's where Pygmalion comes in. Managers can watch talented people give up on themselves, or they can help them hit a home run which will benefit the organization, manager, and employee. So many people haven't begun to tap their full potential—maybe because of a fear of failure. Successful people make things happen; others wait— often a lifetime—for things to happen to them. They don't realize they have to take the initiative, the risk, the chance—and not worry about failing. Managers who believe in their employees and encourage calculated risk-taking put themselves at an advantage.

As you prepare to help your employees take calculated risks, be aware there are three categories of risk takers:

- ❖ **Not on your life**. These people would rather die than take a risk even if it means they'll continue to be unhappy or dissatisfied.

- ❖ **Addicted.** They take risks for the thrill of excitement, (going over Niagara Falls in a barrel) danger, and the unknown. Addicts, whether they are addicted to money, sex, drugs, or thrills, are dangerous to everyone.

- ❖ **Creative.** They pursue risk to improve their lives. They're not gamblers because they take risks only when they have some degree of control over the outcome. Research has shown that people in this category tend to handle stress well, have high self-esteem, and are less controlled than others by irrational fear.

Chances are you have employees in all three categories. If you're lucky, you have a lot of "creative" types. But whether you're a new manager or a seasoned pro, never lose sight of the fact that anyone who hits a home run is also going to strike out a lot. Your employees have got to try for the home run. Don't allow them to be crushed by one or two failures. Use the power of expectation to help them find the best in themselves.

DREAM IMPOSSIBLE DREAMS

One of the most critical tools a manager can use to influence performance is the power of expectation. Most managers underestimate its importance—the best managers create high expectations.

Five key principles summarize the concept of the self-fulfilling prophecy:

- ❖ Managers form certain expectations of people or events.

- ❖ They communicate these expectations with various cues.

- ❖ People tend to respond to these cues by adjusting their behavior to match them.

❖ The result is that the original expectation becomes fulfilled.

❖ This creates a circle of self-fulfilling prophecies.

Consciously or not, we tip people off as to our expectations. Some cues are subtle; others are obvious. But once an expectation is set, even if it isn't accurate, people tend to act in ways that are consistent with that expectation.

In an interview with Jim Ingram, production engineer for Glaxo Wellcome Inc., he offered this perspective: "Anyone can be successful if you can demonstrate that you have confidence in them. All you need to do once they believe in themselves is give them the opportunity to succeed."

Ingram, a manager for many years, shared an interesting example about a production worker on second shift in a new plant. The employees were convinced that they didn't have enough people to start up the production line—it was impossible. Ingram said, "It was like a snowball rolling down a hill—it kept collecting—a chain reaction of sorts." Soon all of the employees believed they couldn't do it. Ingram tried to convince them they could and that they could alter their work plan to account for fewer people and move forward. They still didn't want to try. They were afraid that even if they started operating the line, they wouldn't be running at the efficiencies required.

Of course, they ran the line, and everyone was surprised at how well they did. On a small scale, they had achieved an "impossible dream." But the self-confidence that grew as a result of that experience took the employees to new heights. The lesson for managers is important: One of the most powerful tools for influencing the performance of others is your own expectations.

MAKE THEM FEEL SPECIAL

Believe in people, and they'll believe in themselves. It's a simple truth that's often ignored or overlooked. It's easy to make someone feel special if you make the effort. Harvey McKay illustrates this point in his book *Sharkproof.*

He talks about Jack Kemp, the Secretary of Housing and Urban Development during the Bush administration and Republican Vice Presidential candidate in 1996. Kemp had played football at Occidental College and was a quarterback with the Buffalo Bills before he entered politics.

At the start of one season, Kemp's coach called him into his office for a brief talk. The coach confided in Kemp that each year there was one player he kept his eye on because he saw a special quality in that person. If that player lived up to his potential, he would not only hold the team together and bring it a championship, but he would also go on to greatness as a professional. The coach told Kemp he was that player. He also told him to keep their conversation confidential. Kemp left the room that day on cloud nine and ready to climb mountains for the coach.

He found out later, of course, that the coach had the same conversation with every guy on the team. Why not express the same kind of faith in your employees? Find a way to make them feel special.

RECOGNIZE ASSETS

John Rogers, Chief Petty Officer USN Retired, is known today as Reverend John Rogers. He's worked in two completely different fields, but he's used the self-fulfilling prophecy concept in both.

In the Navy, he supervised a team of men responsible for the electrical maintenance work on aircraft. His people had a huge responsibility—the lives of many others were in their hands. Rogers used the power of expectation because he knew his men could do an excellent job. He helped them over any self-doubt. "I was always there for them and if they had a problem, they asked. I have a 'hands-off' management style, but I checked to be sure what was done was satisfactory. I always told them to do the work as if they were flying in the plane."

After 20 years in the Navy, he retired, went back to school, and earned his Master of Divinity degree. As a minister, he once again was called upon to help others help themselves. "I thought of my job as that of the church 'instigator.' I identified talent that the parishioners didn't see in themselves. I saw the assets that each person had to offer to the church—I encouraged them to take their assets and use them to carry out our ministry to others."

Subtle communication, as well as overt actions, tell people what we're thinking. True Pygmalions are flexible, empathetic, and self-confident—essential qualities that elevate them above the average manager. If you're using the power of expectation at all on a regular basis, you're already a few steps ahead in the managerial game.

To get an even bigger lead try to:

* ❖ Include employees in decision making.
* ❖ Ask for their opinions—often.
* ❖ Let employees tell you stories of their successes—and listen.
* ❖ Tell them they're important to the business and why.
* ❖ Encourage them to try new things.
* ❖ Praise people who don't expect it.
* ❖ Reward them for their achievements.
* ❖ Build self-confidence in them every chance you get.

KEEP THEM ON YOUR RADAR SCREEN

Samantha Renfro and Kathryn Janus, director and associate director, respectively, of MBA Career Services for Goizueta Business School of Emory University, face a twofold challenge. They're responsible for managing a team of employees, as well as their customers—roughly 285 graduate students. "I believe we owe to our employees the right to make choices and then allow them to take responsibility for those decisions," said Renfro. They both believe that they don't need to micro-manage but simply "keep employees on their radar screen."

"If someone seems discouraged and says 'I can't do this,' I ask them to think about what it would take to make it work. I offer employees, as well as students, encouragement and praise and let them know they have my support—that I'm available to help in any way I can," said Janus.

Neither woman believes in giving responsibility without authority—they don't want anyone to feel used. "I've been there in the past as a cog in the wheel with no credit or feeling of empowerment to do my job," added Renfro. Their employees know they don't interfere unless there's a problem. "They might not be approaching something exactly the way I would, but that's OK because what they're doing is fine," explained Renfro.

By keeping employees, as well as students, on their radar screen, Renfro and Janus have just enough contact to share the power of expectation with both groups. They've got them in sight and are consciously aware that everyone needs to feel successful.

Approximately 25% of the population are international students. Emory graduates are among the brightest, but like anyone else, they need to know that they're doing the right things. Renfro, Janus, and their staff work hard to assure that students reach their academic goals, have a supportive learning environment, and find top-notch jobs upon graduation. "Our team of employees meets weekly so that everyone can give an update on what they're working on. It helps to keep us in sync. It also helps us do a better job in meeting the needs of our students," said Renfro.

"The power of expectation is a tremendous force that every organization should use. It's what helps people believe in themselves—and that can only mean benefits like high morale for the manager as well as the entire organization," added Janus.

OFFER APPROVAL AND ACCEPTANCE

Productivity is closely tied to employee morale, and morale is a reflection of how people see themselves. If you can improve your employees' perception of themselves, you can improve their morale and, therefore, boost productivity. Managers need to let employees know they're winners—something that's difficult to do if we're busy telling them they've failed.

We're all eager for approval and acceptance; we sometimes go to extreme lengths to be noticed and appreciated. Take a child, for example, who's not getting enough attention, who doesn't feel appreciated;

he may get so desperate that he resorts to extreme naughtiness just to attract attention. Even punishment is preferable to being ignored.

Employees are no different. Sometimes people want your attention so badly they will find a way to get it one way or another. For example, Trent worked for a manager who helped him change from a nervous and insecure man to one who was promoted three times in 16 months. He was eager to please his boss but was difficult to manage. He was intelligent and anxious to do well. His boss liked him, although he was slow in getting work done. He procrastinated, and his manager often thought it was intentional just to get attention. It backfired.

The manager was a sensitive and astute individual who refrained from making derogatory remarks toward the employee. Instead, he worked one-on-one with him to help him reach the next level of achievement. He also addressed his procrastination and made it clear he had to stop putting things off or he would never be promoted—he might even lose his job.

Pygmalions have a way of popping up when least expected. Fortunately, there was one there for Trent. The Pygmalion mentored him and helped him believe in himself. He also helped him correct a problem that would have held him back professionally for the rest of his career. The Pygmalion was Eddie Blank.

LIFT SELF-IMPOSED LIMITATIONS

People often tend to restrict themselves with self-imposed limitations. It's an easy trap to fall into. In an interview with David Allison, region manager for Siemens Medical Systems, Inc., I discovered a Pygmalion who had this to say:

> "I joined Siemens just about the time they purchased another company. I inherited a number of employees. As I got ready to hire new people from outside the company I found that some of the existing employees from the business we bought had something to say. They were supportive to the management team, but in speaking with sales candidates, they discouraged them from taking the job."

Allison found that some of the people from the organization that was bought by Siemens told his new sales representatives that the sales goals were unreachable. They asked the new employees why they left their last jobs and told them that they had just set themselves up for failure. Some of the new sales people felt like they had made a mistake by joining the company. One new employee in particular, frightened by the reception he received from the existing work force, began to have doubts about his ability to sell.

Allison believes that self-imposed limitations are similar to breaking a four-minute mile—no one thought it could be done until it was. He set out to change the paradigm of the existing sales team. He told his new employees that he knew they could do it—that the sales numbers were realistic and attainable.

The good news is that at the end of his first year, the new employee mentioned above was the #1 salesperson in the company. He not only reached his goal, but surpassed it. Those who had said he couldn't do it were at 75% of their goal and rationalized their failures. They made excuses for the rookie's success—that it was beginner's luck or that he just had a great sales territory. In reality, the employee succeeded because he had no self-imposed limitations to hold him back. He also had the support of his personal Pygmalion, David Allison.

TAKE THE BULL BY THE HORNS

"Take the bull by the horns" is the advice of Bonnie Stewart, manager of employee relations and staffing for Peachtree Software. Stewart's been with the company for over 15 years and is a proud and successful Pygmalion. She shared a story about an employee who wanted to be promoted from supervisor to manager. The decision maker was not convinced that the employee was the best person for the job. Discouraged, the employee wanted to give up. Stewart saw the opportunity to help someone believe in himself. She asked him what made him think he could do the job—he convinced her he was qualified. Then, she suggested he "take the bull by the horns" and convince the decision maker too. She soon began to see a difference in his attitude.

Although she's not his sole source of support, she's there to encourage and bestow the power of expectation. The employee also had a staff of people who worked for him who felt he deserved the promotion.

Stewart found that by expressing belief in people, the word got around. Employees know that she is willing to listen, willing to help. They also see the positive Pygmalion in her.

If you want to see the power of expectation work for you and your employees, consider the following:

- ❖ Invite employees to voice their opinions, complaints, and suggestions.

- ❖ Look for ways to praise employees' successes.

- ❖ Help employees recognize their own strengths.

- ❖ Point out ways each employee's unique talents contribute to the overall effort of the department and organization.

Unlike modest expectations, if you expect the best and communicate that expectation, you will trigger an infectious enthusiasm that will help retain winning employees.

HAVE A GAME PLAN

Managers with high expectations for themselves impart the same to their employees. But when employees fail, even though they understand expectations and are doing their best, it's time for the manager's assistance.

In an actual case, an employee in the field of advertising sales was struggling to meet her goals. She had lots of rejections and became depressed about her future with the company. Her supervisor, John Snellen, manager of sales and marketing for Skyline South, was an encourager. He wouldn't let her give up. He convinced her she was a good sales representative, and, together, they developed an action plan.

First, they identified everything she did well and enjoyed. One of the things she liked to do was meet people. They set a schedule of networking activities that included chamber of commerce meetings and regular participation in advertising, sales, and marketing association events. Snellen helped her recognize her strengths, which included developing friendships—the foundation of successful selling.

They also talked about her weaknesses and what she didn't like. The employee hated cold calling, so they devised a game plan. They set a daily goal of 25 phone calls. She liked record-keeping and detail, so she enjoyed keeping track of her progress. First, she challenged herself to see how many contacts she could make each day with a "live" person versus an answering machine. Second, she estimated how many appointments she could get from those contacts. "It was a 'win/win' situation. We took cold calling out of the realm of personal rejection and made it into a game," said Snellen.

Encouraged and empowered, the employee became an excellent sales representative. "Once she got over the reluctance of cold calling and got her foot in the door, she played on her strength for developing relationships," added Snellen.

Sometimes devising the right game plan is all it takes to enable an employee to meet your expectations as well as their own.

O N MY HONOR...

Pygmalions, in the form of managers, supervisors, ministers, doctors, parents, friends, spouses, group leaders, etc., surround us in our professional and personal lives. I met John Hoyle, a partner with Way Kidd & Associates, Inc., an executive outplacement counseling firm, at a professional association meeting. I had a chance to get to know him during dinner and later invited him to participate in an interview for this book. His sensitivity and caring attitude impressed me. As I got to know him better, I learned that he's a very giving man who encourages others to believe in themselves.

In his work, he counsels executives who have lost their jobs for any number of reasons. He provides one-on-one help with job search tactics as well as, in some cases, strategies to avoid making the same mistake again. Hoyle is a Pygmalion with his executive clients, sometimes working hard to convince an individual that he or she is capable of something previously thought impossible.

He also happens to be a Boy Scout leader. Hoyle describes Scouting as "a wonderful opportunity to be a positive influence on the minds of young men ages 11 to 18." Mothers especially appreciate Scouting because their boys get to know adult men other than their fathers. In some cases, single mothers see Scout leaders as role models for their sons.

He compares his work as a Scoutmaster with the business world. "I believe it's important to impress upon young people the significance of a good work ethic and the importance of honesty." Hoyle envisions members of his troop as leaders in organizations some day. He encourages them and sets the example. He realizes that not all youngsters have Pygmalions in their lives.

"You can't necessarily change a person's life, but as a leader in your organization, you can influence how others feel about themselves and their work," said Hoyle.

N OTHING HAPPENS 'TIL SOMEBODY SELLS

Pygmalions are among us. They're ready to share the power. Sometimes, it takes a Pygmalion to jump-start a career or a person who has low self-esteem. One such individual is H. Lincoln Jepson, president of New Jersey Machine Inc., a manufacturer of product labeling machinery. Better known as Linc to his friends and business associates, Jepson feels compelled to work especially close with what he calls "green" sales people.

> "In training new people, I try to inspire and help them overcome the fear factor which will hold the neophytes back from reaching their goals. They all need two things to be successful in sales: self confidence and product knowledge. I try to lead by example and show them how simple it is to deal with people. I know they can do it—now they have to believe it."

Jepson enjoys helping others become experts at what they do. He teaches them how to put their customers at ease and open the door to a sale by finding out what the customers need before telling them what they've got to sell. Teaching the basics of selling and boosting self-esteem is what makes Jepson a dynamic Pygmalion.

He draws an analogy between new sales people and an elementary school class. The leader can mold new people to fit the organization just as the teacher can work with children who are impressionable and usually eager to learn. He reminded me of the old expression: "Nothing happens 'til somebody sells." Until that happens, it can be a long and tiresome road for both the manager and the employee.

GET OUT OF THE WAY

Pygmalions know how to get out of the way and give employees space. In an interview with Robin Rittenhouse, owner of a Minuteman Press printing business, I found that's exactly what he does. Once his employees understand what's expected and demonstrate competency, he lets them excel.

"I give a lot of responsibility as soon as I see that the employee can handle it. I also reinforce good performance with immediate and frequent feedback," said Rittenhouse. With one employee in particular, he found that expecting more and more has helped the individual become increasingly self-confident.

He never loses his temper when things go wrong. He doesn't berate his employees either. "If there's a problem, they know I'm not happy but we work through it and make sure it doesn't happen again," added Rittenhouse.

He's a firm believer in showing trust—once they've earned it, he's quick to get out of the way.

AND THEY WIPED THEIR MINDS CLEAR

Jackie Lewis, project manager for a software product development group with a Fortune 100 company, is a Pygmalion who shared this story.

A senior analyst led the team of software engineers who reported to her, until cutbacks eliminated the analyst's position. A project came up which required integrating a new system. The programmers who worked for her had little confidence that they could get the work done without the guidance of a senior analyst. Her response was, "I wouldn't ask you to take on this responsibility unless I knew you could do it and neither would my supervisor."

The 6-person team accepted the challenge, started the 9-month project, met the schedule, and had no major disasters. They were rewarded with promotions and recognition.

Lewis had moved to another job within the company two weeks before the team finished the project. However, she kept in touch with the other managers and found out that not only were the programmers pleased with themselves, but they didn't even remember their initial reluctance to try something they feared. "It was like they wiped their minds clear of doubts. I thought that was significant," said Lewis.

She also believes that a lot of what transpired happened because of people with positive attitudes who pulled together to meet expectations. Although she made no mention of personal credit for their accomplishments, I have no doubt that Lewis herself was the positive Pygmalion behind their success.

SUMMARY

It's natural to form expectations, and we communicate expectations about what will happen or how others will behave in many ways. We also often prejudge either positively or negatively. We tend to feel comfortable with people who meet our expectations, whether they're high or low. We tend to be uncomfortable with people who don't meet our expectations—again, whether high or low. Most people behave according to the way they're treated. Some ways managers consciously or unconsciously use to communicate with employees include:

- ❖ Praising lows more often than highs for marginal or inadequate efforts.

- ❖ Praising lows less often than highs after successful efforts.

- ❖ Calling on lows less often to work on special projects, state their opinions, or give presentations.

- ❖ Seating lows in low-prestige office areas far away from the manager.

❖ Interrupting lows more often than highs.

❖ Criticizing lows more often than highs for making mistakes.

❖ Waiting less time for lows to state their opinions.

❖ Requiring less work and effort from lows than from highs.

❖ Paying less attention to lows in business situations (maintaining less eye contact and smiling less often).

❖ Giving them less information about what's going on in the department or organization.

❖ Not supporting lows in failure (i.e., providing less help or giving less advice when employees really need it).

❖ Providing lows with less accurate and less detailed feedback on job performance than highs.

J. Sterling Livingston summed it up like this: "A manager often communicates most when he believes he's communicating least. For instance, when he says nothing, when he becomes 'cold' and 'uncommunicative,' it usually is a sign that he is displeased by a subordinate or believes he is 'hopeless.'"

The way you treat your employees is the key to high expectation and high productivity. Jimmy Johnson, coach of the Miami Dolphins, put it this way: "You've heard me say it before: Treat a person as he is, and he will remain as he is. Treat a person as what he could and should be, and he will become what he should be."

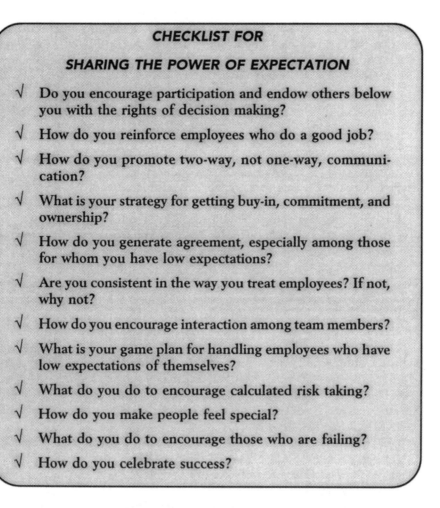

CHECKLIST FOR

SHARING THE POWER OF EXPECTATION

√ Do you encourage participation and endow others below you with the rights of decision making?

√ How do you reinforce employees who do a good job?

√ How do you promote two-way, not one-way, communication?

√ What is your strategy for getting buy-in, commitment, and ownership?

√ How do you generate agreement, especially among those for whom you have low expectations?

√ Are you consistent in the way you treat employees? If not, why not?

√ How do you encourage interaction among team members?

√ What is your game plan for handling employees who have low expectations of themselves?

√ What do you do to encourage calculated risk taking?

√ How do you make people feel special?

√ What do you do to encourage those who are failing?

√ How do you celebrate success?

Additional Reading

Bell, Chip R. *Managers as Mentors—Building Partnerships for Learning.* San Francisco, CA: Berrett-Koehler, 1996.

Blanchard, Ken, John P. Carlos and Alan Randolph. *Empowerment Takes More Than a Minute.* San Francisco, CA: Berrett-Koehler, 1996.

Deeprose, Donna. *How to Recognize and Reward Employees: A Worksmart Guide.* New York, NY: AMACOM, 1994.

Dinkmeyer, Don and Daniel Eckstein. *Leadership by Encouragement.* Delray Beach, FL: St. Lucie Press, 1996.

Dinkmeyer, Don and Lewis Losoncy. *The Skills of Encouragement—Bringing Out the Best in Yourself and Others*. Delray Beach, FL: St. Lucie Press, 1996.

Fisher, Bob and Bo Thomas. *Real Dream Teams—Seven Practices Used by World-Class Team Leaders to Achieve Extraordinary Results*. Delray Beach, FL: St. Lucie Press, 1996.

Gower, Stephen M. *The Art of Killing Kudzu—Management by Encouragement*. Toccoa, GA: Lectern Publishing, 1993.

Hale, Roger L. and Rita F. Maehling. *Recognition Redefined—Building Self-Esteem at Work*. Exeter, NY: Gray Publishing, 1993.

Kushel, Gerald. *Reaching the Peak Performance Zone*. New York, NY: AMACOM, 1994.

McKay, Harvey. *Sharkproof*. New York, NY: Harper Business, 1993.

Overholt, Miles H. *Building Flexible Organizations: A People-Centered Approach*. Dubuque, IA: Kendall/Hunt, 1996.

Plunkett, Lorne C. and Robert Fournier. *Participative Management—Implementing Empowerment*. New York, NY: John Wiley & Sons, Inc., 1991.

Ralston, Faith. *Hidden Dynamics*. New York, NY: AMACOM, 1995.

Richfield, Frederick. *The Loyalty Effect: The Hidden Force Behind Growth, Profits, and Lasting Value*. Boston, MA: Harvard Business School Press, 1996.

Schuster, John P., Jill Carpenter, and Patricia Kane. *The Power of Open-Book Management—Releasing the True Potential of People's Minds, Hearts, and Hands*. New York, NY: John Wiley & Sons, Inc., 1996.

Sibson, Robert E. *Maximizing Employee Productivity*. New York, NY: AMACOM, 1994.

Spitzer, Dean R. *SuperMotivation—How to Energize the Company from Top to Bottom*. New York, NY: AMACOM, 1995.

Stack, Jack. *The Great Game of Business*. New York, NY: Doubleday/Currency, 1992.

Stamp, Daniel. *The Invisible Assembly Line—How to Boost White Collar Productivity in the New Economy*. New York, NY: AMACOM, 1995.

Wendover, Robert W. *Two-Minute Motivation—How to Inspire Superior Performance*. Naperville, IL: Sourcebooks Trade, 1995.

$ MA BELL DID IT 4

(Communicate)

"Along with sharing vital information quickly and honestly with employees, management must be as skillful at listening as they are at lecturing in order to create credible corporate communications."
—Lawrence Tabak

● ●

Establish easy-to-use channels of communication if you want to boost morale in your organization. This advice comes from Robert Half, president of Accountemps, a New York-based temporary staffing service.

Communication has two equally important channels: formal, which includes downward, upward, and horizontal communication; and informal, which is usually referred to as "the grapevine." A good manager knows how to communicate in both channels. The grapevine is often feared because it frequently carries rumors and half-truths along with factual information. Acknowledge the grapevine's presence and be aware that many employees put more faith in it than the words of the manager.

Have you ever wondered if your communication during formal performance reviews is effective? People need to know where they stand. Are you sure staff members understand what's expected of them the next time around? Are employees discouraged when they leave appraisal meetings, or do you see a renewed energy and commitment to get the job done? Often, it's not what is said, but how it is said, that makes the difference in employees' morale.

Your actions also affect employees. Body language and facial expressions let the receiver know how you really feel. Frowns, shrugs, gestures and posture, if interpreted negatively, may prove disastrous.

How you treat employees is the proof of your intentions. For example, speaking up on behalf of an employee who has a problem and needs a friend can contribute to the success or failure of a team member.

Good communication also means listening, but it's got to be more than a casual process. Most people aren't particularly good listeners. Some don't know it, but they're at the root of many breakdowns in communication. It's just as important to understand as to be understood. Businesses prosper when employers listen.

There are also many benefits to good listening. You will:

❖ Gather more information.

❖ Get a better understanding of problems.

❖ Build rapport with your employees.

❖ Find it easier to give a good response.

❖ Be a better manager.

You can use language as a powerful change-creating force. Good communication requires thinking, doing, observing, talking, listening, reading, and writing. Keep your team informed and avoid getting stuck in a no-win communication situation. Make a habit of giving frequent feedback and asking for input. Make working for you fun.

MISSION POSSIBLE

When employees of companies, especially small companies, hit the ceiling early in their careers and top out in terms of pay increases, how do you keep them motivated? For an answer to this question, I spoke with Joan Burkhardt, assistant controller for Horizon Media, Inc., a 100-person company that buys broadcast and print media.

In January, 1996, the company was looking for better ways to solve problems. Burkhardt was instrumental in preparing a presentation to be shared with the Horizon Operating Committee (HOC). The title of the presentation was "Middle Management Empowerment." The HOC liked the initial ideas and asked for more detail, which she provided in March. In July, the "Middle Management Empowerment" concept was approved.

The first meeting, with a voluntary committee of ten employees representing all areas of the company, was launched with the theme music from *Mission Impossible*. Their motto became "mission possible." They started with lots of ideas to make for a better work environment. They all agreed that if they felt like they could make a difference and by doing so, invest in their future, the monetary compensation was secondary.

"I believe in this—it's hard work, but the employees are committed. In some ways, it's like a laboratory test. There are many unknowns, many things to evaluate. Although we're still experiencing growing pains, we're moving in the right direction. The committee members leave meetings, which they attend on their own time, supercharged. Even an hour later, they're excited about the promise of mission possible," said Burkhardt.

Bill Koenigsberg, president and CEO, is behind the effort 100%. He added,

"In today's technologically driven environment, the work force is running faster than ever to stay competitive. Companies that are going to succeed need to provide their employees with 'emotional ownership' in an effort to move everybody in the company in the same direction. Through empowering middle management groups, we have found that our mission is shared and directed by all levels of the company, and, in many instances, this group provides the momentum to move us forward."

The results of their efforts in reducing the high cost of low morale are still speculation. However, from the smiles on the faces of the committee members, along with their renewed energy, it's evident that good things are happening and rubbing off on others in the company. When mission impossible becomes "mission possible," everyone's a winner.

THINK IT OVER...

Effective leaders are not afraid to reveal who they really are and what's on their minds. This can be difficult even when you see your people every day, but becomes even more difficult when employees are dispersed over large geographic areas.

Ron Nantz, senior property manager for AT&T, has had responsibility for as many as 1,000 culturally different employees located in a multitude of cities across 14 states. Nantz found it virtually impossible to see many of his people on a face-to-face basis more than a few times a year. This gave him only minimal opportunity to relate to them in a personal manner.

Nantz began searching for a way to regularly communicate with his people in a positive way. E-mail and memos just did not cut it with him. He knew how much he hated having to read the mountains of "official" correspondence that crossed his desk. He believed that his team felt the same way about it. He decided that he would have to come up with something "unofficial," interesting, and humorous if he hoped to get more than a small percentage of the "troops" to read what he had to say.

He came up with something called "Think It Over" that was based on his interest in quotations and the thought-provoking messages they often contained. Each week he would search for quotations (the more humorous the better), then write a little editorial providing his people with his interpretation. He strove to make the message appropriate to the issues in the workplace, but also dealt with life issues. In doing so, he revealed himself, his values, beliefs, successes, and shortcomings.

For example, two of his memos to staff were simply this:

THINK IT OVER...

"Whatever you are, be a good one."
—Abraham Lincoln

My late Dad was always saying, "Whatever's worth doing is worth doing well." He was a stickler for ensuring that you were doing your best at whatever task you had to do—even if you did not particularly enjoy the task.

I believe that all that we do is a reflection of the type of person we are. Pop did too.

If your result is sloppy and incomplete, then your attitude is sloppy and incomplete. If, on the other hand, your result is high quality and error-free, then your attitude is the same.

We invisibly sign all of our output, and the total of our output creates our reputation. What kind of reputation to you think you have?

THINK IT OVER...

"No one can say of his house, 'There is no trouble here.'"
—Oriental proverb

I've said this once or twice before, but I think it bears repeating. We all have our troubles. Life is not perfect for anyone.

I think sometimes we look over the fence at our neighbor and think maybe he or she has it better than we do. That may be true in some areas, but in others we are probably the one's who have it better. Things have a way of balancing out.

The key, I believe, is to accept the fact that things that cause unhappiness happen throughout our lives. Those of us who deal most positively with our attitudes about these things will generally be happier than those who don't.

There's also something else that's good to remember. Almost always, there's something to be learned from our bad experiences. If we take the lesson, we can usually make our lives better in some way. If we do not, we may find ourselves having the same bad experience at a later date.

Finally, I am reminded of something my late father used to tell me when he knew I was worried about a potential difficulty. 'Never trouble trouble 'til trouble troubles you,' he would say. That's probably still good advice.

The popularity of staying in touch in this manner has spread beyond Nantz's own organization. He frequently gets calls from people in other groups who want to be added to his mailing list. As Nantz travels, he often sees his communications on cubicle walls, bulletin boards, and in special notebooks which his people have created. One of his employees who volunteers to work in prisons uses Nantz's material to get his points across to the inmates. Sunday school teachers do the same in their classrooms.

Nantz believes that this somewhat informal approach to communicating has enabled him to get closer to his people. This closeness has created an "esprit de corps" that would have been more difficult to achieve had he relied solely on infrequent face-to-face sessions with his team.

GIVE CRITICISM IN THE HELPING SPIRIT

Criticism is difficult for most people to accept. It's also not easy to give. Often, it's not *what* is said, but *how* it is said. A popular but bad approach is the "sandwich technique," where the critic "sandwiches" the negative comments between beginning and ending words of praise. Employees soon learn that when a manager starts with praise it will lead to criticism. This method creates conflicting messages. It's comparable to a pat on the back before a kick in the pants.

Positive criticism is given in the helping spirit and designed to help the employee change. Unless you want the individual to quit, or you plan to terminate, all criticism should be encouraging with the goal of improvement.

A classic example of constructive criticism is found in the following letter written by Abraham Lincoln during the Civil War. He was trying to find generals capable of quickly defeating the Southern forces. The letter has been quoted by many authorities on criticism.

Dear General Hooker:

I'm placing you in charge of the Army of the Potomac.

However, there are some aspects of your performance with which I am totally dissatisfied. Let me mention only one of them.

Hooker, you have been too ambitious for command. In this fashion, you have done a great disservice to your brother fellow officers and to the United States Army.

Now, Hooker, beware of unbridled ambition. But you are brave, you are skillful, you do not mix politics with your profession as a soldier, for which I admire you.

Now, Hooker, beware of unbridled ambition, but go forward and give America its desperately needed victories.

—Abraham Lincoln

The point is that President Lincoln told General Hooker where he stood. The objective of criticism is to let others know where they stand as accurately as possible. Never gloss over self-defeating behavior. Be specific, timely, and direct. Don't immediately jump on someone when a mistake is made, but don't wait too long either.

The ability to give criticism without causing defensiveness is the hallmark of an effective leader. It takes practice, but it's achievable. The impact on employee morale is significant especially if the criticism is handled poorly.

MAKE LEARNING EASY

There are many way to communicate with employees, but communication can be a problem when they're not in the office on a regular basis, and you've got materials they need to study. Sharon

Wood, training manager for Conceptual Systems, has responsibility for a group of trainers who are on the road more than they're on site. They spend many hours in their cars driving from one location to another. Wood encourages them to borrow audio and video tapes from the company library. She's always looking for new materials of interest to her staff and welcomes recommendations. "They like learning at their own pace, and that's fine with me. We have tapes on management, training, and even self-help, which is especially popular."

Several companies that offer a variety of audio and video tapes for sale are:

- ❖ American Management Association   1-800-262-9699
- ❖ American Media Incorporated   1-800-262-2557
- ❖ Business Advantage, Inc.   1-800-305-9004
- ❖ Coastal Human Resources   1-800-285-9107
- ❖ Excellence in Training Corporation   1-800-747-6569
- ❖ The Crisp Catalog   1-800-442-7477
- ❖ Video Arts   1-800-276-6569

STAY "CHECKED-IN"

Olga Santo-Tomas, account vice president with a national brokerage firm, stays "checked-in" with her employees. She makes a point of asking for feedback, but, more importantly, she takes time to listen. She's also careful not to let group discussions turn into lengthy gripe sessions. "I try to stay current with what people are thinking and doing. That way I feel comfortable giving them as much freedom as they need to be constantly challenged." She works in a tight-knit sales organization that demands a lot from everyone. She knows the employees well and makes a special effort to find out what's going on in their lives.

Because she stays "checked-in," she also recognizes the various payoffs that the employees want from their work, which include the following:

- ❖ Responsibility.
- ❖ Friendship and a sense of belonging.

- ❖ Job security.

- ❖ Opportunity to learn new things.

- ❖ Recognition.

- ❖ Interdependence to achieve their own goals.

- ❖ A sense of accomplishment.

Santo-Tomas also knows not to treat everyone the same way or reward everyone with the same rewards. People are different, something else she recognizes because she makes the effort to stay "checked-in."

SHARE THE VISION

In a decade which saw the airline industry racked by financial troubles and declining service, Midwest Express has emerged as a shining star. The company has consistently been a profitable carrier, noted for its efficiency, high-quality service, and the "airborne chocolate chip cookie."

Timothy E. Hoeksema, president of Midwest Express Airlines, Inc., gave the keynote presentation at the 1995 fall induction dinner of Beta Gamma Sigma at the University of Wisconsin-Milwaukee. He emphasized that the quality of any enterprise is dependent on the quality of its work force.

> "At Midwest Express, we have 1,500 secrets to success—the tremendous employees who make up our team. We spend a tremendous amount of time in the hiring process, looking for people who share our values. Once we find them and bring them into the organization, we provide them with a tremendous amount of training and recurrent training," said Hoeksema.

Good people and good training are not enough without a corporate vision. Hoeksema said the Midwest Express advertising tagline—"The Best Care in the Air"—is more than a slogan, but rather a summation of their business philosophy, which stresses that:

- ❖ Service to the customer is paramount.

- ❖ Honesty and integrity are fundamental.

❖ Respect for the individual is essential (between co-workers as well as in dealings with customers).

❖ A flexible attitude is necessary (especially in an industry marked by extreme competition and volatility).

TRY TOASTMASTERS

You're probably familiar with Toastmasters International, a wonderful organization which I was a member of for ten years. It offers a variety of experiences to a diverse group of people who seek to improve their communication skills.

Perhaps you've never considered the benefits of an in-house club or its value for you and your employees. Distinguished Toastmaster, Jim Bednarczyk, an agent for American Family Insurance, started such a Toastmasters club. In 1984, he encouraged one of the AFI offices in his area to consider Toastmasters as a perk for employees. The company went along with the idea and launched a club with fifteen charter members. "Over the years, the benefits to the company have been tremendous," explained Bednarczyk.

"Learning to speak in front of others gave employees confidence that they were able to transfer to their jobs as underwriters and adjusters. They became better at communicating with each other, as well as with difficult claimants. They also developed leadership skills because of the officer positions they held. Many were promoted and attribute that success to their Toastmasters experience."

The group has grown to almost 30 members. Every other week, they meet for one-and-one-half hours on company time in the training room. They are financially backed by AFI, who pays each individual's annual dues.

Today the club is still going strong, even though a number of people are gone. Downsizing had an impact on the survivors, who have bonded and committed themselves to better communication among themselves and their customers.

BE ACCESSIBLE

Get out from behind the desk and talk to employees about more than "official business." Walk around. Take time to talk about anything that's on their minds. Get to know them professionally and personally. Be accessible physically and mentally.

I once worked for a manager who was physically accessible but mentally tuned out. She often permitted a staff member or telephone call to interrupt one-on-one meetings—even annual performance appraisals. Morale suffered. Her frustrated direct reports felt she was the least accessible person in the company. The sad thing was she didn't know it.

Nothing's so important that you need to allow interruptions when meeting with employees. To do so sends the nonverbal message that neither the employee, nor what's taking place, is important.

Communicate upward, downward, and laterally. Listen at all three levels. Be accessible. Your employees will respond accordingly.

GIVE EVERYONE A SAY

Most people have a need for self-expression. Even cave dwellers knew that economic survival depended on cooperation and good communication. You have a right to be heard and understood and should respect that same right for others. Feedback and acknowledgment on the manager's part demonstrates or confirms understanding and a willingness to be open to new ideas.

Joan E. Rush, president of Joan E. Rush & Associates, a human resource consulting firm, believes in giving all employees an equal opportunity to share ideas when possible. She feels it's very important to hold team meetings every month and include top management, as well as entry level personnel.

> "I think it's crucial that people feel important in what they're doing for an organization. When I look back on my career, there were times when I was excluded from a meeting or decision that directly affected me and the way I did my job.

It bothered me tremendously and made me feel unimportant because I felt I knew my job better than anyone. In fact, I felt insulted because no one ever asked for my input. I believe not asking for a worker's ideas or opinions about their own jobs is a mistake," said Rush. "Many times an employee has an idea for a better way of doing the job if someone will just take the time to listen."

In her consulting practice, she makes it a policy to solicit suggestions from clients and seminar participants. All of her seminars and training programs are interactive and fun, with everyone feeling they played an important role during the day. This is the major reason Rush is recognized as a superb trainer and consultant.

SPEAK FROM THE HEART

In order for communication to be effective, it must be planned, well-organized, sensitive, and reflect the quality of the organization it's representing. Employees demand that employers put their hearts into what they say.

According to Hyler Bracey, co-author of *Managing from the Heart*, you need to follow five principles when communicating:

1. HEAR and understand me. Employees expect you to hear and understand them. That doesn't mean you automatically agree with them, but you do care enough to understand. The hidden benefit: employees are much more apt to really listen to what you say to them.

2. EVEN if you disagree with me, don't make me wrong. Employees will stay enthusiastic if you gently point out flaws in their areas, commend their initiative, and ask them to keep thinking about a problem.

3. ACKNOWLEDGE the greatness within me. Notice what people are doing well and say something about it. Praise produces immense benefits.

4. REMEMBER to look for my loving intention. Most employees want to do well. Even if you grossly disagree with an employee, acknowledge that person's good intentions.

5. <u>T</u>ELL ME the truth with compassion. Most of us want to be told the truth. But we want it delivered in such a way that we can accept it, which means communicating it with caring feelings.

MAKE THEM DECISION MAKERS

Badger Meter, a $140 million, 90-year-old public company that manufacturers utility metering products, has high morale and low turnover, according to Jeff Byers, personnel manager.

"There aren't a lot of layers of supervision so our employees have the opportunity to get involved in many different assignments. Multi-disciplinary teams evaluate problems and the status quo. Strategic thinking leads them to new concepts that directly impact profits," said Byers.

Badger Meter has 1,000 employees in the United States, Mexico, and Europe, and everyone is a decision maker. The company believes it's important to encourage participation for the good of the employer as well as those they employ.

Making decisions is inevitable for every human being. Look before you leap. Stop...think...then start. Plan your work, and work your plan. Like it or not, rich or poor, man or woman, young or old, professionally as well as personally, you are constantly confronted with problems.

The next time you're faced with a problem, help yourself and your employees by following these steps:

❖ State the problem clearly.

❖ List possible causes.

❖ Select the cause that seems most likely.

❖ Brainstorm for solutions.

❖ Evaluate each proposed solution.

❖ Decide on the best solution.

❖ Develop an action plan.

Successful managing is the direct result of your ability to creatively meet and solve the problems you encounter. Whether you are faced with a technical problem or "difficult people" issue, you have to use problem-solving skills and teach your employees how to be decision makers.

CLARIFY EXPECTATIONS

"To the degree that employees understand what's expected, to the same degree they can succeed." The late behavioral psychologist, Kurt Einstein, Ph.D., shared this truth with thousands of managers.

When there's a gap in understanding, employees turn into "performance pygmies," according to George Odiorne, professor of management at Eckerd College. They're often blamed or punished for preventable failures.

For example, in my personal experience, I recall a man who worked for me who missed deadlines and didn't meet the job's expectations. I soon realized that I was at fault. His priorities were different than mine. My expectations weren't clear. I found out later he was often confused, but too embarrassed to ask. The problem was corrected by defining expectations and following up regularly. He was an excellent employee who would have quit or been fired because I failed to explain what I expected.

KEEP THEM INFORMED

Many businesses go through change successfully. Whether it's rapid growth or a major downsizing, the role skillful communication plays in transition can't be underestimated. Managers are ultimately responsible for what happens, although some do a poor job of letting staff know what's going on.

One of the leaders in employee communications is Eastman Kodak Company. They start at the top in communicating with employees. The president insists that honest information reach all levels. Managers are held accountable for getting the word out to their employees.

Bob Chaet is vice president and general manager for the southern area. He shared some of the ways the company keeps people informed.

"Our employees are empowered to award 'Quality Bucks' to each other for extra effort or a job well done. We encourage people to bestow awards on individuals in other divisions of the company as well. Every quarter, the bucks go into a drawing. Fifteen names are drawn to win prizes. It's one of the many ways Kodak promotes communication."

Another example is the company newsletter that is published twice each month. In addition, a quarterly report lets employees know how the company is doing financially.

Chaet, after being named to a new position, had to tell southern area employees about changes in the benefits and bonus plan. Kodak gave them plenty of time to adjust and made sure everyone understood why the changes were taking place.

With the focus on customer, employee, and shareholder satisfaction, there's no room for communication breakdown. Chaet put it like this: "Whether formal or informal, what we say and do to get the message across can make or break morale. It all starts at the top."

ENCOURAGE FEEDBACK

Asking for feedback sends the message that you value opinions and that you are willing to make changes based on input. Be sure, however, that you listen to what employees say. Be ready with a response and express your appreciation. Take action on their suggestions and involve employees in the change process. Afterwards, follow up and get additional feedback on how you're doing.

There are many ways to solicit honest feedback from employees. In preparing questions for even an informal survey, you may want to include some or all of the following questions:

1. When do you feel most free to discuss a tough problem you may have?

2. What, specifically, in your opinion, could be done here to improve employee relations?

3. What are we doing well as a department? As an organization?

4. What could we improve upon?

5. Do you feel that I change my mind too often and alter your assignments after you've already started working?

6. How can I help you develop your skills?

7. What are the main obstacles to getting the job done in your specific area of responsibility?

8. Do you feel free to tackle problems without interference from me?

9. Do I step in too quickly, or not quickly enough?

10. When I redirect your efforts, do you usually feel helped or criticized?

11. Do you get enough feedback from me, especially positive feedback?

I've already used these questions with my staff to evaluate the department as well as myself and found employees willing to offer their ideas. If you have a good working relationship with your employees, you'll get a lot of information. You may not always like what you hear, but don't hold it against them, or you'll never get honest feedback again.

EXPLAIN THE "WHY"

Just as customers want to know "why" your product or service is best, employees want to know "why" they're asked to do certain things. Jim Tietjens, manager of special sales for Rawlings, a sporting goods manufacturer, explained, "Our customers want to know where the merchandise is being shipped, how, when, and 'why' if something goes wrong. Just because a truck pulls away from the warehouse doesn't mean the job is over." He keeps in touch with his customers to assure quality service. He makes it easy to do business with him. Tietjens calls it "out-hustling" the competition.

His customer-oriented focus goes further. "Education and communication is the key to being a good manager. People need to understand the business. For example, when a new assistant joined me, I felt it was important for her to know all of the 'whys' behind the type of sales we make," said Tietjens.

Many of his sales are to "middlemen" who resell Rawlings bats, balls, gloves, etc. to the end-user. In many cases, their product is purchased and given away to attract more business for their buyers. For example, a Pizza Hut promotion with Rawlings' basketballs increased restaurant sales for their customer.

Tietjens says he meets with his team daily if necessary. He wants to assure a positive end result. He reminds them never to promise what they can't deliver. Motivated and knowledgeable employees are prepared to serve their customers, especially when they're asked "why."

BUILD THE LISTENING HABIT

Personal contact between management and employees promotes a feeling of good will and often allows a knowledgeable manager to quickly respond to concerns. It involves taking time to walk around and ask people how things are going. It means keeping an open-door policy.

The validity of employer responsiveness as a motivator was proven in a 1927 study, a classic in industrial psychology, conducted at the Western Electric Hawthorne plant. The company was attempting to measure which environmental factors contributed to high productivity and lowered employee complaints when they made an interesting discovery. Employees had complained of insufficient lighting. After a minimum wattage was met, the company varied the lighting in one area of the plant. They didn't tell people when they increased or decreased the wattage, only that the lighting was being studied and improved. Productivity increased. People responded to the attention and concern regardless of any actual physical change.

In spite of the amount of time we spend listening, most people are not particularly good at it. Research studies show that people in general are only about 25% efficient; they miss 75% of the content. Yet most people think they listen well.

Learn how to listen. Consider the following tips:

1. Hear the employee out.

2. Resist distractions.

3. Keep an open mind.

4. Don't fake attention.

5. Practice listening.

The Greek slave Epictetus, who taught in Rome in 90 A.D., said, "Nature has given to men one tongue, but two ears, that we may hear from others twice as much as we speak." This advice is still applicable today.

USE HUMOR TO GET YOUR MESSAGE ACROSS

"You don't have to be the good humor man (or woman) but humor is a part of any successful business. Just be careful not to poke fun at someone other than yourself," said June Cline, nationally recognized motivational speaker, humorist and owner of Court Jesters Club. Advice which Cline offers in her entertaining presentations includes the following:

> Schedule a humor break each day and assign volunteers to take turns telling a humorous story or a joke—as long as you or the situation are the "butt" of the joke. It's a good way to keep people communicating with each other, as well as relieve stress. Cline refers to embarrassing moments as "idiot episodes." "We all have them, why not get a laugh or two? Fact is funnier than fiction, and it's always funnier after the fact," said Cline.

> Humor bulletin boards are entertaining and provide a similar release. Invite employees to post their favorite cartoons, jokes,

and silly articles for everyone to enjoy. This is also a great technique to find out what some of the challenging office issues are.

Try attaching a cartoon or funny anecdote to your next memo. It'll break up the boredom often associated with reading the reams of correspondence you get. It may even get your message across better.

Hold a crazy hat, ugly tie, or a "right foot" day where everyone wears the right shoe on the right foot and a mismatched shoe on the left foot. It's a great way to get everyone involved and communicating. It may put them in a better mood, too.

One of her favorite humorous encounters was with a radio station in Colorado that had recent layoffs. She arrived for her interview, found yellow crime tape everywhere, and was startled to see a chalk outline of a body on the floor. A sign said "Downsizing crime scene," making fun of the situation, not management.

A "typical of a woman" comment made in the boardroom of another company prompted the offended female employee to arrive at the next meeting wearing a bath robe, hair rollers, and mudpack on her face. Everyone got the message as well as a good chuckle.

Incorporate humor into what you do because it:

❖ Helps fight stress.

❖ Promotes creativity.

❖ Improves communication.

❖ Fulfills human social needs.

❖ Breaks up boredom and fatigue.

❖ Eases conflicts.

❖ Helps fulfill the need for attention.

CONSIDER A SURVEY

Employee opinion surveys can provide valuable information on employees' attitudes about their pay, jobs, and the organization that employs them. In *Managing the Equity Factor*, Richard Huseman and John Hatfield maintain that the following case study proves a critical link between good communication and employees' attitudes.

In the study, a multinational corporation identified ten locations where morale was high and people seemed satisfied. They also chose ten locations where dissatisfaction was the norm. Their objective was to find the differences between the top ten and bottom ten locations.

The results revealed that employees at the top ten locations had better perceptions of their pay than employees at the bottom ten. The latter employees felt they were underpaid, when in actuality there were no differences in pay scales. Researchers looked at other questions in the survey and discovered that responses to only one of the nearly 150 survey questions distinguished between the top and bottom locations. The level of communication between employees and their immediate managers accounted for the difference in responses.

USE PERFORMANCE APPRAISALS AS COMMUNICATION TOOLS

In most organizations, performance appraisals create fear, embarrassment, and uncertainty. Many managers don't feel comfortable doing appraisals. Consequently, their employees don't know what to expect. Yet appraisals, if used correctly, should ensure clear communication of the employer's expectations and perception of the employee's performance. The consensus is that performance appraisals do not deliver all of their potential benefits to either employers or employees.

Further, "Fifty percent of all performance appraisals are never done! Of the 50% that *are* done, 50% are not done on time!" These facts come from Jim Hackett, president of The Bunker Hill Consulting Group, Boston, MA. He said, "When managers fail to provide a timely performance appraisal, they are telling their people one thing—I don't care about *you* or your *future*."

Hackett views the performance appraisal as a communication tool. The major purpose and benefits of this tool, according to Hackett, are that it:

❖ Lets employees know exactly how they're doing against the predetermined expectation.

❖ Shows employees their strengths and weaknesses.

❖ Lets employees discuss the various aspects of their career with you.

❖ Gives employees a chance to air their grievances.

❖ Gives managers opportunities to provide learning experiences.

❖ Provides *meaningful action plans* that employees identify as their own because of the role they have in developing the plan with their managers.

❖ Recognizes the employees' progress toward planned goals.

Performance appraisal is a basic responsibility of every manager, but often the pressures of day-to-day operations make annual appraisals a low priority. Start by making a commitment to the task. Many organizations make performance appraisal part of a manager's objectives.

During the appraisal, define job goals with employees. You can't measure results if goals are fuzzy. Prioritize the goals. Make goal setting a collaborative process. Always involve the key stakeholders—the people who must implement the goals. It's the manager's responsibility to ensure that the employee's goals are compatible with the group goals.

Hackett offers the following formula for using performance appraisals as communication tools:

$$(S+A+E+T)\ M^2=R \text{ or}$$

Skills plus *Attitude* plus *Energy* plus *Training* times *Motivation* squared (yours and the organization's) equals *Results*.

TAKE INVENTORY

Take inventory by measuring the quality of your communication with employees. Read the following questions and circle either A (for Agree) or D (for Disagree).

A D   1. My employees feel free to talk to me about anything.

A D   2. My employees know what I expect of them.

A D   3. I honestly take time to listen and focus on understanding.

A D   4. My employees are not afraid to disagree with me.

A D   5. I coach my employees toward improvement.

A D   6. I'm honest with my employees at all times.

A D   7. I recognize and reward employees when appropriate.

A D   8. I evaluate performance on an ongoing basis and address problems as they arise.

A D   9. I'm aware of the specific challenges my employees face on the job and let them know I understand.

A D   10. I set a good example.

Now count up the A's you circled. A 10 means you have excellent communication with your employees; 9 or 8 is good; 7 or 6 is above average; 5 or less—you need improvement.

TRY "ROLESTORMING"

You've probably heard of brainstorming, as well as roleplaying. Put the two together and get "rolestorming." Its goal is to improve creativity and communication.

In a rolestorming session, each member or the team assumes the role of another person—someone not present—and then brainstorms 20–30 ideas based on that person's perspective. The actual rolestorming follows.

First, employees share their own ideas. Then, they assume new identities and discuss ideas they think their supervisor, peers, or direct reports might come up with. For example, suppose the topic is communication. Each participant chooses a person to imitate, then says something like: "My person would favor more frequent communication," or "The person I'm thinking of would like to see all teams interact better with each other."

Rolestorming increases the number of ideas generated by up to 75%. Employees get excited about the process, and everyone benefits. Some of the other advantages include better quality ideas and the fact that everyone participates without feeling their ideas are off-the-wall.

The problem with traditional brainstorming is that people are reluctant to give their craziest ideas—usually their most creative. In rolestorming, which allows employees to attribute their suggestions to someone else, the floodgates of ideas opens. Anyone with a wild or unconventional idea can express it without others knowing that it was really his or her own.

WHY DO YOU *SEE* IT THAT WAY?

Communication involves being able to listen. Most people have gotten into the habit of antilistening behavior. Research shows that when we listen for a long time without doing any talking or responding, our listening efficiency begins to drop drastically. Finally, our minds drift off to other topics or what we plan to say next.

To overcome some of the pitfalls associated with poor communication, Linda Jackson, president of Resources & Solutions of JEL Enterprises, Inc., a business resource center for human resource training and development books, cassette tapes and employee development materials, had this to say: "For me, part of listening is asking questions to get people thinking. I ask the question, 'What do you *see*?—not feel.' I think in terms of images. I see my role as someone who asks questions so listeners can expand their thinking and, as a result, share ideas."

Jackson uses this technique with staff, customers, and suppliers. When she asks "What do you *see* as the best way to approach this problem?" or "What do you *see* in the future for this product?", she really wants to know. "I probe for the big pieces, the whole picture—that often comes with the 'how' and 'why'-type of questions," said Jackson.

HEAR WHAT EMPLOYEES ARE *NOT* SAYING

Appreciation breeds commitment. But before you can truly appreciate your employees, you have to know them. Nonverbal cues to feelings surround us, but we don't always recognize the signs. Most people hide their true feelings at the risk of being ridiculed, especially at work.

Body language, whether it's an expression on the face, subtle movement, or even a change in breathing rate, can signal a problem. Part of your job as a manager is to interpret the meaning of nonverbal cues. You also need to keep in mind that culture, social status, economic position, and geographical differences affect the unspoken language.

You can see nonverbal communication in the face and neck, midsection and hips, legs and feet. Prolonged eye contact, wrinkling of the nose, a smile, and compression of lips all provide cues. Outstretched hands, an index finger to the face, and pushing away with interlocked fingers provide hints of what people are thinking.

Nonverbal communication can disclose as much as verbal communication. In many instances, because certain nonverbal signals are involuntary, a person's body language may give a more honest indication of what he or she is feeling.

Although you are more likely to accept an employee's statement when the body language is consistent with what's being said, inconsistencies are not necessarily negative. Employees will display a wide variety of body language, and you must identify those that occur most often and interpret those cues to better understand employees. Once identified, you can use the information to manage more effectively.

As a manager, you should be aware that *you* are also sending nonverbal messages to your employees. Does your body language signal honesty, consistency, and a willingness to listen? Or do you give the impression that you can't be trusted, are inconsistent, or too busy to be bothered with a problem?

The most common deficiencies of nonverbal communication by managers are:

- Not smiling enough.

- Expressing confusion or doubt when presented with conflicting information or bad news.

- Not showing enough interest in what employees are saying.

- Failing to ask for and accept criticism from staff about your management style.

DON'T DISCOURAGE SMALL TALK

The word "communicate" appears in Webster's dictionary between "commotion" and "community." We all have experienced the commotion generated by poor communication in an organization, and we know equally well that effective communication can build a community of thought and feeling that withstands many of the problems in the workplace.

In speaking with Marian Scopa, operations manager for H.C. Brill, Inc., a manufacturer of bakery ingredients, she mentioned a familiar form of communication called "small talk."

"It takes a while for a team to jell and trust each other—to feel comfortable to ask questions without being judged. To help with the process, I don't discourage small talk. Chit-chat about the weekend's events, the new grandchild, or a good recipe promotes comfortable relationships, which, in turn, helps build the team," explained Scopa. She said there was a time when she frowned on what appeared to be time wasted by employees visiting in the breakroom when not on break or talking over a cool sip of water at the drinking fountain. "A certain amount of small talk is healthy for the organization and team as long as it doesn't get out of hand," said Scopa.

S UMMARY

Communication links all the managerial functions. There are none that a manager can fulfill without communicating. Research has shown that managers spend between 70 and 80% of their time sending and receiving information. Some communication is effective, and some is not; but it's still a two-way process—both parties must share responsibility for its success or failure. Communication has been described as an art, not a science, but it can be learned.

Personal power and your ability to communicate go a long way toward keeping the channels of communication open between you and your employees. Whether you're communicating the organization's culture on how employees should treat one another or offering positive feedback to a person who needs extra encouragement, you can boost morale at the same time.

Overcoming barriers to better cooperation is essential for high morale. Often, the manager gets caught in the middle of disagreement between employees.

In working to improve your message to your team, consider the following:

❖ **Be accurate**. A misplaced word or unclear explanation may lead to confusion.

❖ **Be impartial**. When explaining something, try to keep your personal feelings out of it. Remain neutral and give employees a chance to form their own opinions.

❖ **Be precise**. Try not to say anything that would confuse the listener, especially when giving directions.

❖ **Be aware**. Physiological and environmental factors, as well as cultural values, can influence the things you say and how other people perceive them.

There will be times when you may be accused of showing favoritism. An individual may feel picked on. Another may feel like the scapegoat for something gone amiss. Make the best use of your communication skills in working through these kinds of problems. Give people time to vent frustration but don't let it turn into a gripe session.

Morale and motivation also enter the picture. Too often we view motivation as something that one person can give to or do for another. Motivation is an inside job. You can't force it on someone else, no matter how hard you try.

Problem-solving and decision-making also fall under the heading of communication. Remember, your objective is reaching a common goal, not embarrassing someone or moving in a direction contrary to the organization's strategy. Focus on the present and future, not the past—something that's too late to change.

There will be times when you must almost demand that people listen—you will hold them accountable for what they hear. Many people are tuned into WIIFM—"What's In It For Me?" Let them know what you expect.

Of course, some managers are better natural communicators than others. Unfortunately, some managers assume they know how to communicate, and they don't work at improving their skills. Frequently, those who think they're doing a good job are actually only average, or even below average, in skill level.

Visual media, gestures and actions, and spoken and written words are all forms of human communication. There's no form of written communication that can substitute for face-to-face meetings. The barriers to good communication will always be there due to human differences and organizational conditions, but they can be overcome. After all, Ma Bell did it.

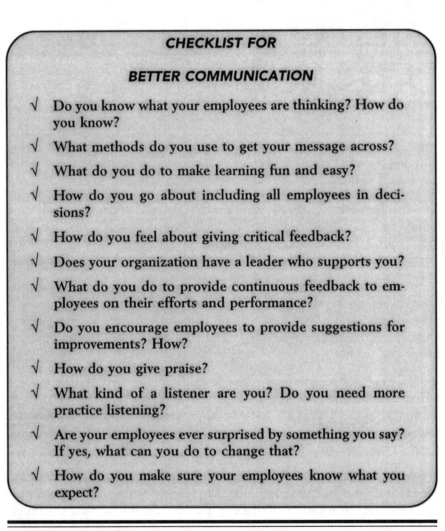

CHECKLIST FOR

BETTER COMMUNICATION

√ Do you know what your employees are thinking? How do you know?

√ What methods do you use to get your message across?

√ What do you do to make learning fun and easy?

√ How do you go about including all employees in decisions?

√ How do you feel about giving critical feedback?

√ Does your organization have a leader who supports you?

√ What do you do to provide continuous feedback to employees on their efforts and performance?

√ Do you encourage employees to provide suggestions for improvements? How?

√ How do you give praise?

√ What kind of a listener are you? Do you need more practice listening?

√ Are your employees ever surprised by something you say? If yes, what can you do to change that?

√ How do you make sure your employees know what you expect?

Additional Reading

Alessandra, Tony and Phil Hunsaker. *Communicating at Work*. New York, NY: Simon & Schuster, 1993.

Bickman, William. *Celebrating the Human Spirit in the Workplace*. Chicago, IL: Irwin Professional Publishing, 1996.

Bradford, Lawrence J. and Claire Raines. *Twentysomething—Managing and Motivating Today's New Workforce*. New York, NY: MasterMedia Limited, 1992.

Charvet, Shelle Rose. *Words That Change Minds—Mastering the Language of Influence*. Dubuque, IA: Kendall/Hunt Publishing Company, 1995.

Consalvo, Carmine. *Team Building Blocks—Practicing Group Collaboration.* Amherst, MA: HRD Press, 1995.

Edwards, Mark R. and Ann J. Ewen. *360-Degree Feedback: The Powerful New Model for Employee Assessment and Performance Improvement.* New York, NY: AMACOM, 1996.

Hargrave, Jan. *Let Me See Your Body Talk.* Dubuque, IA: Kendall/Hunt Publishing Company, 1995.

Harris, Jim. *Getting Employees to Fall in Love with Your Company.* New York, NY: AMACOM, 1996.

Hickman, Craig, Craig Bolt, Marlon Berrett, and Brad Angus. *The Fourth Dimension: The Next Level of Personal and Organizational Achievement.* New York, NY: John Wiley & Sons, 1996.

Klubnik, Joan. *Rewarding and Recognizing Employees-—Ideas for Individuals, Teams, and Managers.* Chicago, IL: Irwin Professional Publishing, 1995.

Langdon, Danny. *The New Language of Work.* Amherst, MA: HRD Press, 1995.

Lipman-Blumen, Jean. *The Connective Edge: Leading in an Interdependent World.* San Francisco, CA: Jossey-Bass, 1996.

Marks, Sharon F. *It Pays to Praise.* Alexandria, VA: Miles River Press, 1996.

Maurer, Rick. *Feedback Toolkit—16 Tools for Better Communication in the Workplace.* Portland, OR: Productivity Press, 1994.

McGhee, Paul E. *How to Develop Your Sense of Humor.* Dubuque, IA: Kendall/Hunt Publishing Company, 1994.

McLagan, Patricia and Peter Krembs. *On-The-Level: Performance Communication That Works.* San Francisco, CA: Berrett-Koehler Publishers, Inc., 1995.

Mendes, Anthony. *Inspiring Commitment—How to Win Employee Loyalty in Chaotic Times.* Chicago, IL: Irwin Professional Publishing, 1996.

Palston, Faith, Ph.D. *Hidden Dynamics—How Emotions Affect Business Performance & How You Can Harness Their Power for Positive Results.* New York, NY: AMACOM, 1995.

Stiles, William H. *Tactics of Persuasion.* Dubuque, IA: Kendall/Hunt Publishing Company, 1994.

Stone, Florence M. and Randi T. Sachs. *The High-Value Manager: Developing the Core Competencies Your Organization Demands.* New York, NY: AMACOM, 1996.

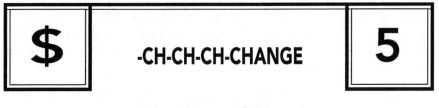

$ -CH-CH-CH-CHANGE 5

(Take Charge Of Change)

"Change is stressful. Times like these can get on your nerves. But it's during the tough times that you have a chance to really grow, and to prove yourself. Here's an opportunity for you to become a corporate hero."

—From *Business to UnUsual—The Handbook for Managing and Supervising Organizational Change*

• •

One of the major problems facing managers is employee resistance to change. Reduction in output, chronic complaining, hostility, tardiness, and absenteeism, along with turnover, are signs of resistance. Most employees view change as a threat to security. Managers, by understanding why employees feel threatened, are better able to develop a plan for eliminating the threat or turning it into an advantage. Threats come in the form of possible loss of something that's highly valued: job security, acceptance, self-esteem, etc. With the turn of the century, many changes will take place to profoundly affect the lives of everyone in the workplace. Changes in the composition of the work force occur as women continue to play a major role in the labor market. "Baby Boomers" will intensify competition among qualified candidates. The acceptance of minorities and the disabled will gain momentum. Employers will hire more older workers, retired military personnel, and part-timers in an effort to meet staffing requirements.

Employees, educated and armed with the best knowledge and technologies, will command higher salaries, better benefits, and more leisure time than ever before.

Increased government regulations will affect not only businesses, but people employed by those businesses. Employment practices regarding hiring, firing, and wage-and-salary issues will be scrutinized more closely.

Managers will bear the ultimate responsibility for handling change. Some will fail to meet the challenge, while others will take charge with a promise of new opportunities. The first step in directing the influence of change is to make sure that all management systems are flexible and geared to embrace change rather than fight it. Grumbling and blaming others sends a message to your employees that you're not ready to accept responsibility as a leader for what is about to take place. If you're not prepared, you can't expect your employees to be either.

Complacent organizations usually have the most problems handling change. They resist suggestions that old methods are out of sync with today's business climate. The advent of computers is a good example. Some businesses resisted. Others had managers who, although they didn't understand computers, jumped in and learned. These organizations moved beyond those who didn't want to tackle something new.

In his book *The Renewal Factor*, Robert H. Waterman, Jr., speaks of change:

> "There was a time when people were factors of production, managed like machines or capital. No more. People will not tolerate it. While capital and machines either are or can be managed toward sameness, people are individuals. They must

be managed as such. Renewing companies treat *everyone* as a source of creative input."

Managers must pitch, hit, and field—often all at the same time—even in the face of change. By meeting change without hesitation, you have a significant impact on morale. Diagnosis is the first step toward treatment. You can make a conscious decision to manage change or let it manage you.

OFFER "INPLACEMENT"

In February, 1986, Wells Fargo Bank announced plans to purchase Crocker National Bank. The first hint of the acquisition's effects appeared in San Francisco's financial district where a Crocker building faced a Wells Fargo building. In an office window, Crocker employees put up an APPLAUSE sign. Wells Fargo employees quickly responded with a WELCOME! sign. The next Crocker sign said: CAREER OPPORTUNITIES? This time the Wells Fargo response was slow. The sign had simply a question mark written on it.

Buyouts and downsizing create more uncertainty than any other events. Anxiety and hostility often surface among those who remain. Some start looking outside for other jobs. Most are determined to stay where they are.

Retained employees need career development. William Bridges, author of *Surviving Corporate Transition: Rational Management in a World of Mergers, Layoffs, Startups, Takeovers, Divestitures, Deregulations, and New Technologies,* is an advocate of helping employees replan their futures. He calls it "inplacement."

The reduced work force that came as a result of corporate restructuring of the 1980s and 1990s is forcing organizations to make the most of those employees who remain on their payrolls. "Inplacement" is helping businesses and its employees work together to maximize productivity by taking on new challenges and interesting job responsibilities within the company.

Today managers are under more pressure than they've been since the Great Depression—it's their responsibility to help employees who have gone through a major change get their minds off the past and focus on the future. However, retraining takes money and a big commitment to remaining employees. Many organizations are not willing or don't have the money to put forth the effort. Individual managers often take on the responsibility without the support of their employers. The more you can do to help the survivors progress, the more productive they will be.

ASK FOR ADVICE

Most organizations facing major change are in one extreme or the other. They either have no idea how to handle it or have a detailed plan in place.

Why not get your employees involved? When my former employer braced for a change that involved moving from a 50-year-old building to a state-of-the-art facility, we almost had a riot. Old-timers wanted no part of the future. I looked at numerous alternatives for easing the pain of change but couldn't find the solution.

One day it occurred to me that the employees had the answer. All I had to do was ask. It turned out they needed to grieve. We decided to give each employee a disposable camera with a 24-exposure roll of film. The last day at the old office and plant, they used their breaks and lunchhour taking pictures and "saying goodbye." They had a great time. We also passed out felt-tip pens and invited them to write comments on the walls—anything but obscenities. Their farewells included words such as:

"We'll miss this old place, even the leaks in the ceiling."

"Goodbye, good luck, see you at the new digs on Monday."

"It's time to say goodbye. I promise I won't cry.
It's time for something new. Even though I'm blue."

Simple messages from a dedicated work force helped end a chapter in their lives as well as prepare them for the move. Of course, it didn't take long for them to accept what they couldn't change. They were soon delighted with their new and modern surroundings.

TAKE CARE OF THE "ME" ISSUES

Change brings uncertainty, complexity, interdependence, and pressure. When all of these factors fall on the manager's shoulders, the transition can be a difficult one—especially if the managers face the same future.

Dial Page, a paging services provider, knows first-hand the trauma associated with change. A competitor acquired them, and immediately identified 180 positions as surplus. They directed Jim Crofts, human resources manager, to work with employees whose jobs were eliminated.

The company offered a good severance package and perks that tied people to long-term success with respect to stock options. Money, however, isn't everything. According to Crofts, the first thing they did was take care of the "me" issues. "Naturally, everyone was concerned for their jobs. The company took the position of being honest about everything. When we didn't know what would happen, we told them. They took our word at face value. We never were untruthful," said Crofts. Low morale was not a problem despite the disruption of the downsizing.

The layoffs affected corporate offices, as well as the field operations. Crofts also lost his job after heading up an outplacement effort for everyone else. "The 'me' issues were also my personal concern. However, I knew those above me were being honest too. It was the key to managing change for everyone," added Crofts.

When asked about the success of placing their employees, Crofts said, "We worked with over 400 companies in our community. We made contacts in person and by mail. Just about all of our people found other employment. Some had to relocate. Most found positions that were equal to or better than the jobs they had with Dial Page." Crofts became the new vice president of human resources for US Personnel, a privately owned staff leasing company.

GET RESISTANCE TO CHANGE OUT IN THE OPEN

In the 1980s, many companies restructured and downsized their work forces. They believed that a lean and mean organization would emerge from the change, with people grateful to have jobs. They hoped that resistance to change among the remaining employees would dissipate. Unfortunately, that was not the case; suspicious employees waited for the other shoe to drop. Blame, if there's any to place, is with the managers who did a poor job of bringing resistance to change out in the open.

There will always be some people who resist even the most subtle of changes. A manufacturing company with 350 employees prepared to hire an additional 600 people. They didn't give much thought to how almost tripling their size would impact the existing population. As the plans unfolded, resistance among the existing employees grew stronger. Seasoned pros ostracized new employees. Turnover among new hires was high. It cost the company an enormous amount of money to continuously hire new employees, only to quickly process terminations. It became a vicious circle.

Resistance to change isn't all bad—up to a point. However, when an underground movement works to destroy the good that comes from change, it's a costly problem. Whether an organization is facing change due to rapid growth, a major downsizing, or something else, change still causes chaos. It's a powerful psychological event that can be frightening to your employees as well as yourself.

Waiting for change to balance out or normalize is unrealistic. Discussing the reasons for change and what the future holds, if known, is the best method for addressing the problem. Remember, the loss and grief associated with change leaves scars.

A useful framework for communicating change utilizes a four-step approach:

1. Accept the fact that employees have the right to hear the bad news as well as the good. Honesty is always the best policy.

2. Get employees involved in making the changes. Get their verbal input as well as their physical assistance, if necessary.

3. Recognize that the grapevine is a significant force in a changing environment. People use the rumor mill as a source of information. The grapevine gains power when management restricts the flow of important information.

4. Managers in changing environments have two acceptable positions: Either they already have established a direction and communicated it clearly to employees, or they're working on doing so.

When it comes to change management, direction and honesty create efficiency of effort and focus on key opportunities. Without it, wheels spin, false starts occur, and good intentions are diffused.

LITTLE THINGS MAKE A DIFFERENCE

Edith Fork is a mechanical engineer by trade. She's employed as a designer for IBC Engineering Services, Inc., a privately owned firm that designs mechanical systems for buildings.

Fork has been a part of an exciting growth process since the day she started. She and her colleagues have not only accepted change, but have embraced it. "Contrary to what most people would expect, rapid expansion has *positively* impacted morale. There's a sense of excitement in working here. We hire talented people who share the vision we have for the business," said Fork.

I asked her why she felt so strongly about the company. "The owners are generous. If we need something to do a better job and they feel it's reasonable and affordable, we get it." For example, because they grew so fast, they had a need for better computers, as well as printers. The employees presented their proposal. Management made a decision to get new computers and a new printer—something that would help them do a better job. The employees agreed to defer additional printers and printer accessories a while longer.

"We also had to expand the office to accommodate more people. We had a chance to voice our opinions on decorating ideas, color of carpet, etc. It was a little thing, but it made the employees feel good," added Fork.

Because they're hiring so many people, the owners are paying a $500 bonus to employees for each person they refer who's hired.

Fork finds working for a growing company that was once small, challenging and fun. She's also appreciative of the little things that help ease everyone through the throes of transition.

VALIDATE THE POSITIVE RESULTS OF CHANGE

Many organizations experience change as they increase in profits and people. One such business is Delaware North Companies, Inc., an international holding business with subsidiaries primarily in the food service industry. Jill Kelly, manager of human resources, was instrumental in implementing a series of major changes in the human resources function.

As project manager, she worked closely with a consultant to evaluate corporate human resources functions for change. They asked 50 of the top people in the company what they wanted from Human Resources. The end result—a totally different structure. They divided Human Resources into teams, and each team now supports a different subsidiary. They still maintain speciality areas but have become a hybrid of specialists and generalists. Human Resources even created their own newsletter that markets their services internally. They implemented Lotus Notes software, and the entire company has converted to Lotus Notes. "In a way, we've become leaders for the rest of the organization," said Kelly.

Through these changes and many others like them, the human resources department has evolved into a 28-person staff headquartered in Buffalo, with an additional 16 people in other locations throughout the country. They support roughly 20,000 employees.

In response to a question about how change impacted the morale issue, Kelly said, "All of the changes definitely impacted morale. Everything was different at first—reporting relationships, lots of new people, etc. But we are seeing the good results of change and hope to validate the positive impact with a survey. Change has people thinking, and communicating better. We also provide training, so there's plenty of learning outside of what takes place here at the company."

DELEGATE, ESPECIALLY DURING CHANGE

Change is the responsibility of managers at all levels. In addition, they may face the pressure to contain expenses—yet increase output—during the change process. Some managers try to be all things to all people. Many times they fail.

During times of change, it's especially important to get employees involved. By delegating, you help them share in the responsibility for change.

Thousands of businesses have faced major changes. In many cases, change has been painful and demoralizing. Delegating responsibility and encouraging employees to participate in the change movement has helped many managers move toward new frontiers.

Strategies for delegating during critical periods of uncertainty include:

❖ Set a clear and simple objective.

❖ Know each person's talents, as well as the skills he or she must improve upon, so as not to delegate to someone who can't do what you ask.

❖ Be specific about how much power and authority employees will have.

❖ Establish controls, such as a budget, a deadline, and when and how a formal review will take place.

❖ Give employees a way to measure their own success. How will you both know they've done a good job?

❖ Schedule regular updates regarding progress.

Most futurists say change will be tomorrow's steady diet. About the only thing that will not change very much is the importance of people to your organization. Learn how to delegate during change, and you'll reap the rewards for yourself as well as your employees.

GET BUY-IN

When an organization is losing more money than it's making, it inevitably leads to change. In the case of B/E Aerospace, Galley Products Division, a $100 million company in Jacksonville, FL, not only were they losing money, but most of the employees didn't know it.

The company builds the products that go into interiors of commercial aircraft, such as seats, seatback trays, serving carts, etc. Larry Huser, vice president and general manager, joined the company in 1996 and recognized the problem immediately. "We had to go back to ground zero and rebuild the company," said Huser. They brought in a consulting firm and made changes in key areas. They worked in teams, and the employees took charge. In eight months, they had a dramatic turnaround in profitability.

"Our people got back to basics. We didn't add 57 robots or lower wages to reach our goal," added Huser. The employees received feedback from the top down that if they didn't make major improvements in cutting costs, the company might not survive. Everyone got behind the effort and committed 120% of their energy to turning the company around.

"Management never held back. We were honest about the good news as well as the bad. Even our most senior employees who had little to lose were eager to buy into helping the company move forward," explained Huser. They capitalized on people wanting to do a good job and feel good when they went home at night. Employees became hungry for change when management made it clear they believed the problem could be fixed. Employees agreed and accepted the idea, and they are once again in the black.

PLAN FOR THE CHANGE REACTION

The phrase "The old way's the best way" isn't always right. It's not always easy to plan for change, so it's important to have a strategy when it occurs. Unfortunately, businesses often react to change with gut feelings, rather than with a plan based on sound objectives.

When change is inevitable, you may have responsibility for sharing the bad news. Here are some questions you will want to ask yourself as you prepare your strategy for introducing change:

- ❖ What is the change?

- ❖ Why is it being made?

- ❖ Who will be affected?

- ❖ When will it go into effect?

- ❖ How will it be implemented?

When you know the answers to these questions, but before you communicate the change with employees, there are several things you will want to keep in mind:

- ❖ **Share only the facts**. Tell only what you know. Don't speculate or interject "what if?" dialogue. Be honest in explaining possible problems the change may cause.

- ❖ **Be positive**. This time is difficult for everyone. You will only make matters worse by interjecting your own bitter feelings.

- ❖ **Allow time for adjustment**. People need time to accept the change—good or bad.

- ❖ **Follow up**. Everything may seem to be going smoothly after a change is announced, but there could be some hidden problems. Some employees may be suffering in silence. Be sensitive. Follow up.

There's no such thing as spontaneous recovery. The healing process is often long and rocky. Managers have a responsibility to keep their employees informed with the most honest and up-to-date information available. Anything less is unacceptable. A well-thought-out strategy will help you ease the pain of something new, better known as "change."

THINK LIKE "ONE" COMPANY

The magnitude of change—downsizing, rightsizing, whatever you want to call it—faced by U.S. industries in recent years has been staggering. And, contrary to expectations, restructured companies have had to struggle to regain their competitive edge while battling low morale and immense resistance to moving ahead. There's often a kind of post-restructuring hangover, and low morale is common among restructured firms.

Any company that buys the competition and doubles in size faces major challenges. When the parent company of an off-price retailer grew from $3 billion to $6 billion in sales with the purchase of another retail operation, they learned quickly the value of efficiently managing change.

Today, they think like one company because they've worked hard to blend the corporate culture. However, it took a plan to get to this point. They eased through a major transition with the help of "state of the company" talks. They worked tirelessly to keep all associates informed on the company's progress and goals. They recognized the importance of keeping employees' and customers' needs a priority, even when going through change.

At their corporate office, perks they provide include an on-site health club, golf clinic, and day care center. They have outings on company time—they swim, play tennis, line dance, give away door prizes—it all changes with a new theme every year. Anyone left behind to handle the business is later given a day off with pay. It's not hard to see why their company culture is described as "associate-oriented."

Although there are still some rough edges, they're settled down and see themselves as one company now. They still keep people informed concerning the reasons behind executive decisions.

Most reorganizations involve dramatic changes. New people arrive while familiar faces leave, but business goes on. A fundamental change in culture is expected. It's how the message is delivered and received that will make the difference in how employees accept all that follows.

BEAT THE DOWNSIDE OF DOWNSIZING

The magnitude of change impacting U.S. businesses is staggering. Millions of jobs were dropped from payrolls during the past ten years. Then, just when it seemed to be slowing down, takeover fever took over, and downsizing eliminated more jobs. Contrary to expectations, reorganized companies have had to struggle to regain a competitive edge. Many businesses have found themselves mired in low morale. Some face an overwhelming employee resistance to moving ahead. Why is this happening? Consider this example. The corporate directive of a Fortune 500 company said they needed to eliminate one-third of the work force. Management had only a short time to plan for the layoffs. Unfortunately, someone obviously got creative.

They called the employees into the company cafeteria. Each employee received a sealed envelope with the instruction not to open it until told to do so.

Employees were not concerned as they were often summoned for special announcements—even a surprise bonus check. Many anticipated such a bonus check inside the envelope. Everyone was totally unprepared for what awaited them.

When employees opened the envelopes, they realized they had been tricked. Two-thirds of the envelopes contained a blue piece of paper. One-third held the dreaded pink slip. The results were disastrous.

This true story is a sad commentary on how downsizing is sometimes handled. They had no strategy; the company and the employees—even those who stayed—lost.

Here are some suggestions for beating the downside of downsizing:

❖ Discuss your proposed plan with other decision makers.

❖ Make sure your plan includes benefits for the employees and the organization.

❖ Plan and practice what you're going to say to employees.

❖ Ask for feedback.

❖ Be ready for resistance and a negative impact on morale.

❖ Have a plan for implementing the change.

❖ Follow through and make sure people aren't struggling with the emotional aftermath; if they are, get them help.

Change of any kind—whether it's fiercer competition, lagging productivity, technological obsolescence, or a change in the way managers in your organization must manage—requires a strategy. It's particularly needed during downsizing or times of rapid growth. A straightforward and logical strategic plan will work if you take the time to evaluate the pros and cons and decide how you will approach your employees with the news.

ANTICIPATE HIGHS AND LOWS

JM Family Enterprises, Inc., a premier provider of quality auto-related products, went through a period of rapid growth in the early 1990s. According to Kurt Koehler, director of staffing, in order to effectively address change, an organization must analyze the change process and identify potential highs and lows in the associate population.

> "We restructured and relocated a portion of our financial services operation to a centralized facility in Mobile, AL. The reorganization involved changing the corporate culture, reassigning job duties, moving associates to a new location, maintaining operations during the transition, and taking care of the people who could not relocate with us. Our associates were grouped into three categories:
>
> ❖ Willing to relocate.
>
> ❖ Unable to relocate.
>
> ❖ Undecided.
>
> "Associates were invited to attend 'option' meetings. A meeting was designed specifically for each option. The associates could attend any or all of the meetings offered. Group meetings were followed by individual sessions with company management. Generous incentive and compensation options were offered to each group. Company management continued the associate meetings every quarter until the transition was completed," said Koehler.

He believes that continuous attention to the associate population provided the key to the smooth transition. "Whether experiencing rapid growth or staff reduction, the fact that the organization is undergoing significant change creates anxiety in the associate population. Growth and reduction can create the same issues," added Koehler.

Their situation impacted morale significantly, and the results were cyclical. Some associates were pleased to leave their old location for new challenges. Others were not. Some looked forward to new job responsibilities—others were upset at the thought of change.

> "It was a multiple reaction—like lighting a pack of firecrackers at once. We took five months to plan and introduce the move. Once the announcement was made, associates and management worked through the emotional highs and lows together and created a smooth transition. The financial capital required to create the physical change was not significant compared to what was at stake had the transition been unsuccessful. The attention to the associate population was the key," explained Koehler.

ACCEPTANCE IS A FOUR-STAGE PROCESS

Survival means coping with change. Change can be disconcerting—even frightening. Given a choice, most of us would rather stick with what we know than have to adjust to the unfamiliar. It's only natural.

When initiating change, you can expect employees to move through a four-stage process—not unlike the grieving process humans go through when facing a death or other major loss.

> STAGE 1: SHOCK. Unless there is a hint of change—something heard through the grapevine or suspected because of subtle differences in the way things are being done—most employees will be shocked.

> **What can the manager do?** Be sure everyone is well-informed. Be honest and to the point. Clarify misconceptions if you can.

STAGE 2: DENIAL. A normal response is: "This can't be happening to me. What am I going to do?" People are obviously upset with the organization and possibly their manager.

What can the manager do? Let them know that you will help them through the change. Emphasize the positive factors and the signs that are stable and not likely to change.

STAGE 3: UNDERSTANDING. Although they may not be ready to accept the change, they are beginning to understand the reasons behind it.

What can the manager do? Allow them opportunity to vent their feelings. Answer questions and appreciate their sense of loss.

STAGE 4: ACCEPTANCE. Grieving takes time—acceptance even longer. It will take time for them to digest what's happening. Eventually they will move toward acceptance.

What can the manager do? Listen. Involve them in preparing for the future. Get their support. Show them you have accepted change too.

Dave Curtis assisted his employees work through the four-stage process of change when the company decided to relocate it's corporate headquarters to Houston. Although most everyone was given the opportunity to move, less than 25% accepted the offer. As expected, there were many distraught employees. "It was a very stressful time. Our employees felt like there were only two ways to look at the world—good and bad. As they began to work through the four-stage change process, I think everyone saw light at the end of the tunnel," said Curtis.

Managers are no strangers to change. Whether introducing a product, system, procedure, or strategy, you can expect resistance. Rapid growth and downsizing are a more difficult challenge. Anyone looking forward to the day when they can depend on stable conditions are living in a fantasy world. Change is a way of life and implicit in a free enterprise system. Learn to accept it—help your employees do the same.

GIVE THEM TIME

Change in American industry has been transformational—causing major chaos, in many cases. Managers have the responsibility to communicate change. They often feel the pressure to contain expenses while increasing profitability, which makes it even more difficult. The net result of change is that managers must cope with greater uncertainty, complexity, interdependence, and pressure than at any time in history. Managing change would be easy if everyone reacted to it in the same way. Unfortunately, change impacts each person differently.

Garner's, Inc., a small, food cooperative located in a rural community, was forced to meet change—like it or not. Customers appreciated the products that were offered as much as they liked being treated as top priority. Eight part-time employees and one full-time manager worked at the co-op. Then the day came when the business could not survive. The competition would force them to close within six months.

It was very difficult for everyone to accept the negative impact of change. The owners were anxious to move forward and cut their losses. The employees seemed to accept the inevitable. Yet, in reality, they were very distraught—they suffered in silence and kept their feelings hidden. They loved the store and hated to see everything come to an end—they were like a family.

Despite the promise of a small severance pay and good references, the employees felt devastated. They had difficulty accepting the uncertainty surrounding their future. "I didn't want to see what we had worked for disappear, but we had no choice. Our employees were dedicated and generous, sometimes volunteering time in the store when sales were slow. They invested so much in their jobs. I felt terrible," said Arnie Babcock, owner. "I understood how they felt and tried to help them the best I could."

These are the suggestions Babcock offered for helping employees handle the feeling of loss of control, of sadness, and of grief:

❖ **Always be honest**. Deception will destroy all of the good in a relationship.

❖ **Help employees manage the pressure**. Put yourself in their place. Don't overlook anything. How do you think they feel? The owner or manager is ultimately responsible for handling change.

❖ **Control your own reactions**. If you can't do anything about the change, accept it and help others do the same.

❖ **Allow them time to grieve**. Loss of any kind is difficult. Give them space. Give them time.

R EINVEST IN EMPLOYEES

When your organization suffers cutbacks, how do you manage morale problems? Pep talks, games, and incentives are often not enough to turn a business from failure to success. Changing the culture from a defensive stance to forward movement takes time. This is where reinvesting in employees comes in.

The difference between investing in employees and reinvesting is this:

❖ *Investing* is done in a healthy business for future growth. Employees view these investments as a sign of good times. They include things like a company cafeteria, fitness facility, day care center, or extravagant parties.

❖ *Reinvesting* spends resources saved or earned through other actions.

When reinvesting, a business allocates a portion of the resources saved through a cost-reduction action (such as a layoff) to the work environment and remaining employees.

This takes the yields of employee sacrifices and returns them to the employees. However, only through a clear message of reinvestment can management successfully ask employees to make sacrifices.

In order for an organization to be successful with the reinvesting concept, several things should be considered.

➡ First, define the objectives of reinvesting. Reinvesting should never be done to simply ease the pain of guilt or to satisfy personal needs. Investments have an expected return. One objective might be an improvement in employee morale, with an expected return of increased productivity. It may keep good people with the organization.

- Also, it should start at the top. Management must demonstrate full support for reinvesting. Financial commitment, as well as time invested, will make or break reinvesting.
- Finally, the organization must decide what kind of reinvesting is the most needed and valuable to employees. For example, is a 401K program more important than an extra day of paid vacation for everyone? Is a service award dinner more valuable than changing all vending machines to "free vend" once each month? There must be a process for deciding where to spend the money.

Reinvesting isn't a new concept. It's been around at least a decade, and its popularity is growing. After all, if you had to lay off 300 people for an estimated annual savings of $2.5 million, you could reinvest one-half million and still save $2 million. On a smaller scale, a $20,000 savings with a reinvestment of $5,000 still saves $15,000.

If approached carefully, reinvesting—even during times of significant change—can be a valuable motivational tool in sustaining morale among the survivors.

DIVERSIFY

Building an organization capable of adapting to an ever-changing environment may require diversification of products, services, or the way you do business. A key element in the success of any company is the ability to respond to change.

Changes can be a result of many factors, both internal and external. External factors that have affected the transportation industry include deregulation, rising fuel costs, narrow margins and driver shortages. In an interview with Kathleen Coakley, president of C. H. Coakley & Co./

Mayflower, she said her company is diversifying now in preparation for change in the future.

> "In addition to hiring, training, and promoting quality personnel, some of the other measures that we have implemented include: redirecting our services into less 'seasonal' lines of business, acquiring an additional 500,000 square feet of real estate to accommodate commercial storage clients, contracting 'owner-operators,' expanding our business record retention division, and developing a full-service printing company. Diversification affords our company the ability to create synergies between profit centers, enhance the 'bottom line,' and weather changing markets," explained Coakley, who is in business with her brothers, Chuck and Mike.

The Coakleys see change as continuing and resulting in a positive impact on their company. "We are well-positioned for the year 2000. We have an excellent business mix, no debt, a positive cash flow, room for expansion, and can react quickly to the needs of our customers," added Coakley.

To build an organization capable of adapting to a changing environment, they strive to do the following:

❖ **Hire the right people**. Hire dynamic and innovative thinkers who are not only open to change, but can also foresee, initiate, and facilitate change.

❖ **Continue to educate members of the organization**. Explain the nature of the business to employees and emphasize the need to be willing to adapt to it. Equip them with the knowledge to make immediate, sound decisions.

❖ **Treasure the company's history and embrace its future**. Many companies are rich in history and tradition. Sharing this legacy helps people develop "roots," a sense of belonging, and an appreciation of the past. Historical perspective adds insight. Furthermore, understanding the natural progression of the company can help people view change as a reasonable, ongoing process.

❖ **Communicate**. Work to improve listening skills. Empathize, encourage, and support. Keep employees current and involved. Foster pride, unity, and cohesiveness. Anticipate change.

❖ **Be forthright, direct, honest, and sensitive.** Be consistent in business practices, policies, and dealings. Be fair, develop trust. Have integrity.

C. H. Coakley & Co./Mayflower doesn't claim to have all of the answers to manage change. But they certainly are on the right track. In 1995, they earned Mayflower Transit's highest honor bestowed upon agents who are in the top 5% of the organization. Criteria include quality, sales, operations, and outstanding service.

After my interview with Kathleen Coakley, I was not surprised to learn of their extraordinary achievements. Although she is quick to give the credit to her brothers and employees, she is undoubtedly one of the forces behind the company's enormous success. Management is focused but also diversified in its thinking. This combination has made the company, whose history can be traced back to 1888, a model employer.

CHANGE COMES IN FAMILIAR PACKAGES

In 1991, a European company hired me to conduct a retained search to find a president for their North American division. The employees already employed by the company had an immediate concern. They wanted to know whether or not the new leader would make major changes—including replacing them with his or her own choices. The owner rejected the single, interested internal candidate, and hired an outsider. As feared, many people lost their jobs with the obvious impact on morale.

A different example involves Lands' End, a large apparel-catalog retailer. As reported on August 30, 1996 by Robert Berner of *The Wall Street Journal*, they made a significant change in 1994—Chairman Gary Comer booted the outsider he had hired to run the business. He replaced him with Michael Smith, a "thirtysomething" insider who had never worked anywhere else. He started with Lands' End as a college intern and stayed with the company after graduating in 1983 with a degree in marketing. "People trusted me and knew I did not have any hidden agendas," Smith said. Soon, profits began to soar.

So far, Smith receives much of the credit for the company's success. He stepped up without disturbing the tightly knit culture of the 7,000-employee company. Some say being an insider is an asset as he seeks to change the company.

Change often comes in familiar packages—sometimes for the best. Don't overlook people in your organization who could make a difference in profitability as well as morale.

SUMMARY

A hundred years ago, we had no radios, televisions, airplanes, microwave ovens, or antibiotics. There were no telephones, elevators, automobiles, automatic dishwashers, or shopping malls. Who knows what will take place in the next 100 years?

Change causes turmoil. Change can leave people feeling angry, scared, confused, or depressed. Yet, it's really not change that creates reactions like these. It's fear of the unknown. Most people resist altering well-established habits. It's simply easier to stay in one's comfort zone than to try something unfamiliar.

Help your employees adapt to change. Consider the following:

❖ Change as little as possible—just enough to meet your objectives.

❖ Conduct a cost-benefit analysis of the change before implementing.

❖ Determine previously unanticipated possible consequences.

❖ Conduct a pilot study.

❖ Have a realistic time frame—too much too quickly spells disaster.

❖ Decide how you're going to judge results.

❖ Have a plan for dealing with unexpected problems.

❖ Be sensitive to the impact of change on your employees.

You will always have change as well as the organizational problems that go along with it. Sooner or later, it will affect morale. In order to handle the transition successfully, you should be sure your employees understand the reasons for change. Change takes commitment and confidence. It means building a climate for change that welcomes and manages change. It means protecting employees with assurance of protection from economic loss. Rumors, resistance, and restlessness are difficult to avoid. Often the people issues seem secondary to the organizational issues, but they really go hand in hand.

Effective leaders have the qualities necessary to take charge of change. In the sixth century BC, Lao-Tzu described the profile of a successful leader, one who can manage change:

> *The superior leader gets things done with very little motion.*
>
> *He imparts instruction not through many words,*
>
> *But through a few deeds.*
>
> *He keeps informed about everything,*
>
> *But interferes hardly at all.*
>
> *He is a catalyst,*
>
> *And although things wouldn't get done as well,*
>
> *If he weren't there,*
>
> *When they succeed, he takes no credit.*
>
> *And because he takes no credit,*
>
> *Credit never leaves him.*
>
> *—Lao-Tzu*

As leaders, you can manage change or let it manage you. Be a change agent, make an effort to minimize surprises, and remember that people want the truth, even if it's bad news. Regardless of the pressures, skip the power plays; work to avoid the breakdowns in communication. Remember, people resist change because of threats to relationships and personal anxiety. In many cases, people are their jobs—they identify so closely with what they do that any change can be devastating.

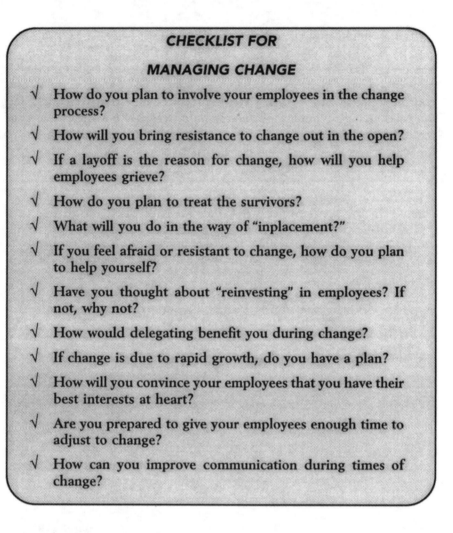

CHECKLIST FOR

MANAGING CHANGE

√   How do you plan to involve your employees in the change process?

√   How will you bring resistance to change out in the open?

√   If a layoff is the reason for change, how will you help employees grieve?

√   How do you plan to treat the survivors?

√   What will you do in the way of "inplacement?"

√   If you feel afraid or resistant to change, how do you plan to help yourself?

√   Have you thought about "reinvesting" in employees? If not, why not?

√   How would delegating benefit you during change?

√   If change is due to rapid growth, do you have a plan?

√   How will you convince your employees that you have their best interests at heart?

√   Are you prepared to give your employees enough time to adjust to change?

√   How can you improve communication during times of change?

Additional Reading

Albrecht, Karl. *The Northbound Train—Finding the Purpose, Setting the Direction, Shaping the Destiny of Your Organization.* New York, NY: AMACOM, 1994.

Albrecht, Steve. *Crisis Management for Corporate Self-Defense.* New York, NY: AMACOM, 1996.

Amatt, John. *Straight to the Top and Beyond.* San Diego, CA: Pfeiffer & Company, 1995.

Barger, Nancy J. and Linda K. Kirby. *The Challenge of Change in Organizations: Helping Employees Thrive in the New Frontier.* Palo Alto, CA: Davies-Black Publishing, 1995.

Barner, Robert W. *Crossing the Minefield.* New York, NY: AMACOM, 1994.

Birchall, David, and Laurence Lyons. *Creating Tomorrow's Organization: Unlocking the Benefits of Future Work.* London, UK: Pitman Publishing, 1995.

Blohowiak, Don. *How's All the Work Going to Get Done?: How to Manage the Challenges of Churning Out More Work with Less Staff.* Franklin Lakes, NJ: Career Press, 1995.

Carr, Clay. *Choice, Change & Organizational Change—Practical Insights from Evolution for Business Leaders & Thinkers.* New York, NY: AMACOM, 1996.

Dolan, John Patrick. *Movers, Shakers, and Changemakers,* 2nd ed. Dubuque, IA: Kendall/Hunt Publishing Company, 1994.

Downs, Alan. *Corporate Executions: The Ugly Truth about Layoffs—How Corporate Greed Is Shattering Lives, Companies, and Communities.* New York, NY: AMACOM, 1995.

Galpin, Timothy J. *The Human Side of Change—A Practical Guide to Organization Redesign.* San Francisco, CA: Jossey-Bass Publishers, 1996.

Herman, Roger E. *Turbulence! Challenges & Opportunities in the World of Work.* Akron, OH: Oakhill Press, 1995.

Illes, Louise Moser. *Sizing Down: Chronicle of a Plant Closing.* New York, NY: Cornell University Press, 1996.

Jeffreys, Shep J. *Coping with Workplace Change.* Los Altos, CA: Crisp Publishing, 1995.

King, Deborah A. *Learning to Live with Downsizing.* Roswell, GA: EMI Publishing, 1996.

Martin, James. *The Great Transition—Using the Seven Disciplines of Enterprise Engineering to Align People, Technology, and Strategy.* New York, NY: AMACOM, 1995.

Tomasko, Robert M. *Rethinking the Corporation—The Architecture of Change.* New York, NY: AMACOM, 1995.

Whiteside, John. *The Phoenix Agenda.* New York, NY: John Wiley & Sons, Inc., 1995.

Wilson, Thomas B. *Innovative Reward Systems for the Changing Workplace.* New York, NY: McGraw Hill, 1994.

Woodward, Harry. *Navigating Through Change.* Burr Ridge, IL: Irwin Professional Publishing, 1994.

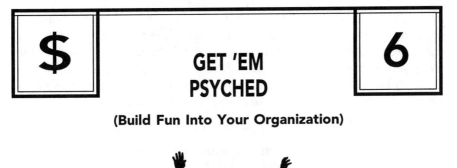

$ 6

GET 'EM PSYCHED

(Build Fun Into Your Organization)

"Fun is not the most important contributor to performance, motivation or creativity, but it's a helpful feature to consider."
—David J. Abramis

• •

For some people, working 8 to 5, 3 to 11, or 11 to 7 is just a way to make a living. They think in terms of "another day, another dollar." Managing such a work force is no easy task. It's difficult to get passionate about people who are just putting in their time and pushing you to your limits. Thankfully, they are in the minority in most organizations.

Employers are often more interested in understanding what gets employees excited about work than about any other factor related to performance. Two recognized motivational approaches are "extrinsic" and "intrinsic." *Extrinsic motivation* involves the use of external rewards such as increases in pay, promotions, and praise. *Intrinsic motivation* involves arranging the job and the work so that it's interesting, challenging, and fulfilling; the nature of the work provides the rewards.

The late consultant, Dr. W. Edwards Deming, drew an analogy. In intrinsic motivation, those who bond with the company will pick up a nail in the parking lot although it's not their responsibility. Someone who may not see the nail will benefit by avoiding a flat tire. Extrinsically motivated employees won't pick up the nail because that's not their job. Why should they help someone who is a potential competitor? Participants in Dr. Deming's seminars came up with the following reasons for poor motivation. Do any of them apply to your organization?

- ❖ Lack of direction, unclear goals and objectives.

- ❖ Lack of time, resources, and equipment necessary to achieve goals set for workers.

- ❖ Arbitrary decisions by the boss.

- ❖ No indication that employees' contributions are valued.

- ❖ Conflicting organizational goals within the company.

- ❖ Deadline anxiety.

- ❖ Staff not valued by line organization.

- ❖ Hierarchy tries to run technology it doesn't understand.

- ❖ Short-term objectives conflict with long-term objectives.

- ❖ Inconsistent application of policy.

- ❖ Poor training.

- ❖ Specifications constrain creativity.

- ❖ Pressure for results; organizational fear.

- ❖ Company and union adversarial relationship.

- ❖ Red tape.

Studies conducted by the University of Chicago Industrial Research Center of over a half-million employees show that 2–4 out of every 10 people find fault with something in their work environment. Getting those same people psyched isn't easy.

In addition, fewer layers of management means fewer promotions. Keeping people happy when the traditional career ladder has lost some of its rungs is tough. Progressive organizations use creative ideas to get top performers to stay with the company. Lateral moves, more responsibility, paid sabbaticals, and raises tied to performance, not seniority, have provided a cure in some cases.

The best strategy for winning employees' cooperation isn't just about fun and entertaining diversions; it's about encouraging not only the fast-trackers, but the slow and tenacious as well. Look for the good qualities in everyone, especially those who are discouraged, bored, or unwilling. Focus your energy on motivating the rest of the team, and you may also win over some of the dissenters too.

Employees come in all shapes and types. Some are like the energizer bunny; others are quietly effective. Before you can get 'em psyched, you have to know what to get 'em psyched about. Share your vision, encourage them to contribute ideas on how to reach company goals, and then help them do it.

It's easy to forget that a manager's responsibility goes beyond attending meetings, preparing a budget, and solving problems. Building and maintaining a motivated team takes patience, energy, and know-how. It also means teaching others rather than doing it yourself, making the job interesting, and keeping everyone informed.

CONSIDER AN R&R FUND

When a stockbroker at Dean Witter Reynolds Inc. has a bellringer day, everyone wins. The successful broker puts $5 into the R&R fund with a maximum contribution of $25 in one month. Three to four times each year, they use the money for social activities that include all employees. Functions have ranged from cocktails, hors d' oeuvres, and dinner in a fine restaurant to a cruise complete with bayou music and a scrumptious Cajun buffet.

Jo Ann Corrao, vice president of investments, sees this morale-building activity as a big plus for business. The brokers are happy to contribute to this relatively inexpensive way to raise money for extra fun. They know that the support of everyone in the office is critical to their success. Their way of rewarding team effort is very effective in keeping morale high.

LEARN TO HAVE FUN

When it comes to laughter and good times, Southwest Airlines has an edge. For over 25 years, Chairman Herb Kelleher and his team of fun-loving employees have made Southwest a great place to work.

According to an Associated Press article that appeared in *The Atlanta Journal/The Atlanta Constitution* on May 18, 1996, Southwest Airlines was among the top ten "100 Best Companies To Work For In America." *Fortune* magazine rated it among the most admired corporations in 1995 when 124,000 people competed for 5,473 jobs.

What makes them stand out? It's been described as "a love affair between labor and management." How did that happen? It started with an idea doodled on a cocktail napkin—the rest is history.

Today, the corporate culture is one of altruism, hard work, humor, and fun. Kelleher is the chief of partiers. He's been known to impersonate Elvis, complete with a white jumpsuit and gold chains, and Corporal Max Klinger from MASH. He's dressed as a leprechaun and served Irish coffee to passengers. Wearing a bonnet and bloomers, he sang "Tea For Two" to his staff, and they loved it!

Employees who join in the lighthearted mood by wearing Mickey Mouse T-shirts and giant pink bunny ears, and flight attendants who give safety instructions in rap are part of what makes this organization different.

Southwest has no seat assignments and no "first class section." If you're connecting with another airline, plan to carry your own bags. Bring your own snacks and don't expect a meal. A typical greeting sounds like this:

> "Good morning ladies and gentlemen. Those of you who wish to smoke, please file out to our lounge on the wing where you can enjoy our feature film 'Gone With The Wind.'"

Fun and games? Yes. But they also make money—lots of it. In 1995, their 23rd profitable year in a row, they made a record $182.6 million.

Southwest Airlines may be unconventional, but they've never had a problem finding or keeping good people.

SHOW APPRECIATION

"Employee Appreciation Day" is a big hit with employees of Pick 'N Save grocery stores, a subsidiary of Roundy's. Linda Yergens, front-end operations manager, is an 18-year veteran. She says employees love this special event, which occurs three times each year. "Each person receives discount coupons which can be used that day. Employees also get a 5% discount on *everything* they buy. In addition, the names of all employees are entered into a drawing for small prizes like T-shirts, mugs, and 5-pound hams. Supervisors visit all stores to keep the excitement and momentum going.

Yergens is responsible for eight stores in her area. At their annual meetings, they draw the name of one employee from each location. All eight winners receive a free lunch. Of these eight winners, one wins a trip for two to Las Vegas, and the other seven get a 13-inch color television. Stores in other areas hold similar drawings once a year.

Although it doesn't cost a lot of money, it's a way to say "thanks" that has made a difference in turnover in a traditionally high-turnover industry.

GIVE US THIS DAY

Thousands of companies have said "yes" to "Take Our Daughters To Work Day." This public education program, sponsored by the Ms. Foundation for Women, was launched in 1993 in response to research findings on the adolescent development of girls. Studies by Harvard University researchers, the American Association of University Women (AAUW), and the Minnesota Women's Fund indicate that during adolescence, girls often receive less attention than boys in school and in youth-serving programs. They also suffer from lower expectations than do their male counterparts.

The annual Take Our Daughters To Work project is celebrated as a crucial show of support for the self-esteem of adolescent girls everywhere. More than 5 million girls, ages 9 to 15, are expected to accompany a parent to work in 1997.

During this special day, girls get a glimpse of their own future potential. They learn about employment opportunities outside the home. They have the chance to see work as an integral part of the lives of women and a good reason to plan for future careers. They'll learn about life options and what it takes to succeed. Mothers, fathers, teachers, aunts, uncles, and neighbors will show girls that women can achieve in the world and will talk to them about the promise of education.

A recent Roper Starch Worldwide poll confirms that Take Our Daughters To Work Day is one of the most popular, well-known, and highly regarded programs for girls in the country. The poll reports that more than 140 million Americans are aware of this event. Ninety-two percent of those people think the day is a positive experience for girls.

PROVIDE EDUCATION AS AN INCENTIVE

On May 20, 1996, *Time* magazine ran an article entitled "Doing Well By Doing Good." One of the companies featured was Fel-Pro, a privately held company that makes gaskets, sealants, and lubricants for cars. They provide their employees with many special perks. *Working Mother Magazine* has put them on its "Best Places To Work" list for ten consecutive years.

Fel-Pro is committed to education. They have a tuition reimbursement program for all employees and pay bonuses to those who earn degrees. Employees' college-bound children get $3,500 in scholarship money. They also contribute toward tutoring costs for employees with children who have special needs.

Fel-Pro invests in its work force because management believes that, in the long run, the investment leads to lowered costs and increased market share.

REWARD THEM WHEN THEY LEAST EXPECT IT

Most people enjoy a pleasant surprise from time to time, but an employee who gets a special reward when not expecting it is likely to be a loyal employee for a long time. Ron Hawes, M.D., always looks out for his medical staff. "When you give them a Christmas bonus, for example, it's almost a rite of passage, and it becomes an entitlement. But when you reward them when they least expect it, they never forget it," said Hawes.

He rewards employees who go the extra mile with a gift basket, dinner for two, or a cash bonus. "I believe that money is still the most versatile gift to give. I don't always know what people would enjoy the most, so money allows them to select something they can use," added Hawes.

Elsie Sanders concurs. She and her husband retired and bought an existing business in the community where they both grew up. "I like to surprise my employees. It might be something as little as a $20 gift certificate to a music store or a day off with pay. I believe that my people work hard and do whatever it takes to satisfy the customers. They love the surprises as much as I enjoy giving them," explained Sanders.

Most people treasure the times they are rewarded for something they said or did. Sometimes, rewards come simply through praise—other times, a gift might be more appropriate. The sooner you reward someone, the more it means. Spontaneous rewards reinforce the exhilaration the employee experiences in the first glow of success or accomplishment. If you reward them when they least expect it, it's all the more meaningful.

GET CASUAL

Many organizations have gone casual. According to a survey of 752 white-collar workers conducted by San Francisco-based clothing maker Levi Strauss & Co., casual dress has a positive impact on the workplace. The majority of respondents (81%) report that casual dress improves morale. Eighty-seven percent say that "dressing down" has a positive effect on productivity.

Casual day once a week is the most popular. Some companies report they have casual day only once a month or just occasionally. Thirty-five percent of the companies allow casual dress all of the time. Nine out of ten employees, including senior management, participate.

Although some people believe the professional atmosphere is lost when there's a casual dress policy, the majority are highly in favor because of its positive impact on morale.

MAKE SAFETY COUNT

At Robert Bowden, Inc., a privately owned manufacturer and distributor of building materials, safety and recognition are synonymous. Their safety incentive awards program is company-wide. They set a monthly accident goal that's based on the prior year's data, so it's achievable. (The goal is never zero accidents because they've found that's unrealistic.) Both the department and the division must reach the goal in order to earn breakfast, lunch, or a special gift.

"Our tight reporting and management system eliminates the risk of injured employees not reporting accidents. We want to know if anyone's hurt," explained Mark McCann, training and safety coordinator.

Their employees have learned the value of a safe work environment. "The incentive offered adds to the efficiency and fun," said McCann.

HOST A GAG NITE

Fun is part of what makes a business successful. When people feel good, they want to be productive. At OHMEDA Pharmaceuticals Products Division, it's no exception. Bob Oberg, district sales manager, has a great time with his team at Gag Nite.

"It's a time for our sales people to get together for an evening of relaxation." Oberg initiated Gag Nite more than 15 years ago. Many of the company's other sales districts have followed suit.

Every year in June, one or two people have the privilege of purchasing a gag gift for each team member. They award the gifts at a special dinner. It's never done to cause embarrassment—just to have a few laughs. Gifts have ranged from a key chain for someone who always loses the car in the airport lot to a gigantic pencil for the person who takes the most notes at sales meetings. They've also awarded an "I love to shop" T-shirt and a book on how to get organized. Eventually, everyone has the chance to host the evening and select the gag items.

"I see my team having fun. Everyone is recognized. We have a nice dinner in a private dining room so we can hoot and holler," said Oberg.

Gag Nite has become as popular as their annual awards banquet and just as entertaining.

OFFER THEM "HIDDEN PAYCHECKS"

Many organizations claim they want their employees to feel appreciated. They offer salary plus benefits; for the average employee, however, there are very few additional perks. Many businesses do a few things like lunch or dinner for everyone, but one company stands out above the others—Quad/Graphics, Inc., a privately owned billion-dollar printing company. In speaking with Claire Ho, corporate spokesperson, I learned more about the thinking behind their generous endowment of employees.

"We do many extravagant things to show employees that we value them. We also believe that it's important to look at the lighter side of life and enjoy the success that we've worked so hard to achieve," said Ho. One of their many slogans is "Work hard, play harder."

Harry V. Quadracci, president and founder, is the driving force behind the energy and high morale in his organization. In 1996, along with 2,500 volunteers, he threw a party in honor of the 25th anniversary of the company's incorporation.

More than eleven thousand employees and their families attended the 12-hour extravaganza, described as an event that put most county fairs to shame. People wandered among the many tents that covered the grounds and enjoyed complimentary food, beer, soda pop, cotton candy, games, and rides. Food included 26,000 Italian sausages, 14,000 ears of corn, 12,000 hot dogs, and 800 pounds of baked beans, as well as potluck-style dishes brought by employees.

The numerous activities for children and adults included swimming, volleyball, a midway, and musical entertainment. The evening closed with a 50-minute video, fireworks, and laser-light show described as one "that left everyone fused into a solid mass and ready to fight for Quad to the end of their days."

As you may suspect, the company doesn't stop at parties. They offer "hidden paychecks" in the forms of an on-site medical facility with no-cost care for employees and their immediate families and access to a network of doctors who offer significant discounts. Employees can apply for interest-free loans to purchase a car or repair an existing vehicle. They're also offer discounted bus services to the suburbs where company plants are located. Two annual holiday parties, one for adults and one for children, are a big hit. On-site day-care services and scholarships in the form of tuition reductions to help defray costs are very popular. "The Management Review," when managers put on a mini-musical production for their employees, provides great entertainment.

"We offer so much more than a paycheck and benefit package because we know that our people are what make the company successful. When morale is high because they're excited about working for Quad/Graphics, everyone wins. And hopefully, should employees choose to leave the company, they leave with good feelings," added Ho.

NAME YOUR CUSTOMER

A company that prides itself on how they treat employees, as well as customers, is Ace Products. Committed to the sale of small household items like kitchen knives, potato peelers, graters, ice cream scoops, and wine bottle openers, their customers are small family-owned hardware and grocery stores, as well as speciality shops. They focus on determining what new products a customer will buy. Unfortunately, it's not a simple task. The outstanding business successes usually result from suppliers seeing needs that the customers themselves have not have recognized. That's the challenge.

Ace Products feels it's critical that their salespeople feel good about the company and its merchandise because if they don't, neither will their customers. One of their approaches to maintaining good morale is to invite each member of the sales team to name his or her best customer each year. That customer receives a cake in the salesperson's name, at the company's expense, along with a handwritten note of appreciation. Mike Williams, president, said, "It's a little thing to do for the customer, but it helps them know we recognize the importance of their business. Our salespeople enjoy deciding on the best customer and having the cake delivered. We're a small company, but we still look for ways to keep our employees and customers happy."

COUNT ON RETIREES

It's no secret that the nation's population is aging, resulting in a growing number of middle-aged and older employees. Many are approaching retirement, and a shortage of talent when they retire presents a variety of challenges to management.

After people retire, they're often never seen again. The company throws a farewell party in their honor, and they soon are off doing other things. That's not the case, however, with a healthcare company in New York that encourages retiree participation, along with regular employees, in quality circles. They've found that active workers can benefit from the retirees' experience. How this organization solved the need for more help with no extra dollars to spend might also benefit your business. Brenda Davis, general manager, said:

> "We were looking for a way to keep our retirees involved since many of them had been practicing physicians and other medical personnel. Although it was agreed that they would not be paid for their time, it didn't matter to them. Once each month, they meet with members of cross-functional teams to review some of the most difficult issues facing healthcare and our facility today. We've found their input to be invaluable. Our current employees welcome the outside advice and have implemented many of the suggestions that have come from the groups."

M ODIFY THE NATURE OF THE WORK

To many people, repetitive work often becomes boring. There are ways, however, to add new elements to a job to make it more interesting. For instance, rather than have an employee do only one part of a large job, expand the assignment to include the complete job from beginning to end. This varies the job, uses a wide variety of skills, and gives the employee a greater feeling of accomplishment. In addition, you can increase the employee's responsibility by providing greater autonomy.

Given the trend today to create self-managed work teams, it makes sense to assign employees to teams where they will complement other team members. Allow them enough time to adjust to their new roles and build on their strengths. Then, ask for their help in training new employees when appropriate.

Consider this example; Jerry hated his job, or at least that's what he told everyone he worked with—everyone except his boss, who didn't see the whole picture when it came to Jerry's dissatisfaction. When the supervisor took time to listen, his employee's negative attitude surprised him. Until recently, Jerry had seemed comfortable with his assignments. His supervisor didn't realize that Jerry was about to explode. The work bored him—in fact, it had never challenged him—because it was the same old task repeated. Obviously something had to change.

And, it did. He and his supervisor decided that he needed more responsibility. The supervisor made Jerry a team leader. His attitude improved, and, before the year was over, he was promoted to lead-worker for the shift. This didn't happen overnight; however, by simply changing the nature of an employee's work, you could find yourself with a whole new perspective on your employee.

B E THERE TO GREET THEM

No one expects the president of a company to personally greet employees when they arrive or bid them goodnight at the end of a second shift. So, would you be surprised to see the CEO meeting and greeting employees on a Saturday or on third shift? Probably, but for one company, it's just a matter of getting 'em psyched. Francis Loeb, managing director of Loeb AG, a department store chain in Switzerland, has a unique approach for improving morale. He personally greets his employees because he wants them to feel valued.

Loeb is not alone in his strategy. I once worked for a man who insisted that managers greet employees on all three shifts, and sometimes, he greeted them himself. It wasn't done on a daily basis but on the spur of the moment or on special occasions. He loved to see the surprised looks on the faces of employees who wondered why the president wasn't home sleeping.

Eventually, the company even organized a contingent of managers and supervisors who volunteered to serve as greeters at company events that spanned weekends, holidays, and off-shifts. It was a benefit to employees as well as to those who got in the habit of making others feel welcome and appreciated.

THE 1212 CLUB

Bowling and golf leagues, baseball teams, tennis and basketball courts, museum trips, canoeing, kite flying, picnics, company cookbooks, shopping trips, Christmas parties, and in-house health facilities are a few of the events, activities, and perks that are sponsored either by Atlas Van Lines in Evansville, IN, or by their employee 1212 Club.

The club is named for the company's street address. I spoke with Pat Walter, assistant vice president of human resources, who told me that the company financially supports the club but that fund-raisers like the cookbook bring in extra money to help defray the costs of special events. "We're a paternalistic organization. People are very sensitive. We offer lots of benefits to our employees beyond the traditional medical and life insurance, etc. Our employees like to spend time together outside of work. In-house programs, like Weight Watchers once a week during lunch, are also very popular."

The 1212 Club elects officers every year, and they make the decisions about what kinds of fun things the club will offer employees and their families. The activities they plan add to the company culture and high morale. As evidence, Walter shared the fact that among their hourly employees, the seniority average is ten years. For managers, it's fifteen years. Many of the clerical and administrative positions are entry level, but turnover is low. Entertaining activities offered in conjunction with the 1212 Club have helped employees maintain a balance between work and family.

DO SOMETHING EXTRA TO REWARD DEDICATION

Recognize staff effort beyond what the organization offers in pay and benefits. Sometimes managers take an employee's long hours and dedication to the task for granted. That attitude can lead to the words "I quit."

Phil Kaplan, vice president, investment and portfolio manager for Smith Barney, Inc., depends on his sales assistant, who also works for three others, to help him meet client expectations. Although she's paid by the company, he also pays her an extra incentive every month and awards a bonus twice a year. Kaplan wants her to know he appreciates her. Birthdays and special occasions never go unnoticed. A small gift or check is his way of saying a special "thank you."

CONSIDER SABBATICAL LEAVE

When you hear the word "sabbatical," do you think of a vacation? The word "sabbatical" refers to a year of rest for the land and is observed every seventh year in ancient Judea. Today, some organizations offer employees sabbaticals for the purpose of study or personal renewal. Do they work? How do they impact the bottom line? For answers to these questions, let's look at what two companies are doing to get 'em psyched with sabbaticals—a popular employee perk.

Wells Fargo Bank in San Francisco has two types of sabbaticals: The Personal Growth Leave program, which is paid for up to three months, and the Volunteer Leave program, which allows up to six months of paid leave. There are eligibility requirements: The Personal Growth Leave program requires a minimum of ten years in the company, and the employee must be in good standing. The Volunteer Leave program requires only three years of service.

The bank receives roughly 40 sabbatical requests each year, most of which they reject. The selection committees must fit the sabbaticals into a budget; more-highly-paid employees deplete the budget faster than lower-paid employees. The selection committees also look for projects that actually require a full-time commitment—those that an employee could do while working full- or part-time are less likely to be approved.

Apple Computers in Cupertino, CA, offers employees a six-week paid sabbatical after every five years of employment. They see it as an opportunity for employees to recharge. Once employees become eligible, they have one year in which to start the sabbatical. They may request an extension for their start date of either one year for business reasons or six months for personal reasons.

An application process helps with scheduling leave times. However, sabbatical leave is company policy, so despite occasional conflicts, employees who have earned paid time-off get it. Apple keeps a computer listing of eligible employees. It helps in planning, especially when a cluster of employees fall into the same eligibility time frame.

The general consensus concerning a sabbatical is that it's a popular benefit from the employees' perspective, but it's expensive for the employer. Whether or not there's a quantified direct impact on the bottom line varies with each program and organization.

1 MILLION DOLLARS FOR YOUR THOUGHTS

A winning idea comes from *Making Successful Presentations* by Terry Smith. The next time you conduct a problem-solving or brainstorming session, give away lottery tickets for each good idea presented.

A company who used this novel give-away approach actually had a winner among its managers. A woman won $1,000 with her lottery ticket and generated so much enthusiasm for the project that she came up with another suggestion that saved her division $1.5 million in 12 months. Who says money doesn't talk?

IT'S IN THE CARDS

Success in management, at any level, depends on the ability to keep good people—to provide an opportunity-loaded environment of goodwill. A company that has definitely achieved this level of rapport with employees is Hallmark Cards, Inc. They believe the key to their low turnover and high morale is the way they treat employees. Their most recent achievements were highlighted in a January, 1996 article that appeared in *Personnel Journal* titled "A Satisfied Work Force Is in Hallmark's Cards."

Honored as one of the ten best companies to work for in America, this family-owned business provides a work-life approach that employees can't help but appreciate. As evidence of the company's ability to maintain low turnover, they boast the fact that 25% of their work force has been with the company 25 years or more. That's over 3,600 employees.

How do they do it?

Irvine Hockaday, CEO, cares about people. The company is generous—since 1956, employees have received, on average, almost 10% of their pay a year in profit sharing. The plan is worth $1.4 billion; Hallmark stock comprises 67% of the plan, making employees one-third owners.

In other areas, new parents can take advantage of a six-month leave; adopting parents receive reimbursement of up to $5,000. The company newsletter, *Noon News*, has been published daily since 1957. In addition, a monthly CEO forum allows groups of employees to speak their minds with no managers present.

Whether it's hosting a celebration for Quarter Century Club members, or providing low-cost "TLC" for a sick child, Hallmark offers a work environment conducive to learning and friendship. Some say "it's in the cards."

CREATE OLYMPIC PERFORMANCE EVENTS

The centennial Olympics offered opportunities for volunteers to experience the event's energy and excitement from opening to closing. One of the volunteers was Gregory P. Smith, internationally recognized consultant, trainer, and president of Chart Your Course International. In an interview with Smith, he shared some ideas on why Olympic Performance Events (OPEs) keep organizations and their people excited about work and what they do.

"I wanted to be a part of the whole magic of the Olympics. That experience supported my research in the area of the difference between low- and high-performance companies. People want to be a part of something greater than themselves. Thousands of people gave 12–18 hours for free doing something significant," said Smith. He believes that some businesses are factories where people mentally punch a clock. They feel no more valued or able to contribute than someone working at a minimum-wage job in a high-stress, high-turnover industry.

During our conversation, Smith referred to his book *The New Leader Bringing Creativity and Innovation to the Workplace*. In his book, he talks about "zest factors" which create high energy and motivation as identified by Robert Schaffer in an article in the *The New York Times*. They are:

❖ A clear and compelling goal.

❖ Success within reasonable grasp.

❖ A collaborate mode.

❖ A genuine sense of fun and excitement.

The "zest factors" are behind the success of every organization. Without them businesses often flounder or fail.

The news media didn't have to remind us that when the Olympics was over, some people went through withdrawal, even a mild form of depression. According to Smith, it's no different when a woman gives birth or when an athlete finishes a competitive event. Something significant has ended.

To capitalize on those times of vitality, energy, and enthusiasm, organizations should create their own OPEs. These OPEs can have a bottom-line impact and help people feel energized. "No business can create a fun and motivational environment 24 hours each day—people would get burned out. But by creating OPEs in your business throughout the year, whereby people look forward to planning and participating, you can't help but maintain high morale," explained Smith.

As long as the events have a purpose, such as to improve profitability, reduce waste, or increase productivity, they are worth the money invested. The big payoff is employees who are committed to the goals and objectives of their organizations.

THE LEADER OF THE BAND

It's often amazing to me how little we know about each other. Twenty-five years ago, I worked for a wonderful man in Alameda, CA. Today, he is the City Manager in Chula Vista. John Goss, known for his good sense of humor and sincere interest in people, is also a musician—something I never knew about him until now.

During high school and college, he played saxophone in a band. He says he took 30 years off before deciding to start playing again. He has his own group now, and they play 20–30 engagements each year. He even gave a solo presentation at a San Diego Padres game last summer. Goss loves music and the relaxation and fun it brings. Four years ago, he decided to try something different and see if he could spark an interest in music among city employees. He started a trio made up of city employees—drummer, bass, and himself on sax. During the Christmas holidays, they entertained employees with carols. Enthusiasm for the music grew, and soon supervisors even recommended members of their staffs who played instruments or sang. Today, they have a total of nine to ten employees who look forward to the excitement of sharing their love for music with their co-workers. "We go to 12 or 13 different locations, including two libraries, a senior citizen center, the police department, city hall, the park services building, a community development building, and the department of public works, to name a few," explained Goss.

They have gospel and opera singers. One employee also sings in Spanish. "It helps get both the left and the right side of the brain engaged. People like to use their creativity, and this is the perfect vehicle to do that," added Goss.

Even though the city does other things to keep employees excited about working there, the special Christmas "show" each year always has everyone talking and wondering what the new season will offer.

HELP THEM REGAIN THE SPIRIT

"It wasn't long ago that the most prevalent business meeting or office communication forum was the sight of two white collars talking with one another in the hallway of the office complex," says Bob Carr, president of Executive Adventure, Inc. "It wasn't unusual for an entire marketing strategy or new product introduction plan to be delivered in the course of information exchange in a 20-minute conversation outside one's office." Bob, along with his team of trainers, helps organizations of all sizes get their employees psyched.

He's found that "when employees are 'empowered' with critical strategic information, when employees are asked to be team players, when officers and front-line workers work side by side in work force design focus groups, giving and receiving of critical corporate communication cannot be left to passive interaction."

Carr accomplishes his client's objectives by frequently taking employees off-site for something as simple as a walk in the woods or as challenging as an outdoor ropes course. One of his most popular activities is having teams design a way to catch a falling raw egg. Teams are given a "budget"—supplies of paper clips, paper plates, rubber bands, pencils, etc.—plus 20 minutes to come up with the best system for catching the egg without letting it break. Activity-based simulations that attempt to reconstruct the workplace atmosphere employees come from are also popular. It helps people see ways they can change for the better.

His goal is for employees to see improved ways to work with each other. "It's people that drive businesses. My company helps them regain that spirit," said Carr.

GIVE THEM OWNERSHIP

Scott Barnes, operations manager for ABB Power T&D Company, has extensive experience in setting up and managing teams. He's worked with teams that had team advisors who oversaw from the sidelines the teams' activities. He's also been involved with teams where someone takes the lead and steers the rest of the members—it's called situational leadership. The important thing is that teams take ownership. Certainly there are different degrees of ownership, but the more committed employees are to their success, the more effectively they will work together.

Even when it comes to problems—the team owns them, too. "I've seen teams ignore problems because it's easier than dealing with them. When there's conflict, they're all responsible and need a mature attitude as a team to get beyond the problem," said Barnes.

It can be very costly when a team has morale problems—when they don't pull together as a unit and take ownership.

Several tips for getting teams psyched are:

❖ Be sensitive to their needs and teach them to be sensitive to each other.

❖ Focus on the future. Effective teams are not satisfied with the status quo. They want to move forward.

❖ Respect confidential information and be sure people know they can trust you.

❖ Don't over-manage. The team needs to resolve the problems and buy into new ideas. Don't under-manage either. They still need support and coaching.

❖ Be sure you have the right mix of talent on the team. Under- or over-staffed teams often fail.

❖ Let them know you value their unique contributions.

Team players and winning managers are a great combination. Pep talks are not enough to launch a team and keep it progressing. The team management style does away with adversarial problem-solving, "win/lose" strategies, and "top-down" communication patterns. It gives team members ownership and can only bring about good things.

SUMMARY

Showering employees with gifts and special events will never replace the common courtesy and respect that everyone wants from an employer. The extra goodies are fun but are most successful when offered as a perk in combination with a positive work environment.

Some businesses make the mistake of believing that these kinds of rewards will smooth over feelings of discontent and create one big happy family.

Wrong! You've got to give people a voice in what they're doing. People want more than money and benefits. Getting 'em psyched isn't easy. However, if you want to offer extra rewards like some of those mentioned in this chapter, but don't know what your employees would like, ask them.

Some additional ideas that organizations use to add fun to their work environment include:

- ❖ Sending flowers or a gift certificate directly to the employee's spouse.
- ❖ Paying for spouses to attend trade shows and/or conventions.
- ❖ Holding a theme party in-house or off-site.
- ❖ Recognizing employees with ribbons or pins for extraordinary customer service.
- ❖ Letting your employees produce a video about what their department does.
- ❖ Establishing a "sounding board" where employees can post their ideas without fear of rejection or criticism.
- ❖ Putting together a company "yearbook" with photos and bits of information that represent highlights of the year.
- ❖ Using "secret shoppers" to award employees with cash on the spot for a job well-done.

Morale is everyone's concern. Many businesses have successfully provided an environment of good morale without sacrificing the company's objectives. Anything can influence morale either positively or negatively. Perhaps some of the ideas offered in this chapter will work for you. Maybe you've gotten some additional ideas of your own as a result of reading what others are doing to "get 'em psyched."

CHECKLIST FOR

GETTING 'EM PSYCHED

√ How do you show appreciation? What could you do differently?

√ Do you provide education as an incentive? If not, would you consider doing so?

√ How often do you reward people when they least expect it?

√ What kind of "hidden paychecks" work for your business?

√ How do you give employees ownership and a sense of empowerment?

√ Do you ever modify the nature of the work when people are bored? If not, why not?

√ What do you do to give your employees something to look forward to?

√ How do you reduce or eliminate barriers to having fun?

√ What kind of a role model are you?

√ What one outrageously fun thing did you do for your employees last year?

√ What will you do this year?

√ What makes working for you and your organization special?

Additional Reading

Belasco, James A. and Ralph C. Stayer. *Flight of the Buffalo*. New York, NY: Warner Inc., 1993.

Carr, Clay. *The Competitive Power of Constant Creativity*. New York, NY: AMACOM, 1994.

Cialdin, Robert B. *The Psychology of Persuasion*. New York, NY: William Morrow, 1993.

Cranny, C. J., Patricia Cain Smith, and Eugene F. Stone. *Job Satisfaction—How People Feel About Their Jobs and How It Affects Their Performance*. Lexington, MA: Lexington Books, 1992.

Garfield, Charles. *Second to None—How Our Smartest Companies Put People First*. New York, NY: Irwin Professional Publishing, 1991.

Herman, Roger E. *Keeping Good People—Strategies for Solving the Dilemma of the Decade*. New York, NY: McGraw-Hill, Inc. 1991.

Holt, John W., Jr., Jon Stamell, and Melissa Field. *Celebrate Your Mistakes and 77 Other Risk-Taking, Out-of-the-Box Ideas from Our Best Companies*. Chicago, IL: Irwin Professional Publishing, 1996.

Klubnik, Joan P. *Rewarding and Recognizing Employees—Ideas for Individuals, Teams, and Managers*. Burr Ridge, IL: Irwin Professional Publishing, 1995.

Matejka, Ken. *Why This Horse Won't Drink—How to Win and Keep Employee Commitment*. New York, NY: AMACOM, 1990.

McCoy, Thomas J. *Compensation and Motivation—Maximizing Employee Performance with Behavior-Based Incentive Plans*. New York, NY: AMACOM, 1992.

McCoy, Thomas J. *Creating an "Open Book" Organization...Where Employers Think & Act Like Business Partners*. New York: NY, AMACOM, 1996.

McNally, David. *Even Eagles Need a Push*. New York, NY: Bantam Doubleday, 1990.

Muchnick, Marc. *Naked Management—Bare Essentials for Motivating the X-Generation At Work*. Delray Beach, FL: St. Lucie Press, 1996.

Nelson, Bob. *1001 Ways to Reward Employees*. New York, NY: Workman Publishing Company, 1993.

Pfeffer, Jeffrey. *Competitive Advantage through People—Unleashing the Power of the Work Force*. Boston, MA: Harvard Business School Press, 1995.

Schlesinger, Len with Bill Fromm. *The Real Heroes of Business...And Not a CEO Among Them*. New York, NY: Currency/Doubleday, 1994.

Shandler, Michael and Michael Eagan. *VROOM! Turbo-Charged Team Building*. New York, NY: AMACOM, 1995.

Smith, Phyl and Lynn Kearny. *Creating Workplaces Where People Can Think*. San Francisco, CA: Jossey-Bass, Inc., Publishers, 1994.

Weinstein, Matt. *Managing to Have Fun: How Fun at Work Can Motivate Your Employees, Inspire Your Coworkers and Boost Your Bottom Line*. New York, NY: Simon & Schuster, 1996.

Wick, Calhoun W. and Lu Stanton Leon. *The Learning Edge*. New York, NY: McGraw-Hill, 1993.

WHO'S ON FIRST?

7

(Is It leadership or Is It Management?)

"There are two kinds of people in this world: those who come into a room and say, 'Here I am!' and those who come in and say, 'Ah, there you are!'"

—Anonymous

● ●

It's inevitable that an organization run by a good leader will have good morale. Whether leadership ability is inborn or learned is a question that has interested management researchers for more than a century. There's plenty of evidence to support both theories. Leadership has been described as an art and as difficult to explain as why Picasso expressed himself as he did. Some of the experts, including Donald R. Keough, past president and COO of the Coca-Cola Company, see leadership as something that can be learned.

In an excerpt from his speech to students at Duke University's Sanford Institute of Public Policy, Keough had a lot to say about the difference between a leader and a manager. He believes that motivated, intelligent people can be trained as managers, but they won't necessarily become leaders. A good leader is more than a manager. A leader can turn work into a challenging vocation. Everyone in an organization run by a good leader knows that what they do is important to the enterprise. A leader is constantly restless, always looking at ways to do something better than yesterday, at what needs to be done, and at how to grow in order to survive tomorrow.

The signs of good leadership appear among the followers. Employees who have reached their potential and are looking for new challenges are often influenced by a strong leader. Max De Pree, in his book *Leadership is an Art*, believes, "The first responsibility of a leader is to define reality. The last is to say 'thank you.' In between the two, the leader must become both a servant and a debtor." Creating an environment where employees are fulfilled can only help the organization reach its goals.

There's no secret formula for becoming a good leader. It's a tough road and not for everyone. It takes a combination of knowing how to lead as well as how to be a friend. Leaders must sometimes make unpopular decisions and that can make life miserable for a while.

Some of the proven qualities that distinguish managers from leaders are the ability to:

- ❖ Envision where the company and its people are going. (Global thinking is a required part of today's business perspective.)

- ❖ Solve problems—particularly when the leader involves others in the solution.

- ❖ Spark energy and creativity in employees.

- ❖ Act as a catalyst for change and embrace the reality of what lies ahead.

- ❖ Never quit, but remain dedicated and keep on learning from mistakes while encouraging others to do the same.

- ❖ Use good judgment, including the ability to separate the important from the unimportant.

There are many ways to lead people, but winning their loyalty by supporting the best interests of your employees is a major part of success. Loyalty is also influenced by how you interact with the individual for whom you work. Set an example: show enthusiasm for your boss, treat him or her with respect, and don't complain about decisions. Lastly, always tell your employees where they stand. No one wants to be surprised.

OFFER SMALL REWARDS

"You can rule by divine right, or you can be a leader and promote an atmosphere of learning, creativity, and positive energy," said Mary Ellen Hiatt, executive director of Southern Home Furnishings Association. "That kind of thinking brings gratification and high morale."

Hiatt strives for an environment where employees look forward to coming to work and doing their best. One of her goals as a leader is to take the hassles out of their day. She also understands that her employees value the gift of time. As a treat, she bestows what she calls "the executive privilege" of an extra 10 or 15 minutes for lunch. She looks for creative ways to reward them. Rewards are often small but meaningful, such as a gift certificate for drycleaning or a car wash.

As a leader, she knows that not every good employee wants a career. She believes that giving those individuals meaningful work develops a strong sense of purpose, which is more important than control for many people. Leaders can influence the high cost of low morale in a variety of ways.

BE A COACH, NOT A COP

It's easy to forget our responsibility to employees who do a good job. Sometimes we become cops when we focus more on discipline and punishment than on helping people maximize their potential. Even though the troublemakers are the minority, they get more than their share of attention. Certain problems are inevitable, and you'll need to learn to live with them. Ignoring trouble isn't the way to lead a team. Be a coach.

Here's how. First, you'll have to find out why things have gone wrong. Address the problem early. Also, consider what irritates you personally. You may find that some things are just annoying and aren't worth addressing, at least not if you want to maintain peace in the organization.

Second, solve the most disruptive problems:

❖ Define all the recurring problems and prioritize them so you can tackle the most difficult first.

❖ Look below the surface; be sure you know the real cause.

❖ Analyze the problem in order to determine who or what is responsible.

❖ Tackle the problem; decide how you're going to handle it and do it.

Third, in coaching a poor performer, expect misunderstanding and denial. Be sure you're accurate, clear, and impartial. Watch for falsely placed blame.

Last, be sure you follow up. Although you have asked for change, you'll find people tend to fall into old habits. Your employees may not always do what you expect, but acknowledge that they are trying. Encourage and reward progress.

Being a cop is a difficult job. It's much more fun to be a coach and help develop winning teams.

BE FLEXIBLE

Besides being secretaries, sales clerks, mechanics, waitresses, accountants, machine operators, engineers, and nurses, employees are parents, homemakers, caretakers, patients, and leaders in their communities. So when obligations arise that interfere with work, what responsibilities do employers have to accommodate employees? After all, employers have businesses to run and employees are expected to work regular hours. Organizations that provide little or no flexibility, however, are asking for problems.

Not permitting time off to keep a doctor's appointment, renew a driver's license, care for a sick child, or occasionally make a personal phone call leads to loss of employee commitment. Several studies have demonstrated that family-friendly flexibility is amazingly effective at reducing turnover. By being understanding when employees are in need, you let them know you care. In turn, they are more likely to offer you loyalty.

Treat others as you expect to be treated. This is the way Mike McGhee, chief of staff of the San Diego Police Officers Association, manages his people. "If they need time off for personal business, as long as someone can cover for them, I try to accommodate them. Because our organization has only eight full-time people, they depend on one another to a great degree, and that's where flexibility comes in."

Sometimes he can't be as flexible as he would like, but as a people-oriented leader, he's willing to stretch to meet employee needs as much as possible.

LEARN FROM THE PAST

Leadership responsibility offers the challenge of day-to-day management, as well as the opportunity to learn from the past and plan for the future. Ken Blanchard speaks to this in a July 1995, *Quality Digest* article entitled "Learn From the Past." In his 1995 book *Everyone's a Coach*, co-authored with Don Shula, former coach of the Miami Dolphins, Shula's philosophy is explained as follows: "Success is not forever and failure isn't fatal."

Blanchard witnessed Shula's positive outlook after a Buffalo Bills-Miami game in which the Dolphins suffered a big defeat. Shula looked drained after the game. The next day, however, he was his usual energetic self. He had put the loss behind him and was totally focused on his next opponent.

Even when the Dolphins had a perfect 17–0 season, the coach kept pushing his players to look ahead and not get too comfortable with winning. "Learn from the past," whether good or bad, but don't live there. Plan for the future, but focus your attention on the present and what you must do to prepare for the next day.

The best leaders are also coaches. Coaches develop potential, which means suspending judgment, listening, and helping others learn from mistakes. Shula's in favor of giving people a fresh start. He's a leader as well as a coach. Leaders help people recover from their failures. Do anything less, and you've lost commitment and their willingness to embrace the future.[1]

Cost Management Services, a national employment consulting firm specializing in unemployment issues and background investigations, has a similar philosophy.

"We empower our employees to make decisions. We also know they won't always be right. The important thing is that they learn from their mistakes," said Ted Richardson, vice president. He and the rest of the management team give their employees the opportunity to "explore the realm of possibilities." "We refrain from pointing fingers and dwelling on mistakes. We'd never tell employees that what they did was stupid. It's water under the bridge. Employees know they can't make the same mistakes over and over, but they know we're behind them in helping them move on and grow," added Richardson.

REWARD RISK-TAKING

Connie and Janet are best friends. They work for XYZ Company in Anywhere, USA. They're afraid if they do something wrong, they'll be fired or at least formally disciplined. They've never had the opportunity to learn from making mistakes, so they're afraid to try new things.

Good leaders understand that everyone makes mistakes. They encourage, support, and reward risk-takers. Here are some guidelines for establishing a healthy risk-taking environment:

* ❖ **Encourage smart risks, not foolish chances.** Help employees search for opportunities in traditional areas, as well as with new technologies. Be sure they are focused on a goal.

* ❖ **Evaluate best- and worst-case scenarios.** Identify critical issues. Assess opportunities against objective criteria to determine the potential return and decide whether the organization can support a negative result.

- ❖ **Celebrate setbacks as well as successes**. You can expect failure when you ask people to take risks. If you celebrate the fact that they tried, they won't be as reluctant to try again.

- ❖ **Set the example**. Don't be afraid to let your employees know that you make mistakes too. People who don't falter once in a while are usually not trying new things.

Use creative risk-taking to improve the status quo. A creative risk is not gambling because it's calculated. It's not taking a risk for the thrill of excitement, such as bungee jumping. Undoubtedly, you know risk takers at both extremes—some take none, and some go all the way. The ideal is a balance between the two. Reward those who are willing to take the chance.

DON'T BE A PRETENDER

Nick Nichols, president of ProMax & Associates, Inc., is a professional speaker, trainer, and consultant. In his new book *Finding the Magnetic Leader Within—Moving from Personal Chaos to Personal Peace*, he talks about the importance of being honest with yourself. "The first time we're embarrassed, made fun of, or made to feel stupid, we put up a front to protect ourselves. As leaders, we often make decisions based on what we think the consequences will be for us in terms of how others judge us," said Nichols.

The most successful leaders have an inner strength and sense of personal responsibility. They understand that the true mark of courage is not how bravely you face the world, but how honestly you face yourself. Are you a leader or a pretender? Are you willing to take responsibility for who you are and what you do or do you share only what you believe others want to see and play the game? Within each of us, hidden deep inside, is a "Magnetic Leader," a core self that consistently tries to guide us in the right direction to do the right thing. Exceptional leaders are those who have discovered this "Magnetic Leader." They make the decisions they feel are right, rather than decisions which they hope others will think are right.

LIGHT THEIR FIRES

If you have a vision, but don't share it, you've lost a powerful management opportunity. The success of many corporations is due largely to the early vision of its leaders.

For example, when Disney World opened, Walt Disney was deceased. They asked his wife to speak. The man who introduced her said, "Mrs. Disney, I just wish Walt could have seen this." She responded with, "He did." Walt Disney had a powerful vision.

Businesses begin with visions. Bill Gates had a vision, as did Oprah Winfrey, Steven Spielberg, and Dr. Shannon Lucid. They all overcame obstacles to get where they are today. Their visions lit fires that couldn't be extinguished.

Consider this. You can't share what you don't have. You can't lead if you don't know where you're going. What do you see for the organization and the people in it in the future? The vision needs to be simple and appealing, or it won't be understood and accepted.

Once you've formulated the vision, let your employees know how they can contribute to make it a reality. Guide them, encourage them, and make sure they have the tools and supplies they need to do the job. Light their fires.

ENCOURAGE TALKING BACK

Small businesses face the same turnover problems as larger organizations. However, the impact of turnover on morale is often greater for the small business.

In the case of Hair Concepts, a salon in Roswell, GA, turnover has never been a problem. I asked owner Laura Wolf about the secret to her success.

"First, I hire subcontractors (hairdressers who rent a booth from me) who fit in with the rest of the group. We're like a family, so compatibility is very important," explained Wolf. "In addition, I'm always willing to listen to suggestions. In fact, I encourage everyone to offer ideas and 'talk back'." For example, the operators asked her if they could have their own telephones if they paid the cost. Wolf had no objections. She also agreed when the hairdressers felt they needed another hairdryer. Reasonable requests are never refused.

Wolf works in her salon beside the subcontractors, and this helps her stay in touch with reality. She recognizes a need for rules, such as children of hairdressers are not allowed in the shop. However, she's quick to add that the rules are common sense. They're in place for the benefit of everyone—the entire "family."

Wolf has discharged only one employee in the three years she's had her business. "She had a lot of problems with her customers which fell on my shoulders because I'm the owner," said Wolf. "I had no choice but to let her go."

She keeps her shop neat, clean, and in tip-top condition. It's a pleasant place to work. Plans for future expansion are under way, and Wolf has total confidence that the record of low turnover will continue as she moves ahead. She's made it easy for people to work with her and the rest of the business family. She's made it easy to "talk back."

CATCH THEM DOING SOMETHING RIGHT

"Praise what you want to raise." "Catch them doing something right." These are two positive ideas that don't always get the expected results. Why? Because managers don't do it enough. Leaders look for ways to reward those who do a good job.

Here's an example. An employee commuted to work two hours each way for almost four years. He reported directly to the president of the company—a man too busy to give recognition. The president demanded a lot and believed that he didn't need to say anything about a job unless there was a problem, in which case everyone knew about it. One day the employee told his boss he had accepted another position closer to home. The president was upset and said he couldn't do without him. He told the employee that he was his right-hand man and that the company had reached a pinnacle of success because of him. He begged him not to leave. The employee, however, had made up his mind.

In reality, the employee wouldn't have left had he received even the slightest recognition. He didn't mind the travel as he was able to read and relax on the train. He just couldn't work for someone who gave no positive feedback. His boss failed to "catch him doing something right" and lost the best worker he'd ever had. Then, one by one, others began to leave and morale dropped. The company eventually lost a foothold in the marketplace. Furious shareholders fired the president.

Take the time and make the commitment to praise your employees, or you may lose your best people, maybe even to the competition.

VIEW PROBLEMS AS "GOLDEN EGGS"

Every job has problems, but they're not always considered opportunities. In some companies, finding and tackling problems is expected and encouraged. However, this isn't the norm.

Most companies find it difficult to view problems as "golden eggs." Dr. Min Basadur, professor of management, McMaster University in Toronto, and Founder of the Center for Research in Applied Creativity, had this to say: "'Golden eggs' offer people in organizations the chance to think more innovatively." He stresses the fact that realizing creative potential of employees at all levels, through training, helps move the business forward. He describes organizational adaptability as:

- ❖ Focusing innovation.

- ❖ Developing innovative solutions to real-world business problems.

- ❖ Significantly improving bottom-line results through corporate innovation.

"When push comes to shove, people go back to efficiency," said Basadur. Leaders need to accept the idea that with creativity comes a certain amount of risk. However, rewards can be great. For example, Basadur was instrumental in helping Frito-Lay achieve a $500 million bottom-line cost improvement by involving employees in using their own creativity.

New product innovation, strategic planning, productivity, employee involvement, total quality management, cross-functional teamwork, and continuous improvement are the result of looking at problems as "golden eggs." Leaders are in a position to open the doors by creatively involving everyone, not just senior management, in doing new things in new ways.

EXHIBIT "FRIENDLY BRAVERY"

Leaders greet everyone—even strangers—with whom they come in contact. Their greeting is enthusiastic, sincere, and always involves positive body language. They smile as they say "hello" and often shake hands. Their behavior is an extension of their personality. It's called "friendly bravery."

Leaders say the incredible aspect of acknowledging people is that, more often than not, those they greet will return the greeting.

Leaders carry this idea one step further. At social gatherings, they introduce themselves to, and begin conversations with, people they don't know. They use small talk to get acquainted and break down barriers. The same holds true for the workplace. A partner in an accounting firm used this approach to gain the cooperation of his peers. He had always kept to himself and that caused suspicion and hard feelings. When he became aware that his attitude was negatively impacting morale in the company, he changed his approach to people.

Build a reputation in your organization for exhibiting "friendly bravery." All it takes is the courage to reach out to others. When you do, you may be surprised at the response.

BLEND STRATEGY WITH CULTURE

Culture is a major part of the fit when it comes to employees. If they don't feel comfortable with the organization and the leader to whom they report, it's a stretch to be successful.

Sue Marks, CEO/president of ProStaff, a full-service staffing company, has two reminders on her desk that help her stay focused on her responsibilities as a leader. They also help her keep in mind the importance of the culture in which her employees work.

The first item is a list of four reasons employees don't do what they're supposed to do:

1. Can't do it.

2. Don't know what you asked to be done.

3. Don't know how to do it.

4. Don't want to do it.

"The leader's responsibility in the first three is related to hiring the right people, setting and communicating expectations, and training and coaching. The fourth point is a motivation issue—if you don't terminate those who lack motivation, they'll poison the rest of the organization," said Marks.

The second item was written by the late Maurice Mescarhenas and is called "The 5 Key Result Areas of a CEO." They form the foundation of a productive environment:

1. Strategic planning/succession planning.

2. Financial performance.

3. Key management system.

   -Responsibilities

   -Results

   -Rewards

4. Internal climate.

5. External relationships/corporate citizenship.

Marks has been challenged since the inception of her business in 1981 to maintain a culture conducive to growth and good employee morale. Within the last few years, ProStaff has doubled in size. She believes it's critical for leaders to stay in touch with what's going on in the business. She still calls on customers and promotes her company.

"In general, people are hired for what they've done in the past. They're fired for who they are. In other words, if they don't fit in with the rest of the employees, you set them up for failure," said Marks. She hires selectively, always paying close attention to cultural fit.

ELIMINATE THE OBSTACLES TO INNOVATION

When leaders lack faith in employees' capabilities, it sends the message that innovation isn't welcome. It's critical that solutions to business problems are sought and determined. An organization that innovates, not once or twice, but continually and systematically, also removes obstacles to new ways of thinking.

To avoid the roadblocks to innovation that some businesses fail to overcome, you'll need to:

❖ Eliminate self-induced fear of failure.

❖ Encourage freedom of expression.

❖ Set goals and objectives.

❖ Ask for feedback.

❖ Avoid penalizing employees for mistakes.

❖ Recognize and reward the talent in your organization.

❖ Emphasize the positive aspects of innovation.

Your organization's ability to sustain innovation and revenue growth depends to a great degree on educating the managers.

BALANCE SKILLS

"Balance the skills of team members, and it's bound to breed teamwork." These are the words of Joel Blumsack, manager of manufacturing support for Silgan Plastics, Inc. He recommends that leaders not put two people who have the same skills on the same team. "Balance your team members so that, for example, you don't have your top two engineers on the same team. My experience has been they buck each other. Everyone can gain from the team approach if they are interdependent," added Blumsack.

To help promote a balance of skills on the team, leaders can do the following:

❖ **Encourage input**. Provide employees with a number of ways to express themselves. Ask for their opinions. Get them talking to each other.

❖ **Provide appropriate training**. Aside from formal education and training, employees need opportunities to learn from each other. You may want to encourage this through pay-for-knowledge programs that compensate employees for sharing their knowledge with co-workers.

❖ **Be responsive**. When an employee expresses concern or asks a question, respond in a timely manner. Updates and timely responses, let employees know their input is valued.

❖ **Recognize achievement**. Never miss a chance to let your employees know you're aware of their successes.

The challenges leaders and their teams face in today's business environment are as bizarre and convoluted as the world encountered by Alice when she stepped through the looking glass into Wonderland. Whether it's the start-up of a new venture, the struggle to establish a niche in the marketplace, or the efforts of a mature business to fend off new competition, people play a critical role in managing themselves and working together toward a common goal. For best results, leaders must learn how to balance the skills of their employees.

L INK PAY TO PERFORMANCE

"Merit Pay" has lost its luster. Companies that grant employees a yearly merit raise often link the increase to the inflation rate. As inflation has fallen, so have annual increases. To most employees, a 1–5% increase doesn't seem like enough compared to the double-digit figures of the 1980s.

Compensation experts say that 75% of all employees see no connection between their performance and what they are paid. If people don't see a correlation, morale suffers, and there's no motivation to improve. It's also a reason U.S. employers have had difficulty meeting the challenge of foreign competition. The American Compensation Association offers this advice to leaders who want to be successful at selling the pay-for-performance concept to employees:

- ❖ Train managers in techniques for measuring and evaluating employee performance.

- ❖ Work to earn a high level of trust from your employees.

- ❖ Measure differences in job performance in a valid and reliable manner.

- ❖ Set pay ranges wide enough (35% or greater) to allow for significant base-pay differences among employees in the same job.

- ❖ Communicate expectations—help employees know and understand the criteria on which you will judge their performance.

- ❖ Make sure that management supports the pay-for-performance system.

Although pay-for-performance is not the solution to every organization's morale problems, it can be very effective as a motivator, especially among hourly employees. Salaried employees tend to focus on rewards other than money. Increased autonomy and special assignments are often more appealing to them.

SHARE COMPLIMENTS

A dynamic leader who believes in passing on the compliments is Andrea Schaffell, vice president of business operations for Turner Entertainment Group. In an industry that's volatile and constantly changing, people often work odd hours and have little overlap with management. It can be a lonely life for many employees.

Schaffell is personally generous with praise, but also makes sure, when she hears positive feedback about her employees and their work, that they immediately get the same good news. "I feel it's critical to the success of any leader to share the good as told by others. Unfortunately, I think sometimes that doesn't always happen, and employees don't get the messages they deserve to hear. It's all part of being a leader and building and keeping good morale."

DON'T CUT CORNERS

One of the fastest ways to cause loss of pride in the product, service, and organization is to ignore the fact that the work is not up to standard. Remember the game Follow the Leader? The same holds true for the workplace. What leaders do is often what they get. Leaders who ignore problems, look the other way when things aren't done right, or deliberately cut corners send the message that quality, attention to detail, and pride of ownership aren't important.

Bill Brininstool, assistant export manager for The Heil Co., one of the largest manufacturers of truck bodies and tank trailers in the world, had this to say: "My staff knows the importance of good quality products and service. When frustration sets in, I remind them that, when in doubt, always treat the customers as you want to be treated."

Brininstool went on to say that in the 1980s, the company wasn't happy with the quality of their products. They were losing out to the competition. The situation forced them to take a new approach in meeting customer requirements. Finally, they put everything that didn't meet the new criteria for quality on hold. The plant didn't meet their production goals, but they had to get tough on themselves in order to survive. They learned not so quickly that to compete in the marketplace, *everyone* had to make a commitment to change, and they did. Cutting corners is seldom productive in the long run.

MAKE THEM BUSINESS PARTNERS

The #1 need of most employees is the respect of their managers. Add to that the authority to handle their responsibilities, and a business partnership is likely to evolve.

Begin by motivating employees with incentives that match shifting employee values. For example, offering more money to someone who's hungry for a challenge is as effective as giving new clothing to someone who's starving. Special privileges, such as an assigned parking space, office with a window, or flextime, don't automatically excite people about their jobs.

Who are these people? Why would you want to make them business partners?

They're the "me generation." They're people of all ages who work for you. They're the young, middle-aged, and senior members of your work force. They come from different backgrounds; they're different races. They represent a puzzling challenge to their managers. Many are under thirty, but not all. They're identified less by age than by attitude. They're on your staff. They work in your offices and manufacturing plants. They impact morale positively and negatively. It's not easy to keep pace with them. They want a say in decisions and, like all employees before them, want success. But they want it now!

Here are a few suggestions for making employees business partners:

❖ **Start with quality employees.** Match their skills to the job requirements. Promote self-development, discipline, and hard work, then reward these qualities.

❖ **Establish a physical, psychological, and social environment.** To do so encourages and supports motivated employees.

❖ **Provide regular feedback.** Don't wait for annual appraisals. Recognize their efforts immediately.

❖ **Help employees chart career paths.** Don't hold them back just because you don't want to go to the trouble of replacing them.

❖ **Empower them.** Give them the authority to match the responsibility.

❖ **Get them involved.** Help them feel a valuable part of the organization.

REDUCE FEAR

Many of today's leaders grew up in the old school where fear controlled employees. The boss's mentality—"it's my way or the highway"—was the rule, not the exception.

Bill Frieder, president of The Mirro Company, a Division of Newell, the world's largest manufacturer of aluminum cookware and bakeware, said, "Leaders need a certain amount of benevolence running through their veins. Instilling fear is never acceptable. Leaders must work to reduce fear and build trust in people and their abilities."

Since childhood days, we've been regulated by fears. "If you don't eat everything on your plate—no dessert." "Do your homework, or you can't watch television." "If you're late one more time, you're grounded." "If you don't brush your teeth, they'll all fall out." Then, there were exams, grade point averages, contests, sports competition, and other hurdles we had to pass to earn rewards.

Think about how fear motivates your actions today. You:

❖ **Got up and to work on time**. If you're late, you're in trouble.

❖ **Showered and used deodorant**. You don't want to offend anyone.

❖ **Ate a healthy breakfast**. You hoped doing so lowered your cholesterol.

❖ **Did enough work to keep from being laid off or fired.** Maybe you'll even get a raise.

❖ **Didn't drink alcoholic beverages during lunch**. Someone might smell it on your breath.

❖ **Sped home hoping you wouldn't get a ticket**. You don't need another increase in your insurance premium.

❖ **Skipped exercise because you were too tired to get out of the recliner**. Maybe tomorrow.

So we, as well as our employees, are motivated by our fears that something we need will be withheld or withdrawn. Employees become actors and try to give the impression they are someone else just to satisfy others.

This fear-generated motivation may work for the individual but not for the good of the overall organization, which loses whatever enthusiasm the employee may have but doesn't want to share under the pressure of fear.

USE YOUR MUSCLES

The flash of a smile is pleasant, spontaneous, and simple. A smile improves one's appearance 1,000%. Nearly 100 facial muscles are behind it, invisibly working together to make it happen.

Brenda Ward, Harry Sanderson, Sue Brickle, and Dennis Foreman know how to use their facial muscles. Each is a dynamic leader who brightens a room upon entry.

Close your eyes. Think of a person *you* know who's always smiling. He or she is ambitious, motivated, and has high self-esteem. Right? Nice vision. Keep going. This person helps others feel good about themselves. People love to be around them. Their energy and smiles are contagious.

Tom Champion, my high school guidance counselor, was one of those special people. Mr. C. always wore a smile—it seemed to come naturally. What I found most amazing was that he knew all 500+ kids in the graduating class by name.

I last saw him at the ten-year reunion—still the same, wonderful person who had inspired so many to do their best. He had smiles and hugs for all of us that evening. I called him Tom. He was the wind beneath my wings. He knew how to use his muscles.

GET THEM INVOLVED

Getting employees involved from start to finish is a mark of a leader. For Beverly DuCharme, project manager, research and development for H.C. Brill, Inc., a manufacturer of bakery ingredients, helping people understand the process and apply what they learn is the key to being a good leader. "I like everyone to know what everyone else is working on. Our employees see a project evolve from raw material onto shelves in grocery store bakeries. There's a feeling of accomplishment when a project is complete. If they have a sense of involvement and support each other, the results are reflected in consumer satisfaction," said DuCharme.

Several tips for keeping employees involved are:

❖ Be sure that each employee completely understands the quality of performance expected of him or her and the related productivity level.

❖ Provide them with the tools they need to do the job.

❖ Address frustrations and problems as they occur.

❖ Don't over-discipline for mistakes, or they will shy away from involvement in the future.

❖ Recognize accomplishments—reward them and keep them excited about being an integral part of the project.

People are a means to accomplishing something. The sooner you get them involved in planning and decision making, the quicker you'll see results. To stay profitable, businesses must constantly improve productivity and product quality, develop new products and services, and meet customer demands, including custom-tailored solutions to problems. Help your employees see that the "business as usual" mentality will no longer cut it. Get them involved.

LAUGH IN THE FACE OF STRESS

Most leaders are confronted by stress to some degree. There are many books and materials available to help counter the negative side of stress; but few have taken the approach of Jeff Justice, president of Corporate Comedy, a company dedicated to bringing humor to the workplace. To fight the daily onslaught of stress in your life, Justice suggests using your sense of humor. Nothing relaxes and refreshes the body like a good hearty laugh. It makes you feel good. There are no bad side effects, and it's nonfattening. The ability to take your job seriously and yourself lightly will go a long way in the battle against stress, according to Justice.

He also suggests that from a psychological point of view, work is nothing but organized stress. So unless you're the chief tester for La-Z-Boy chairs, your job is where you feel life pressing down on you most heavily. It's also where you need to lighten up.

"Did you ever notice that the trees left standing after a hurricane are the ones that bent with the wind? The rigid ones snap in two like twigs. Your sense of humor can help you bend with the gale of stress you face every day," added Justice.

According to Justice, stress busting with humor works by stepping back from a situation and playing up its absurdities. Remember the dream vacation you planned that turned into an episode of "The Twilight Zone?" How about the camping trip from hell or the project that was going to make you look so good except that the harder you worked, the worse it got? At the time, it probably seemed as though the whole world was against you, but two weeks later, you laughed about it with friends. For stress busting, Justice says, "Why wait? Laugh while it's happening."

He also offers these final words of encouragement: "Our island friends in the Caribbean may have a simple solution when they say, 'Don't worry, be happy.' The next time things around you are going crazy, remember—don't tighten up—lighten up."

SUMMARY

Leadership has a lot to do with creating alliances and providing meaning to people's lives. Leaders have open minds. Charles F. Kettering said, "Where there is an open mind, there will always be a frontier." Leaders know how to get the best from people and offer rewards. A strong constitution and a juggler's finesse are assets every leader must acquire. Being a leader is not just a matter of applying a set of rules, but of working with people who have feelings, thoughts, and attitudes. Because leaders accomplish their jobs through others, they must be interested in employees and treat them as individuals. By earning loyalty and respect, they also ensure good morale.

Today's employees are mobile and moving. They're ready to flee from an old-time domineering boss. They are not devotees of a lifelong commitment to even the best leader in the world. Many simply want attention and recognition for a job well-done. This thinking makes leading a tougher job than it has ever been. Employees are better educated, more self-reliant, less afraid of the future, and less afraid of losing their jobs than in the past.

"The deepest principle in human nature is the craving to be appreciated," said William James, psychologist. Yet leaders regularly miss opportunities to satisfy this craving in others, especially their employees.

Winning the prize for best marketing idea of the year is an achievement, but submitting a good idea that didn't win is also worth recognition. Use sincere praise to help employees improve and want to do better. I compare the manager who doesn't give enough praise to the spouse who never says, "I love you." Leaders who miss the chance to offer words of encouragement and praise run the risk of losing someone very hard to replace.

Frankenstein, published in 1912, has been compared to the terror of modern organizational life. It can help leaders understand how they frequently take good people and turn them into cynical, bitter employees. The bright, enthusiastic people who were once positive and excited about their jobs sometimes reach a point where they hate what they do and will even use sabotage to get back at the leaders they see as responsible for their frustration. People have one thing in common with machines—it takes understanding to make both of them work properly. A mechanic can't make a machine work right without understanding *how* it works. That's true of people, too.

As a leader, you will be faced with employees with personal problems, bad attitudes, lack of understanding—but also a willingness to learn. Most people do not want to fail and will try to succeed. Leaders have the power to build a bridge between themselves and their employees. You can meet them halfway or wait for them to cross over. Many will make it, but some will not. Be flexible and keep your eye on the goal. Help your employees cross the bridge.

Endnote

1. Story reprinted with written permission of Blanchard Training and Development, 125 State Place, Escondido, CA, (619) 489-5005.

CHECKLIST FOR

ENHANCING YOUR LEADERSHIP STYLE

√ Do you offer enough rewards? Are they frequent but not so often as to lose their value?

√ How flexible are you? When is it acceptable to break the rules?

√ Do you focus too much on the past, something you can't change?

√ How do you reward calculated risk-taking?

√ How much do you communicate with your employees and by what methods?

√ How effective are you as a coach and counselor?

√ What do you do to help everyone feel a part of the team?

√ Do you praise employees in front of others and give recognition when they do a difficult job well?

√ How often do you use humor to ease tension and stress?

√ How do you let employees feel they are contributing to the overall work flow?

√ What methods do you use to help employees attain their goals?

√ How do you handle critical comments of your own actions?

Additional Reading

Ambrose, Delores. *Leadership: The Journey Inward*, 2nd ed. Dubuque, IA: Kendall/Hunt Publishing Company, 1995.

Bardwick, Judith M. *Danger in the Comfort Zone*. New York, NY: AMACOM, 1995.

Basadur, Min. *A Flight to Creativity*. Buffalo, NY: The Creative Education Foundation Press, 1994.

Basadur, Min. *The Power of Innovation*. London, UK: Pitman Professional, Division of Financial Times of London, 1995.

Blanchard, Ken and Don Shula. *Everyone's a Coach*. New York, NY: Harper-Collins, 1995.

Blank, Warren. *The Nine Natural Laws of Leadership*. New York, NY: AMACOM, 1995.

Clemens, John K. and Steven Albrecht. *The Timeless Leader*. Holbrook, MA: Adams Publishing, 1995.

Durant, Jane. *The Colors of Supervision*. Dubuque, IA: Kendall/Hunt Publishing Company, 1995.

Ginsburg, Sigmund G. *Managing with Passion*. New York, NY: John Wiley & Sons, Inc., 1996.

Glacel, Barbara Pate and Emile A. Robert, Jr. *Light Bulbs for Leaders*. Milwaukee, WI: Schwartz Business Books, 1995.

Harris, Phillip. *High Performance Leadership—HRD Strategies for the New Work Culture*. Amherst, MA: HRD Press, Revised 1995.

Harvey, Eric and Alexander Lucia. *Walk the Talk...And Get the Results You Want*. Dallas, TX: Performance Publishing, 2nd ed., 1995.

Kouzes, James M. and Barry Z. Posner. *The Leadership Challenge—How to Get Extraordinary Things Done in Organizations*. Erlanger, KY: Pfeiffer & Company Publishers, 1995.

Losoncy, Lewis E. *The Motivating Leader*. Delray Beach, FL: St. Lucie Press, 1995.

Rosen, Robert H. *Leading People*. New York, NY: Viking, 1996.

Rothschild, William E. *Risktaker, Caretaker, Surgeon, Undertaker*. New York, NY: John Wiley & Sons, Inc., 1993.

Smith, Gregory, P. *The New Leader—Bringing Creativity and Innovation to the Workplace*. Delray Beach, FL: St. Lucie Press, 1997.

Stack, Jack. *The Great Game of Business*. New York, NY: Bantam Doubleday Dell Publishing, Inc., 1992.

Thor, Carl G. *The Measures of Success—Creating a High Performance Organization*. Essex Junction, VT: Oliver Wright Publications, Inc., 1994.

Welch, Jack. *Get Better or Get Beaten—31 Leadership Secrets from GE's Jack Welch*. New York, NY: Irwin Professional Publishing, 1994.

CLOSE ENCOUNTERS OF THE WORST KIND

(Managing Difficult People)

"A troublemaker is a person who rocks the boat, then persuades everyone else there is a storm at sea."

—Anonymous

• •

Hostile-aggressives, complainers, silent types, whiners, backstabbers, gossips, stick-in-the-muds, and morale busters constitute only 10% of the work force but cause 90% of the problems. It's no wonder that managers get frustrated at the thought of them. Unfortunately, problem employees are a part of every organization—there's no escaping the troublemakers. How you handle them will partially determine your success as a manager.

Negative behavior adversely affects individual and group job performance, and the impact on morale is devastating. It interrupts work, causes stress, and sometimes keeps us awake at night.

When we think of discipline, it's easy to focus on disruptions and conflicts caused by employees. However, rather than wonder how to *make* employees act responsibly, we might ask why they would *want* to behave inappropriately or take on the role of a discipline problem.

Employees are easier to manage when they do what we want them to do. But what's in it for them? Some people are motivated by external forces—fear of criticism, discipline, disapproval, or even termination. Others are motivated by internal needs that are not dependent upon anyone else. Preventing problems is an important part of a manager's job. Signs that a problem is developing include:

❖ Arguments, short tempers.

❖ Bantering that is no longer funny.

❖ Loss of productivity.

❖ Increased tardiness and absenteeism.

❖ Increased accidents.

❖ Sudden change in behavior.

❖ Suspicion that the boss is out to get them.

❖ Loss of enthusiasm.

❖ Sudden loss of cooperation.

❖ Preoccupation with other things.

Even if you recognize a situation before it gets out of hand, you may still have a major challenge in trying to correct the problem. (We're not talking about psychotic or other mental disorders, but common behavioral issues.) Managers aren't shrinks, nor are they expected to resolve conflicts with a paperback version of Freud in their pockets. Common sense is helpful, but success really depends upon identifying the *cause* of the problem. You must find out what's behind the aberrant behavior. It's your only hope for correcting it.

DON'T DWELL ON PAST MISTAKES

Managers are often challenged to put employees' mistakes behind them. This isn't always easy, especially when they're costly. Reduced productivity and losses that impact morale and profits are hard to forget. However, after you've identified what went wrong, decided what you'd do differently next time, and disciplined, if appropriate, it's time to move forward. Unless you want the individual who made the mistake out of your organization, you must work in partnership and focus on the future.

In my seminar *Win/Win Performance Appraisals*, participants are sometimes surprised to learn that during an appraisal, 15% of the time should be used for discussing the past, 25% should focus on the present, and 60% should focus on the future. Dwelling on past mistakes is rarely beneficial. It's the contributions the employee can make to future success that counts.

How you communicate your confidence that the employee, despite the mistake, is a valued member of the team may impact morale for years. We all make mistakes, but no one wants to be thought of as a loser.

When people join my company, one of the first things I talk about is the fact that I expect them to make mistakes. I also ask them to let me know when they do, so that together, if necessary, we can tackle the problem before it gets worse.

For example, a new employee told me that he thought he was in serious trouble. While cleaning his office, he had destroyed more than 50 personnel files. He realized after the fact that they were important. He asked if I was going to fire him.

I was angry but calmly told him employment termination was not the solution. I lived up to my words, and, together, we decided on a plan for reconstructing the information (this took place in the days before computers). The employee learned a lesson, and I benefited in that he didn't try to cover up a potentially devastating mistake that would have made matters worse. He became a dedicated long-term employee who is still with my previous employer today and is respected by other managers and peers as a leader who inspires others to go above and beyond.

DON'T WAIT TOO LONG

It's almost impossible to change difficult employees. You have several choices. You can learn to handle them, tolerate them, or get rid of them before they destroy the morale in the rest of the business.

Redirecting their actions into constructive channels is a strategy that sometimes leads to better-than-average employees. However, it takes time, patience, and employees who are open to changing their behavior. If that doesn't work, you may choose to try discipline, such as a loss of privilege or time-off without pay. In some cases, termination of employment may be the best or only alternative. The problem many managers have is not knowing when to act.

Although you want to avoid hasty decisions, if you wait too long to address problems, they only get worse. For example, Jon Cartwright, vice president of sales for A. G. Sanderson, Inc., admits he waited too long to confront a sales manager. "He was the best producer I had, but he wasn't willing to follow the rules. He was consistently late for meetings, belligerent in front of the other employees, and ignored pleas for help from his staff."

Cartwright waited for the manager to change, but things got worse. When he finally terminated him, the other employees were already disgusted. They had lost respect for their boss, whom they felt had mismanaged the situation.

No one wants a reputation for being a petty tyrant, but when discipline is needed, you're hurting everyone by ignoring the problem. Don't wait too long. It will only get worse.

TRADE COMPLAINTS FOR SOLUTIONS

One of the most useful lessons I learned as a new manager was that when my employees came to me with complaints, they were also required to bring solutions.

I've decided it must be human nature when it comes to dropping bombs on the boss. Maybe it's the employee's way of saying, "I'm not getting paid enough to handle these kinds of problems. You deal with it."

However, how the manager trades complaints for solutions can be tricky. You don't want to give the impression that you're shirking responsibility. You need to make it clear that there's no dumping permitted. Everyone in the organization is responsible for coming up with solutions.

Help employees resolve problems *before* they turn into complaints by:

❖ Giving assignments to the right people.

❖ Defining expectations and including step-by-step instructions if necessary.

❖ Asking for and answering questions before getting started, including explaining reasons for doing something in a certain way.

❖ Discussing time tables.

❖ Knowing what motivates.

❖ Determining who requires "special handling."

❖ Resisting the temptation to explode when employees overload you with complaints.

The best supervision may be no supervision, but it's unrealistic. Successful leaders aren't perfect, but they can make a big difference in how employees view problems. Encourage the use of common sense and keep lines of communication open. Teach employees how to tackle problems before they become complaints.

THINK BEFORE YOU ACT

We all prefer pleasant rather than critical exchanges with people. We're often uncomfortable and awkward when it's necessary to discipline employees. So when employees violate a work rule, it's tempting just to call them in, describe the infraction, and impose a penalty. The best advice is to think before you act rather than regret your actions later.

Bruce Mihalik, operations manager for Quantro, Inc., regrets that he didn't think before acting in one particular situation. He disciplined an employee without following company policy. The employee filed a grievance with his union, and the case went to arbitration. "It was not a pleasant experience. I've always been one to jump the gun when it comes to discipline. I hate seeing problem employees get their way because a manager is afraid to address the problem. I'd rather deal with it immediately. I know I'm too hasty at times," said Mihalik.

Before you begin any disciplinary process, ask yourself the following questions:

- How serious is the offense?
- Are the policies and procedures known to the employee and are they reasonable under the circumstances?
- Can I provide proof that the employee violated the policies and procedures?
- Have I been consistent in enforcing the policies and procedures to avoid the charge of discrimination?
- Have I taken into consideration "past practice"?
- Were there any extenuating circumstances?
- If new to the job, what kind of orientation did the employee receive?
- Can I truly say that this disciplinary action is impersonal and based on verifiable facts?
- Have I followed the organization's discipline policy?
- Do I have the backing of my manager?

Once you've made the decision that discipline is necessary, you must communicate this to the offending employee in a tone that's firm but fair and friendly, yet instructional. Decide what you need to say to the employee about the problem. Be aware that he or she may present a rebuttal in defense, and don't react emotionally if it happens. Think before you act.

GREASE THE SQUEAKY WHEELS BUT...

"Squeaky wheels get the grease" is an expression that most people have heard. Translated, it means—Employees who do the most complaining get the most attention.

Writer William Wilkerson described the anatomy of an organization as having four different kinds of bones or squeaky wheels:

> Wishbones—People who wish someone else would do the work.
>
> Jawbones—Staff members who talk a lot but do little else.
>
> Knucklebones—Employees who knock what everyone else does.
>
> Backbones—The people who actually do the work.

Often, it's the backbones who do most of the work but get little credit. Some employees create a crisis to get attention. Managers who waste time with complainers risk the loyalty of the rest of the team.

Ted was a squeaky wheel who was rewarded because his supervisor didn't know enough to ignore him. He was a combination of a wishbone, jawbone, and knucklebone. He monopolized everyone's time, including the customers'.

Glenn Pence, customer service manager for J. D. Brand Corporation, was so frustrated with Ted, he wanted to quit. His own manager saw the problem and helped Pence work through it. "I felt I was boxed in. That one difficult employee made my life miserable until I learned how to deal with him," said Pence.

Here are some tips for handling squeaky wheels:

❖ Consider the source, but also recognize that some complaints are legitimate.

❖ Get to the root of the complaint before it impacts work performance.

❖ Head off complaints by allowing employees to participate in planning and goal setting.

❖ Explain the "why" when dismissing a complaint.

❖ Remember, 90% of the complaints come from 10% of the employees.

BEWARE OF "BUCKANEERS"

One of the biggest threats to morale is people who buck the system. Some are goof-offs; others simply find ways to shirk responsibility. Still others are overtly antimanagement. The end result—morale problems.

People who are constant irritants mean long-term problems for their organizations. Buckaneers often have the attitude that the organization is never right, the boss borders on incompetent, their friends work for better companies, management doesn't appreciate them, and products or services are inferior.

During her first week on the job as a new manager, she could sense the insanity that filled the office atmosphere when a difficult employee came near. But when he picked up a pair of bookends and threw them at her, she knew for sure. "He terrorized the other employees. I was the new kid on the block," recalled Cloris O'Conner. Even when she found out that the anger the flying bookends caused was not personally directed at her, she still knew she had a problem employee.

Troublesome employees can't be managed like naughty children, even when they act like kids. So what recourse do managers have when confronted with buckaneers?

It's time to take measures to correct the problem. Either they work, or you must remove the problem employee from the work force. After following the progressive discipline procedure, if employees slip back into old ways, either push them into resigning or fire them.

Sometimes an aggressive approach to managing the buckaneers will result in better and more cooperative employees. But don't count on it. The best way to avoid the buckaneer problem is to watch for warning signals during the interview process. Look for a history of antiauthoritarian behavior. Telltale signs also include spotty performance at school, a poor armed services record, and job hopping.

DON'T LET THEM PLAY DEAD

Managers don't always immediately know that they've made a bad hiring decision. Then, when they discover the mistake, it's often difficult to sever the relationship. When employees don't take initiative, shirk responsibility, and obviously don't blend in with the rest of the team, you need to make a decision. What you have are people who have quit but plan to stay—at least as long as you're willing to tolerate them.

Rhona Vogel, president of Vogel Consulting Group, a tax and business advisory firm for wealthy families and closely held businesses, offered this advice: "Don't hire a friend, friend of a friend, or anyone who doesn't match your specific job requirements. If you've made a bad choice, don't tolerate poor performance."

Vogel admits that she's made her share of mistakes during the start-up and growth of her business. One employee in particular was a misfit. Vogel recognized the problem after six months, but, because of guilt, the fact that the employee needed the job, and was a friend's friend, she tolerated marginal performance for two years. "I estimate that between myself and the other staff members, we wasted 200–300 hours training and counseling her. Although everyone wanted the employee to succeed, it never happened. We were fooling ourselves." She eventually had a heart-to-heart talk with the employee before terminating her. "The employee cried for two hours. I felt awful." said Vogel.

Her advice is simple: "If you make a bad hiring decision, don't let them play dead. Cut your losses early, and everyone will be better for your decision, including the misfit."

G ET THE FACTS

Before you discuss a problem with an employee, be sure you get the facts. One of the worst mistakes managers make is assuming they've got the facts, when, in actuality, they're far from knowing the truth.

For instance, I know the owner of a company who was in the habit of soliciting feedback, better known as gossip, from one employee about another. He never validated the information but was quick to make decisions based on what he heard. Employees soon caught on and found out that if they didn't like a supervisor, they could blackball him or her by going directly to the owner of the firm. This destructive behavior hurt many people. Failure to get the facts crippled morale.

If you're certain that a rule is being violated, and you know you've got the facts, meet with the employee. Allow enough time for discussion and be sure there are no interruptions. Remember, it's not punishment; it's discipline. You're trying to help the individual correct a problem, not force him or her to quit.

First, ask if the person is aware he or she is breaking the rules. Get his or her version of the story before you explain what you have heard or observed. If the versions are similar, you can approach the problem from common ground. At this point, don't suggest a solution—ask the employee to suggest something. If it's acceptable, the employee will be more willing to pursue it than if you impose a solution. If it's not, continue the discussion until you agree on a mutually acceptable plan to correct the problem. If the versions are not similar, you have more investigation to do.

Second, before you end your meeting, make sure you get commitment on the plan of action. Plus, employees need to know the consequences of failing to follow through. As a final step, set up a time to meet again. If the situation improves, make sure the employee knows you're aware of the change. Recognize the accomplishment.

PERSONAL PROBLEMS OF THE WORST KIND

A manager's job wouldn't be complete without the challenge of dealing with employees with personal problems. They range from financial problems to alcohol and drug abuse, and everything in between. Every problem imaginable, may be dropped in the lap of the leader. Helping employees solve personal problems can bring improvement in productivity, cost reduction, and morale.

Think about this. Pam walks into your office and asks if she can speak with you in confidence. She and her husband, Brian, have been employed at your company for 14 years. She suspected that he was involved with another woman who also works for the company. When she became aware of his unfaithfulness, she took an overdose of pills, passed out, and woke up in the hospital. That's why she wasn't at work yesterday. She's very distraught and threatens to kill the other woman if you don't do something.

All of the personal problems you encounter may not be quite as dramatic as this one, but you still have a responsibility to find out what you can do to help. You may be fortunate enough to have access to an Employee Assistance Program (EAP). A once unfamiliar resource, EAP is now readily available at an affordable price. The money saved by helping just one employee remain productive could easily pay for most, if not all, of your EAP costs for the year.

Just letting a troubled employee know that you're willing to listen is a big help. However, keep in mind that giving advice can be dangerous. The most effective way to handle less serious situations is to let employees talk and work out the solutions to their problems.

To help employees who have personal problems:

* Give them your undivided attention.
* Never interrupt or argue with them.
* Be patient. They may have trouble putting feelings into words.
* Don't pass judgment.
* Encourage them to solve their own problems.

- ❖ Advise those with more serious problems to meet with an EAP counselor or other professional.

- ❖ Have the names and phone numbers of resources assistance available.

TURN CONFLICT INTO COOPERATION

Conflicts are a way of life—but managers can help diffuse these situations by opening lines of communication and identifying mutually acceptable solutions. After a week or two of making life a little difficult, it may be time to bury the hatchet.

Erin was in constant conflict with Todd. They worked side by side for six years, and everyone thought they had a good working relationship. Then, one day Todd lashed out at Erin, and the battle began. Their manager, Tim Button, was furious but uncertain as to how to handle the problem.

When faced with staff conflicts, you must balance your responsibility to tell people what to do with allowing them the opportunity to work out their own problems. This balancing act has two steps: (1) manage conflicts while looking for solutions, and (2) manage conflicts while considering feelings.

It's easy to think, "This isn't a popularity contest. I'm the manager, and I have the right to straighten out this problem now!" Any time you get a group of people together, the odds are that you're going to run into personality clashes. To sort out facts and feelings when conflict arises, you need to do the following:

- ❖ **Treat every conflict with the appropriate degree of importance.** Some disputes are more serious than others.

- ❖ **Avoid taking sides.** Your role is an impartial leader. Listen carefully to both parties. Paraphrase what you believe you heard to be sure you have the correct understanding.

- ❖ **Seek information from a wide range of reliable sources.** Be sure you have all the facts.

❖ **Don't allow your biases to enter the picture.** Your personal feelings about one or both employees should not be your basis for making judgment.

❖ **Don't ignore the conflict, hoping it will go away.** If you do, you'll lose the respect of your employees and with it, your authority.

❖ **Never be hasty when handing out severe discipline.** You don't want to do something you will regret later.

If you want to balance feelings with solutions, you can take one of two approaches. First, you can help them compromise. For example, two employees are working on a challenging customer-relations issue. They're at odds on how to tackle the problem. A possible compromise is for each employee to suggest their best idea and combine the suggestions for best results. It's a win/win for the employees and the customer. Compromise is a popular solution. The main drawback is that both sides must agree that the compromise is fair.

The second approach involves problem-solving. The seven steps to effective problem-solving that involve both the manager and the employee are:

1. State the problem clearly and specifically.

2. List all possible causes.

3. Select the cause that seems most likely.

4. Brainstorm for solutions.

5. Evaluate each proposed solution.

6. Decide on the best solution.

7. Develop an action plan.

There are days when I'm sure you ask yourself, "Will this conflict ever be resolved?" Managers have faced, and will continue to face one conflicting situation after another. But gradually, as change takes place, conflict subsides, and everyone moves forward. Even close encounters with the worst kind can get better.

DISARM THE ARGUMENTATIVE

There's one argumentative type in every crowd, and usually more than that in every organization and in just about all work settings and industries. Most of us can identify with the problems associated with managing those people. The key to managing people—problem employees, in particular—is to develop a basic understanding of the leverage you have as a manager and the limits of that leverage.

It all hinges on four factors:

1. The manager determines what constitutes desirable work behavior.

2. The manager can give something to or take away something from the employee in an attempt to get more desirable behavior.

3. Focus on the employee's perception, because that determines whether reward or punishment has occurred.

4. If the employee exhibits more of the desired work behavior, the manager can assume that he or she has been rewarded.

It sounds simple enough, but motivation is complex. With problem employees, what constitutes a positive or negative reward is even less clear-cut.

The following strategies are useful in dealing with an argumentative employee:

❖ Address the employee by name, quietly but firmly.

❖ Ask him or her to sit.

❖ Listen carefully to what the employee has to say. Once allowed to vent, the argumentative types usually become easier to handle. Admit it when the person has some valuable ideas.

❖ Don't argue. Instead, managers have two options when deciding how to handle a problem employee.

First, you can do nothing. Sometimes that is the better choice. However, the risks of this are twofold: (1) the problem most likely will continue and will probably get worse, and (2) you'll begin to develop resentment toward the employee. Second, seek to eliminate the problem by causing changes in yourself, the environment, or the employee. When you choose to influence change in others, you want to accomplish three objectives:

1. The problem is resolved, and everyone concerned is satisfied.

2. The employee doesn't lose self-esteem, nor do you.

3. All negative impact on the supervisor-employee relationship is avoided.

LEARN HOW TO NEGOTIATE

"Negotiating is an attempted trade-off between getting what you want and getting along with people."[1] If you decide you want to negotiate with a negative employee, your goal is to settle your differences. However, that won't happen unless both you and the employee believe there's some possibility of persuading the other to modify his or her original position and agree to a mutually acceptable compromise. Negotiation is a process of interpersonal communication.

There are several questions you'll want to ask yourself before entering into negotiations:

❖ What do I want to achieve through negotiating and why?

❖ What do I think the employee wants to achieve and why?

❖ How do I plan to gain cooperation?

❖ How am I likely to react emotionally?

❖ How is the employee likely to react emotionally?

❖ How will I respond to the employee's emotional reactions?

Once you've answered these questions, you're ready for the next step—the actual negotiation with the negative employee:

- ❖ Open negotiations by talking about the problem as you see it.

- ❖ Discuss solutions with the employee.

- ❖ Evaluate the alternatives.

- ❖ Select the best solution.

- ❖ Develop a plan of action with the employee.

- ❖ Follow up to be sure the employee implements the plan.

Most problem employees are frustrated. Even if managers can't eliminate the source of that frustration, they can learn to cope with the resulting defensive and offensive behaviors. Negotiating with a difficult employee isn't easy. It definitely takes planning. However, just because you have a difficult person working for you doesn't mean you have to suffer. Don't accept the role of the helpless victim. Learn how to negotiate.

CARE ENOUGH TO CONFRONT

Greg Henski dreamed about becoming a manager with a Fortune 500 company. He spent years working his way up the corporate ladder. When he was promoted to accounting manager, he made a promise to himself that he would never tolerate poor results or slipshod work. He knew that he not only had the right to issue orders and directives, but that he had the responsibility to do so.

With his new position came the task of managing a staff of 22 men and women, many of whom had been his peers. He thought to himself, "People are my business, my first priority, but will I be able to meet the challenge of managing them?"

He encountered a major problem shortly after his promotion. One of his employees was suspected of copying a vendor's social security card number from an invoice and using it to apply for credit cards in the vendor's name. Henski became aware of the potential fraud, but he couldn't believe what he heard. Upset, he investigated and soon came to the conclusion that the vendor was correct.

Henski was furious. He knew the employee well. They had worked together for almost 12 years. He respected and trusted him. Now he must look the other way or confront the problem.

Aside from all of the legal issues surrounding the situation, Henski cared enough to confront the guilty person. His supervisor offered to handle it for him, but he declined. He knew it was his job to talk to the employee. He listened with an open mind, but allowed no excuses and fired the employee. The vendor decided not to press charges. It was a tough experience for a new manager.

In looking back, Henski had this to say, "It was the most difficult job I've ever had as a manager. The employee was my friend. But I knew I had to confront him because the problem wasn't going to go away. I also had made the commitment to myself when I became a manager that I would always try to do the right thing. In this case, I know I did; I cared enough to confront."

WHEN THE BOSS IS DIFFICULT

I once worked for a company led by a dynamic individual. His charming manner easily closed one business deal after the other. At first, the employees loved this paternalistic pied piper with his warm and engaging gift for getting others to follow him. Then, without warning or explanation, he suddenly began terminating staff members who thought they had earned his respect and loyalty.

The situation worsened; people whispered among themselves and speculated about what would happen next. Eventually, morale reached an all-time low. Some employees quit; others prayed. Those closest to the leader hid their true feelings and wondered if he knew what a monster he had created. No one understood why he had changed—only that he had become the enemy. It was a lose/lose situation. The high cost of low morale reared its ugly head. The cycle of despair that followed devastated the business. Many years later, the company and the leader still struggle to recover.

What's the solution? I learned a long time ago that you are as good as your boss will allow you to become. If you work for someone who's insecure or insensitive to the needs of his or her employees, chances are nothing will change—it may even get worse. I personally learned a lot from my close encounter with the worst kind of boss. I vowed to never be a reflection of what he was. I moved on to bigger and better opportunities.

EMPLOYEE HEALTH PROBLEMS AND ADA

What do you do when an employee becomes difficult because of health problems? Richard Lindquist, corporate human resources manager for G. Leblanc Corporation, a manufacturer of state-of-the-art, world-class musical instruments, had this to say: "I hired someone whom I felt was an excellent choice. About a year later, she started complaining about allergies. She claimed her work environment was making her sick. Naturally, I was concerned—I investigated immediately." She filed a Workers' Compensation claim. What the claim's board found was inconclusive.

"Initially the impact on morale was noticeable. The employee blamed the company, and, given her highly visible position, co-workers were at first sympathetic. However, they later saw a different side of her," explained Lindquist.

The company accommodated her under the Americans With Disabilities Act (ADA). As an employer, you have certain obligations if an individual joins your organization with an existing disability or develops a problem later. Title I of the ADA prohibits employers from discrimination against a qualified employee or job applicant with a disability. This applies to all employers with 15 or more employees and includes private employers, state and local government, employment agencies, and labor unions.

The ADA requires employers to provide "reasonable accommodation," which is modification or adjustment that will allow qualified applicants or employees with disabilities to participate in the application process or do the job's essential functions. Reasonable accommodation also includes adjustments to assure that a qualified individual with a disability has the same job rights and privileges as nondisabled employees.

In the case of G. Leblanc, the company, at substantial expense, enhanced the facility's air conditioning systems for both administrative and production areas. ADA does not, necessarily, mandate expensive solutions in order to meet the "reasonable accommodation" test. However, G. Leblanc was willing to make this investment to enhance morale and productivity.

Comprehensive technical assistance on the requirements of the ADA is available by calling the toll free ADA information line: 1-800-514-0301. Or you may visit your local library and consult an ADA information file.

ACCEPT THE HELP OF OTHERS

If you were young, new to the company, and leading a team of people who were older and more experienced than yourself, would you be the least bit concerned? What would you do if a team member on a project belittled you and made you feel insecure about your capabilities?

Caroline Yarbrough, product manager with SmithKline Beecham, offered this advice: "Try to handle the difficult person yourself rather than immediately go to your supervisor. Confront him or her and let that individual know how you feel. Stand up to the troublemaker. Talk it through, and I believe you will see things improve."

If that isn't enough to make the situation better, she recommended getting help from a mentor. In some areas of her company, new employees are assigned to a mentor, someone to get advice from other than the boss. "Mentors can be extremely supportive and help you make a decision about how to handle a problem and when to get your manager involved," added Yarbrough. She also has found their mentor program useful because problems tend to get resolved without having to disrupt the team process. "You have someone to help you rather than go it alone."

Your organization may or may not have a way to help managers who are struggling with difficult people issues. You may want to consider a mentor program, especially for new managers who can benefit from the friendship, as well as the encouragement and information mentors can offer.

REDUCE THE RISK OF WORKPLACE VIOLENCE

A man discharged from his job at a marble plant after 13 years gunned down his supervisor. The shooting was unusually dramatic because the gunman's father had worked in the same plant for 26 years and had also been fired. For two decades after his firing, the parent often mentioned he wished he had gotten even "with the bosses" over his humiliation.

At a Chrysler Corporation plant, a worker in a "bad mood" shot and killed one employee and wounded three others, including a supervisor. In addition, an employee who witnessed the shooting suffered a heart attack, and another employee went into shock because of the incident.

Being discharged from a job often fills people with a sense of failure, rage, and despair. Workplace violence is on the rise. It can happen anywhere, and it's costing companies every year.

Workplace violence is terrifying and impacts morale like nothing else. When a disgruntled employee goes on a killing spree, it usually grabs the headlines. But such incidents are only the tip of the iceberg that costs employers billions of dollars annually in workers' compensation insurance, lost productivity, safety fines, employee counseling, added security, legal and medical costs, insurance premiums, and low morale.

Employers can take several steps to prevent employee violence:

❖ Conduct comprehensive background checks on the final candidate.

❖ Enhance the work climate. Get feedback from focus groups and employee opinion surveys.

❖ Hire managers with effective people skills and train them to identify and respond to inappropriate or strange behavior.

❖ Make security at the workplace as effective as possible.

❖ Provide an employee assistance program, as well as outplacement and support systems for discharged or laid-off employees.

❖ Establish a pre-crisis plan to deal with potentially violent employees, and train a response team to handle volatile situations.[2]

The workplace, like the home, once was considered a safety zone. No more, according to a study by the Northwestern Mutual Life Insurance Company. Violence is making its way into businesses of all kinds and affects one in four employees. Even for those who escape physical harm, violence has a damaging effect on the work environment. The atmosphere it creates lowers productivity and morale. A prescription for managers—pay as much attention to firing as you do to hiring.

FOCUS ON THE ISSUES

Michele Mendelson, a psychotherapist with Jewish Family Services of Rochester, NY, shared professional as well as personal advice for dealing with difficult people. "When you've got a problem employee, try to get a clear picture of how the difficult person operates. He or she may be bossy, negative, short-tempered, irritable, or self-contradictory. Try to understand what the true issues are, even though you may have personal reactions and speculations," explained Mendelson. She recommends setting aside your own emotions, staying calm, and clearly discussing expectations.

She also believes that because managers have the power, they must make the decisions regarding how to discipline difficult people. For example, employees who are unhappy, feel they're not empowered, and believe their opinions are not heard often become angry. As a result, they incite emotional feelings in others, too. If they don't know where they stand or haven't been disciplined when necessary, they quickly become a problem for the manager.

In addition, the dynamics among team members, or even two individuals, vary with who composes the team or duo. "The complaints of the complainer say as much about the complainer as the person or thing being complained about. It's critical for the manager to recognize this fact and work toward resolving the complaint or problem by starting with the issues," said Mendelson.

TRYING BUT FAILING

One of the most difficult close encounters is managing an employee who's trying—but failing. Bob Luciano, president of Luciano Packaging Technologies, Inc., a consulting engineering firm specializing in packaging machinery and special automation systems, finds this problem especially difficult. "When I've got problem employees, I give them enough rope to either climb it or hang themselves. I do what's necessary," said Luciano. He sees discipline, and even termination, as a popular move with the rest of his employees in terms of morale. "When attitude or initiative is not right, I have no choice," added Luciano.

However, he sees employees who are really trying but not making the grade as tough on the company's morale, as well as on him personally. He even tries to find such employees other jobs.

If you have an employee who is trying but failing, ask yourself the following:

- ❖ Why do I think the employee is failing? What is the evidence?
- ❖ Am I sure the employee understands what's expected?
- ❖ Do I need to start over and place more emphasis on clear communication?
- ❖ Am I providing immediate feedback when there's a problem?
- ❖ Do I follow up in a timely manner?
- ❖ Is the job "do-able"?

If someone is trying but failing, the manager is responsible for finding out why. Looking the other way makes matters worse. You have a business or department to run. If you determine that an individual is not worth saving, the impact on morale, as well as your budget, can be devastating.

FIRE WITHOUT CREATING A MESS

Terminating employment is a painful process for both the employee and the manager. It's something that most leaders dread. Few corporate executions are planned; but tales of thoughtlessness and cruelty during the firing process are common and, sadly, often true.

In addition to the emotional costs of termination, there are considerable financial drawbacks. Boston outplacement specialist Laurence Stybel estimates that the average U.S. company spends at least $25,000 to replace an employee earning $70,000.

If you feel you *must* terminate, keep these guidelines in mind:

❖ Reduce legal risks by following the company policy for terminating.

❖ Respect the employee's dignity.

❖ Protect the organization's reputation.

❖ Minimize disruptions and the impact on the morale of the rest of your employees.

Some suggestions for keeping morale intact as you prepare to terminate are:

❖ **Be sure you're doing the right thing**. When you fire someone, you also fire his or her family. Many people may be affected by your decision. People have committed suicide and murder as a result of being fired.

❖ **Don't fire en masse**. Firing half of your work force at once is devastating to everyone—especially the survivors.

❖ **Don't use your employees as pawns**. Shady tactics lead to low morale. Plus, don't fire through electronic message; telephone or mail is no better.

❖ **Stick to the facts and don't get personal**. Your decision to terminate is strictly business.

❖ **Once you've made up your mind, don't back down**. Even if an employee tries to coerce or threaten you, don't change your mind.

❖ **Be sensitive to the strong emotions that are unleashed during a termination meeting.** Treat others as you would want to be treated.

No thoughtful manager enjoys firing. Nevertheless, every manager must be prepared for those inevitable situations when they must remove an employee from a position for the good of the organization and its remaining employees, customers, and clients. Terminating an employee's employment in a proper manner is a challenging and complex part of a manager's job.

CONDUCT EXIT INTERVIEWS

Find out why employees voluntarily leave, and you can significantly impact your turnover rate. Just be aware that to avoid conflict, many individuals will offer only a superficial explanation for resigning.

Exit interviews, in order to get the truth, should include:

❖ Conducting the interview several days before the employee leaves.

❖ Finding the right time and place. A quiet office and a convenient time is important.

❖ Using a skilled interviewer, preferably from the human resources department.

❖ Encouraging the employee to be frank while assuring confidentiality.

❖ Following a structured interview format with questions that are short, simple, and to the point.

❖ Asking questions that are open-ended, which allow for further questioning.

❖ Making the interview a discussion rather than an uncomfortable grilling for facts and feelings.

SAMPLE EXIT INTERVIEW FORM

Information from company:

Date:_____

Employee interviewed:_____

Interview conducted by:_____

Reason for leaving:

_____voluntary

_____involuntary

_____layoff

_____at-will termination

_____for cause termination (describe cause)_____

_____other_____

Eligible for rehire?

_____yes   _____no

Hire date:_____

Last day worked:_____

Questions to ask employee:

If you are leaving voluntarily, why?

_____moving   _____other employment

_____problems with supervision   _____problems with job duties

_____disability   _____retirement

_____failed to return from leave of absence   _____other

What did you like most about your work at this company?

_____

_____

_____

What did you like least?

_____

Do you feel that you were properly placed in your work position, considering your interests and abilities?

_____yes   _____no

Comments:

_____

_____

Did you receive sufficient orientation and appropriate training as a new employee?

_____yes   _____no

If no, please explain.

_____

_____

Was your job defined and explained to you sufficiently when you were hired?

_____yes   _____no

If no, explain how it wasn't.

_____

Did you receive a written job description? If so, was it appropriate to your position?

_____

_____

Did you receive effective and fair supervision?

_____yes   _____no

Comments:

_____

_____

Did your department function as a team?

_____yes   _____no

Comments:

_____

_____

What did you like/dislike about your supervisor?

_____

_____

_____

Did your supervisor urge you to find better and more efficient ways to do your job?

_____yes   _____no

Please rate your supervisor on the following standards:

	excellent	good	average	fair	poor	unacceptable
Cooperation	—	—	—	—	—	—
Fairness	—	—	—	—	—	—
Gives clear instructions	—	—	—	—	—	—
Recognizes and rewards	—	—	—	—	—	—
Follows policies	—	—	—	—	—	—
Responsiveness	—	—	—	—	—	—
Availability	—	—	—	—	—	—
Attitude	—	—	—	—	—	—
Ethics	—	—	—	—	—	—

Please rate this company as a whole on the following standards:

	excellent	good	average	fair	poor	unacceptable
Cooperation	—	—	—	—	—	—
Fairness	—	—	—	—	—	—
Gives clear instructions	—	—	—	—	—	—
Recognizes and rewards	—	—	—	—	—	—
Follows policies	—	—	—	—	—	—
Responsiveness	—	—	—	—	—	—
Availability	—	—	—	—	—	—
Attitude	—	—	—	—	—	—

If you had two improvements to suggest for the company, what would they be?

_____
_____
_____
_____
_____
_____

If you have suggestions which might improve workplace safety, please comment.

_____
_____
_____
_____
_____
_____

Good exit interviews take time. It's more than just collecting uniforms, locker keys, company vehicles, and processing paperwork. Exit interviews should be done as effectively as selection interviews.

Exit interviews, combined with data from discharges, can help you find many of the causes of turnover. Problems can range from dissatisfaction with compensation and benefits to inadequate tools, supplies, and poor working conditions. It's rare that only one area is behind the reason for resigning.

Turnover within the first six months often means a bad hiring decision. After twelve or eighteen months, it's likely related to career progression. Departments with higher than average turnover often mean a poor manager.

Summarize your findings and develop a graph that can be shared with the management team. Learning why one employee is leaving can help you keep the rest.

WHEN TURNOVER IS GOOD

Maximizing productivity, increasing profitability and hiring winners are the top priorities in today's competitive market. When employees leave, the time and money required to recruit and train replacement employees is reflected in the bottom line.

Every company expects a certain amount of turnover. The assumption is that any turnover is undesirable when, in actuality, the intent of reducing turnover is to retain only the best employees. Turnover may actually benefit the organization and the individual employees who move out of the company to more suitable positions elsewhere. It's possible as you assess why people have left your business, that you find they were people who should not have been hired in the first place.

Results of an employee turnover survey I conducted indicated that employees who stayed with their companies did so because of feelings of accomplishment, interesting work, the opportunity to use abilities and get ahead, and good salary. Those who left emphasized more concern about fair company policies, job security, good working conditions, supervision of others, and status. Those who remained appeared to be most interested in personal growth and what they could do for the organization.

Positive turnover may mean terminating employment when a poor performer fails to meet job expectations. Co-workers often recognize the problem before the manager does. Matters become worse when people who don't do their share of the work are allowed to go undisciplined and everyone else must take on extra work. It causes hard feelings and can lead to low morale.

SUMMARY

Every work environment has backstabbers, complainers, hypocrites, steamrollers, and silent types. Then, there are snipers, morale busters, gossips, and volcanos. They're everywhere and can make even a trip to the restroom a difficult task. Managing people who are underhanded, self-centered, and troublesome can be infuriating and can even damage your career.

So now that you've read about them and ways to manage them, what else can you do to ease the pain and aggravation of managing difficult people? While each type of problem employee should be handled differently, the following do's and don'ts can help you diffuse the most difficult situations you may encounter:

- ❖ DO look at problems in terms of finding solutions.

- ❖ DO recognize feelings, even those of the most hard to manage.

- ❖ DO understand that some problems are unavoidable, as are the people who "own" the problems.

- ❖ DO find out which employees are your allies, which are adversaries, and which are neutral.

- ❖ DO determine what's causing the problem.

- ❖ DO care enough to confront.

- ❖ DON'T withdraw or ignore the problem individual.

- ❖ DON'T be afraid to discipline when appropriate.

- ❖ DON'T focus all of your energy on the one person who's difficult and ignore all of the rest.

- ❖ DON'T compromise your work ethic to appease others.

- ❖ DON'T blame yourself.

- ❖ DON'T let problem employees get to you.

You may sometimes feel like you're between a rock and a hard place. Maybe you have even gotten caught in the crossfire between two or more employees. Remember, you're still the manager and in charge of what happens in your department or organization.

There is a tale of Gothic horror that strikes fear in the hearts and minds of managers everywhere. It's how to manage hard-to-manage employees. Let's face it—some employees are monsters and will never change.

CHECKLIST FOR

HANDLING DIFFICULT PEOPLE

√ Do I talk to problem employees tactfully so they are motivated rather than demoralized?

√ Do I tend to dwell on past mistakes rather than focus on the future?

√ Have I let them "play dead" and not take action soon enough?

√ Do I give too much attention to the troublemakers?

√ Do I always think before I act, especially in disciplinary situations?

√ How will I know when turnover is for the best?

√ How do I go about getting the facts when there's a problem?

√ What's the best way to handle an employee's personal problem?

√ Am I satisfied with the way I handle employees who argue with me? If not, what can I do differently?

√ What am I doing to reduce the risk of violence in my organization?

√ How can I fire someone without creating a mess?

√ Do I conduct exit interviews? If not, why not?

Endnotes

1.   Roger Fisher and William Ury, *Getting to Yes.*
2.   Source: Society for Human Resource Management, Alexandria, VA.

Additional Reading

Blank, Renee and Sandra Slipp. *Voices of Diversity*. New York, NY: AMACOM, 1994.

Brinkman, Rick and Rick Kirschner. *Dealing with People You Can't Stand*. New York, NY: McGraw-Hill, Inc., 1994.

Charney, Cy. *The Manager's Tool Kit—Practical Tips for Tackling 100 On-the-Job Problems*. New York, NY: AMACOM, 1995.

Daniels, Aubrey C. *Bringing Out the Best in People*. New York, NY: McGraw-Hill, Inc., 1994.

Deems, Richard S. *Fear of Firing*. Franklin Laeks, NJ: Career Press, 1995.

Edwards, Mark R. and Ann J. Ewen. *360° Feedback—The Powerful New Model for Employee Assessment & Performance Improvement*. New York, NY: AMACOM, 1996.

Elbing, Carol and Alvar Elbing. *Militant Managers—How to spot...How to work with...How to manage...your highly aggressive boss*. Burr Ridge, IL: Irwin Professional Publishing, 1994.

Fisher, Kimball, Stephen Rayner, and William Belgard. *Tips for Teams—A Ready Reference for Solving Common Team Problems*. New York, NY: McGraw-Hill, 1995.

Grote, Dick. *Discipline without Punishment—The Proven Strategy That Turns Problem Employees into Superior Performers*. New York, NY: AMACOM, 1995.

Kaye, Kenneth. *Workplace Wars and How to End Them*. New York, NY: AMACOM, 1994.

Labig, Charles E. *Preventing Violence in the Workplace*. New York: NY: American Management Association, 1995.

Mann, Rebecca B. *Behavior Mismatch—How to Manage "Problem" Employees Whose Actions Don't Match Your Expectations*. New York, NY: AMACOM, 1996.

Marshall, Edward M. *Transforming the Way We Work*. New York, NY: AMACOM, 1995.

McAdams, Jerry L. *The Reward Plan Advantage—A Manager's Guide to Improving Business Performance Through People*. San Francisco, CA: Jossey-Bass Inc., Publishers, 1994.

McGee-Cooper, Ann. *Time Management for Unmanageable People*. New York, NY: Bantam Books, 1994.

McGill, Ann M. *Supervising the Difficult Employee*. Burr Ridge, IL: Irwin Professional Publishing, 1994.

Morin, William J. *Silent Sabotage—Rescuing Our Careers, Our Companies, and Our Lives from the Creeping Paralysis of Anger and Bitterness.* New York, NY: AMACOM, 1995.

Tjosvold, Dean. *Learning to Manage Conflict—Getting People to Work Together Productively.* Lexington, MA: Lexington Books, 1993.

Walsh, James. *Rightful Termination—Defensive Strategies for Hiring and Firing in the Lawsuit-Happy 90s.* Santa Monica, CA: Merritt Publishing, 1994.

Wisniski, Jerry. *Resolving Conflicts on the Job: A Worksmart Guide.* New York, NY: AMACOM, 1993.

$

ALL ABOARD

9

(Orientation and Training)

"Trainees learn only 16% of what they read; 20% of what they see; 30% of what they are told; 50% of what they see and are told and 70% of what they see, are told and respond to; and 90% of what they do."

—Joe L. Whitley

● ●

Even though not all turnover is bad, its impact is always disruptive. The best ways to reduce turnover are by better employee selection, improved communications, well-trained managers, and a good orientation and training program.

The first 90 days of employment are especially important. You've worked hard to hire talented people who will help you reach your goals. Just be sure that they are "oriented into the mainstream" and not left "disoriented" and faltering to find their own way. Busy managers don't always allocate time for new hires. Often they are passed off to someone in the department who may or may not want the job of showing new employees around.

Whether your company offers a comprehensive month-long orientation program or a basic, one-hour overview of the operation, the manager is ultimately responsible for ensuring that new employees get a good start. Several agenda items fall into the first hours on the new job. One is getting acquainted with fellow employees; another is becoming familiar with job responsibilities; a third is learning the ropes.

It's ideal to spread orientation over several days, weeks, or months so that new employees have time to absorb everything they learn. The first few days may include a tour, a lot of paperwork, policy review, and instructions. Help new employees learn unwritten rules, customs, and idiosyncrasies that are not in the book. Encourage questions.

Information overload is a risk that comes with orientation. Too much to learn during the first few days on the job can be discouraging. Most people are not likely to remember names and details of the new responsibilities if presented quickly in a short period of time. Give them permission to ask questions and make mistakes.

Regular follow-up by the manager is important. Remember that most new employees are anxious and want to make a good first impression. Too much information in the beginning can be a stumbling block that some will not overcome. They will handle their frustration, and sometimes, embarrassment, by quitting.

Issues such as location of breakrooms, restrooms, and use of special features on the telephone are important and should be covered upon the new employees' arrival. It's also nice when new employees have a buddy with whom to have lunch. Details like these can make the difference between a person who quickly feels accepted as a member of the team and one who sits on the bench hoping to be called in to play. Businesses that have a mentor system have found that matching experienced employees with new hires can assist in a smooth transition into the new environment and job. It's important, however, that employees volunteer to help and not be forced to participate in mentoring. A good mentor will take some of the burden off of the manager by helping the new employee with day-to-day questions. The more personable and knowledgeable the mentor, the better likelihood of a positive transition.

Some companies require all employees to take a course in sensitivity training. This helps them get along better with co-workers and also interface more effectively with new personnel who are sometimes seen as a threat.

Videos, employee handbooks, and mission statements are part of the orientation process for many businesses, but they don't take the place of a warm welcome from the manager and co-workers. The personalized touch may last for only a few months, but it's worth the investment when new hires become valued, long-term employees.

After employees are integrated into the workplace, you need a system for maintaining relevant job abilities. Organizations that recognize the need for lifelong learning are more likely to have employees who are motivated to meet the demands of the job. Whether you decide on group training or individual instruction, emphasis should always be on progressive learning.

Planning is important. You will want to think about the objectives and contents of the training, as well as who will be the best instructor. The ability to use various instructional techniques such as case studies, illustrations, visuals, humor and creative training ideas, will contribute to the success or failure of each training endeavor. The need for ongoing education is never over. Managers should be observing employees as they use the ideas they've learned. They should also help employees build confidence and lend support. For without the backing of management, even the best training is doomed to failure.

As you read this chapter, consider not only what you do or plan to do for new employees, but how you expect to keep people up-to-date and in step with new trends in your industry.

USE TRAINING AS A MOTIVATOR

Organizations that invest in employee development enjoy significantly higher market values than industry peers. They also, according to researchers, make significantly larger productivity gains than those who don't invest in training.

While the impact of employee training may not be immediately visible, short-term gains, such as greater customer satisfaction, reduction in waste, and improved efficiencies, are indicators of future financial performance.

Ben and Sue Russo, proprietors of Sarah's Place, recognize the benefits of training even in a small family-owned business. The Russos are not alone in their thinking. Research supports what they're doing.

> "Our employees are encouraged to sign-up for employer-paid training. Our cooks, for example, have the opportunity to attend a two-day class on meal preparation and presentation. Although they follow recipes, without a doubt the privilege of attending impacts morale. When our employees are happy so are the customers," said Sue Russo.

In a study done by the U.S. Labor Department's Office of the American Workplace, in conjunction with Ernst & Young L.L.P., they found that (1) there's a definite relationship between training and participation programs (they both lead to reduced turnover and lower overhead costs), and (2) on-the-job training is most effective when combined with teaching employees how to make good decisions and empowering them to do so.

All successful organizations know the value of training. For more and more businesses, the issue is not whether they should embrace training, but what to offer and how to best present it to employees. People who feel they're growing, learning, and accomplishing something, get the same satisfaction as athletes on a winning team.

VIEW EMPLOYEES AS INVESTMENTS

Employees are investments. When you make an investment—whether it's a house, a car, or a major purchase—you take time to research. It's no different when you hire new employees. Human investments need care and training.

Some organizations don't provide new hires with the basic information needed to do the job. Frustration takes over, and, combined with a lack of direction, may create morale problems that eventually lead to termination.

It can be a frightening experience to start a new job with no friends and unclear expectations from the manager about what needs to be done. Eliminate that problem. Help new employees get off to a good start by providing orientation to the co-workers and the job. Invest time and whatever else it takes to help new employees feel accepted and part of the team. People are your most valuable asset.

RECHART CAREER PATHS

Price Waterhouse L.L.P. has taken steps to assist employees in redirecting careers without having to leave the company. Their old rule was: "Take 12 steps up the career ladder within 12 years to make partner or look for another job."

With clients demanding specialized skills, the company realized they had a talent crisis. A new approach to career opportunities has improved retention. The company's goal today is to challenge employees at all levels by keeping the work exciting. Turnover has fallen from the industry average of 25% to 18%. The secret to their success is offering employees more control over their careers in three plateaus:

- ❖ Foundation.
- ❖ Mastery.
- ❖ Entrepreneurship.

This is one example of how organizations have shifted their thinking when it comes to alternatives to traditional career growth. What are you doing to build intellectual capital for the future of your employees?

TEACH THEM THE BUSINESS

Carol Hayes-Budd has two full-time jobs, but she still manages to create an environment of predictability, one where clients know what to expect from a well-trained staff. She owns C. C. Hayes, a film directors' talent agency. She's also the General Manager of Vuja de´, a company that handles the creative side of editing television commercials.

Her philosophy is to help people feel part of what's going on beginning with their first day on the job. She personally trains new employees and has found that taking an active role in orientation reduces turnover. "For small businesses, it's especially important to keep costs down," said Hayes-Budd.

During orientation, for example, she takes office personnel (such as a receptionist, as well as a producer) on out-of-town sales calls. They have dinner with clients and have an excellent opportunity to build rapport. One of her producers actually bid on two jobs while on an orientation trip. "It gave the producer another perspective in that she realized she can get out of her office and generate business anywhere she goes," said Hayes-Budd. Her receptionist got the benefit as well. All customers now interface with employees who are ready to assist them because they understand the business.

NO MATTER HOW GOOD THE PRODUCT...

Managers play a vital role in selecting, orienting, and training employees. It should be a priority. In addition, managers should recognize the need for their own training and development and take advantage of every opportunity to learn and grow with the business.

Employee development involves the need for managers to constantly assess the skills and potential of employees so that they can perform better both now and in the future. Training is not exclusive to rank-and-file employees. Every manager should recognize the value of education in order to avoid obsolescence or status-quo thinking.

In an interview with John Shingler, vice president of worldwide conferences for Holiday Inn Worldwide, he told me one of the organization's top priorities is training. "The company is in the service industry—no matter how good the product, there is no value unless we can supply high quality customer service. It's a continuous training cycle. We cannot afford to become complacent."

Without proper job training, employees often feel incompetent, become frustrated, and may leave. With consistent education, the possibility of retaining employees increases, as well as the possibility of deriving other benefits, such as:

- ❖ Consistently high quality work and customer service.

- ❖ Increased job satisfaction.

- ❖ Higher morale.

- ❖ Less waste and lost productivity.

- ❖ Improved communication.

- ❖ Better employee self-image.

- ❖ More time for managers to manage.

Holiday Inn Worldwide doesn't claim to have all of the answers to the training issue. Shingler admits, "Training may not be where it needs to be, but our focus continues to drive it as a priority."

What are you doing in your organization to instruct and guide the development of your employees toward acquiring knowledge, behavior or skills, and attitudes to meet the needs of your customers? No matter how good the product, success will always be "just around the corner" for those who ignore the need for training.

DON'T LEAVE THEM BEHIND

National Data Corporation, the leading provider of value-added information systems and services for the health care and electronic payment systems market, believes in new-hire orientation and ongoing training. New employees get an overview of the company and its products and services immediately upon joining the company. They spend four hours with members of the human resources department and additional time in their individual business units.

Donna Thiraveja, manager of employee training and development, had this to say about training: "We want employees to know that the company cares enough to invest in their development. We give them a sense that we're not leaving them behind."

NDC offers a formalized personal growth program that consists of three stages: a pre-workshop assignment for both manager and employee; a one-and-a-half- to two-day, facilitator-led workshop; and a post-workshop discussion. A key benefit of the program is that employees and their managers work together to reach agreement on job requirements, employee strengths, and employee development areas—resulting in improved employee performance and job satisfaction.

For the technical side of training, the company formed a training and development committee with the major purpose of advancing and enhancing careers of technical professionals. For example, they've had sessions on the Internet and client-server technology. Additionally, NDC's modular management development program is "action learning" based. That is, managers actually put learning into practice at work.

Thiraveja describes her training philosophy as one aimed at providing the newest information in the most interesting format so that everyone feels part of the organization and its future.

DEVELOP TOMORROW'S LEADERS

Organizations who recognize staffing requirements before the need arises have an edge. Those who do something about it are leaders in their industry. McDonald's Corporation is one of those companies. A January 1996 article by Gillian Flynn appeared in *Personnel Journal* describing some of the reasons behind McDonald's success.

They want their employees to grow with the business. And rightly so, as their plans for expansion include 1,500 or more new restaurants each year through the end of the decade.

Consequently, the company offers new employee orientation through its Crew Training Program. Their Management Development Program continues the education. McDonald's is also known for Hamburger University, where professors teach management and restaurant operations courses to owner/operators and managers from around the world. Translators and electronic equipment allow them to communicate in 20 languages.

Their McJobs program matches and offers extra support to people with physical and mental disabilities. It sometimes includes customized training to assist individuals who need special help.

McDonald's ReHIREment program targets older workers and teams them up with a partner to help them quickly learn the new job.

One of the company's objectives is to get commitment from employees. They've achieved this goal, as evidenced by the opening of 17,000 restaurants in 86 countries. Every eight hours, somewhere in the world, another McDonald's restaurant opens. Education and training are part of what make it possible.

BE SURE THEY GET WHAT THEY NEED

Another organization that has experienced tremendous growth credits its orientation program with maintaining high morale. Remuda is an eating disorder treatment facility designed to meet women's medical, nutritional, and psychological needs. They blend these components with a biblically-based, nondenominational Christian perspective. Remuda's clients are bulimic, or anorexic, or both.

The facility, licensed by the State of Arizona, hires nurses, therapists, technicians, and administrative staff. They require employees to meet specific guidelines and earn continuing education credits. They compete for the best available people. Cindy Logan, director of human resources, has been there four years. When she started, Remuda employed 33 people. Today, they employ over 220.

Their paid orientation programs, which range from one to four weeks, commence the day the new employees start work. Everyone attends a brief three-hour orientation in the human resources department. New hires complete paperwork and go through an in-service program on how to use the phone system. "When employees are new, so often they get thrown into a job without orientation. From then on, it's a constant battle to learn what to do. Many people are afraid to ask questions because they think they are expected to know," said Logan. She believes in giving them all of the tools they need beginning with day one. They're encouraged and also allowed flexibility to learn at their own pace.

Remuda wants their staff to be able to speak about their facility and truly understand all facets of the services provided. The library is filled with books and audio tapes so that employees can learn more about psychology and eating disorders. There are 100 one-hour video tapes, and everyone is encouraged to review at least 80% of them, as well as pass a written test with a score of 80% or better. A graduation ceremony every December honors those who have finished viewing the tapes.

In addition, they learn about infection control, quality management, and grounding techniques for dealing with patients who become agitated and may become a threat to themselves and staff members.

Even a therapist, with a minimum of a graduate degree, completes a four-week orientation program, which Logan insists impacts morale. "We want everyone to know they're connected and wanted as a valued member of the team," added Logan.

"At the rate we're growing, we had no choice but to develop a comprehensive orientation program. It's had a major impact on morale and retention," said Logan.

HAVE 20/20 VISION

Metropolitan Property and Casualty Insurance Company restructured their new orientation system and named it *20/20 Vision: Focus from the Start*. They identified six elements for their orientation program to be successful.

1. **Informal structure.** Since each department has different needs, they decided that each would establish its own schedule of events within a broad orientation framework that encompasses the new employee's first 6 to 9 months on the job.

2. **Self-development role for the employee.** In focus groups, they determined that employees wanted more say in their future. The new orientation program emphasizes the employee's self-development role.

3. **Minor time demands on the supervisor.** Supervisors made it known that an orientation program that was too time-consuming would lose its impact. They also suggested that mentors would be helpful. The company combined the two ideas and developed a system that provides the new

employee with coaching from the supervisor and support from a mentor.

4. **Directly supports job training.** They found that orientation would fail if not perceived as an essential part of the job. *Focus from the Start* is aimed at enhancing the new employee's ability to learn and perform the job. They consider it the most critical aspect of the orientation process. By getting trained quickly, there is a direct impact on productivity and a recognition that the orientation system adds value and makes a difference.

5. **Payoff for the employee and the supervisor.** The payoff for the employee is enhanced learning and supportive socialization that lead to satisfaction with the job and the company. For the supervisor, there's a sense of more rapid learning on the job, enhanced teamwork, and opportunities for early sharing of problems so that they may be quickly resolved.

6. **Success-oriented.** The orientation has to provide a path that leads the employee to a feeling of achievement and success. *Focus from the Start* provides benchmarks for the employee to assess how thing are going.

The most effective orientation approaches for Metropolitan Property and Casualty Insurance Company seem to exist in centralized or large office locations, where having many new employees enables ongoing meetings. They quickly recognized that centralized approaches would not meet the needs of the more than 150 locations around the country. In their smaller offices, many months separate the hiring dates of new employees. Also, outside of the home office, there are no human resource professionals on the field office staffs to coordinate the effort.

MAKE IT INFORMAL BUT MEANINGFUL

Any organization that's growing at a rate of 30–40% per year faces many challenges. Among them is providing orientation for new hires. One company that's met the problem head-on is CompUSA, Inc., a distributor of computers and related products and services. According to Mel McCall, senior vice president of human resources, last year, the hundreds of people they hired throughout the 40 states where the company has stores included over 70 experienced retail managers. These managers participated in a formal, fast-track training program to prepare them for a General Manager position created through the opening of 30 new stores.

Managers completed a formal training program designed to give them the technical skills and knowledge of the business required for a successful General Manager. However, the management team realized this extensive external recruitment made it difficult to effectively communicate the vision, values, and developing culture of the company.

To facilitate the communication of this critical information, the company developed a four-day orientation session for these key managers. Two sessions with 35 participants each were conducted at the corporate office in Dallas, Texas.

The program included presentations from each of the officers describing their vision and strategic plans for their areas of responsibility. One full day was devoted to the company's philosophy and practices involving team members. Each of the seven senior officers spent a minimum of four hours with each group. They also dropped in throughout the week and participated in "after hours" events. Their focus throughout the week was to communicate the company's philosophy, values, and the company strategy for accomplishing its mission. The sessions included some formal presentations, but mostly were informal discussions and question-and-answer periods.

The final session was a scheduled "debriefing" for participants. "We spent several hours soliciting feedback from the group to ensure we had accomplished our objectives for the session. We were very pleased with the participants' comments and the degree of understanding of the business they had gained during the week," explained McCall. The informal but highly organized program was so successful that it's now part of the formal training for all new management recruits.

LINK TRAINING TO CORPORATE INITIATIVES

Motorola is one of the world's leading providers of wireless communications, semiconductors, and advanced electronic systems and services. They won the first Malcolm Baldrige National Quality Award in recognition of superior company-wide management of quality processes. The company links all employee education to corporate initiatives.

In a presentation to the Atlanta Chapter of American Society for Training and Development (ASTD) in May 1995, Bill Wiggenhorn, senior vice president of training and education, and president of Motorola University, shared his perspective on education.

> "Our mission is to be a catalyst for change and continuous improvement in support of the corporation's business objectives. We will provide for our clients the best value in leading-edge training and education solutions and systems to be their preferred partner in developing a 'Best-in-Class' work force."

Motorola University began in 1981 as the Motorola Training and Education Center. During the 1980s, Motorola University's charter was to help the corporation build a quality culture. They developed an internal training design system to meet this challenge. The 1980s also brought the establishment of corporate-wide training plans and training investment policies.

By the end of the decade, Motorola University had expanded its operations both in the United States and around the world. Their training centers are called "people factories."

Motorola believes the key to successful training and education is:

❖ Top-down commitment and involvement.

❖ Policies that set expectations and are tracked.

❖ Solid prerequisite skills for the work force.

❖ Curricula that forms an integrated system to deliver consistent messages.

❖ Linkage of programs to corporate initiatives.

Donald K. Conover, retired vice president of education and training for AT&T, summed up the Motorola philosophy in the March 18, 1994 issue of *Business Week* magazine: "The intimacy between education and business strategy is tighter at Motorola than any place I know."

IF YOU WERE EXPECTING A PACKAGE...

United Parcel Service provides extensive new-hire orientation and training. They have over 335,000 employees worldwide and make sure that everyone gets the information they need to understand their jobs and serve the customer well. In an interview with Lea Soupata, senior vice president of corporate human resources, she said one of the popular sayings in new-hire orientation is: "If you were expecting a package, how would you feel if you didn't get it on time?"

Training is crucial at UPS. Upon joining the company, service providers have three weeks of orientation aside from the "how to's" of doing the job. Training emphasizes customer satisfaction and behavior that's appropriate and necessary for employees to model—friendliness and efficiency count for a lot. New employees quickly learn that they are an advertisement to the customer. Therefore, safety, appearance, and attitude are extremely important. "It's critical that employees understand the value chain and the role they play from pickup to delivery," added Soupata.

Regardless of their particular job, everyone learns something about the company history, legacy, traditions, and culture. According to Soupata, employees in different positions get more or less of this information depending on their need to know.

The peer training program has been especially successful as peers teach portions of the new-hire orientation. They explain details of the job and talk about how they feel about what they do. New employees get the inside scoop.

Their successful company goes beyond the first building block of orientation training—they use continual education. Employees take particular classes depending upon the business strategy of the company and their departments, as well as their specific needs. According to

Soupata, quality initiatives and enhanced service features require more and more ongoing training.

When asked how the investment in training impacts morale, she said, "There's no doubt that people feel more confident in their jobs, and that translates into higher morale. People are recognized for their knowledge. It's especially important because of the extensive contact with the public."

CONSIDER A MENTOR PROGRAM

Once new employees are introduced, taught the ropes, and are given time to adjust, does a manager's responsibility end?

Not exactly.

Human maintenance is important. The fact that people reach a satisfactory production level doesn't mean they're going to stick with you without further attention.

Businesses go to a lot of trouble to keep equipment running but often overlook the needs of people and what keeps them motivated, especially during the first few months on the job. A mentor program offers a successful strategy for helping new people ease into the workplace.

Peers assisting peers can help reduce problems. Employees hesitate to tell a supervisor, "I don't understand," or "I made a mistake," or "I'm not happy here." But they may be willing to share their thoughts with a mentor or friend who lends support, encouragement, and understanding.

In addition to the mentor program's value for new employees, it provides an additional benefit for the employees who serve as mentors. Hanley Bell Associates assigns a mentor to all new employees. These mentors are employees who have volunteered to be a buddy to a new employee. The one-year assignment offers the satisfaction of helping others integrate into the hectic but people-sensitive environment. Owner Joe Heisler explains, "Our turnover is significantly lower because we've learned the hard way that everyone who leaves costs us thousands of dollars. Our team of employees decided that they'd rather have that money in their paychecks or in bonuses. Everyone pitches in—almost every employee has mentored someone, and that's impacted morale and profits."

A final note—beware of mentors who grumble along with new hires! They're no help to anyone.

S HOW THEM HOW

When you think Disney, do you think magic? You're not alone if you do. If you've been one of the millions of visitors to a Disney property, you've probably noticed the employees or "cast members" as they're known. It takes a lot of people to make it happen. According to an article published in *Corporate University Review*, May/June 1996, by Lynn E. Denford, Disney anticipates hiring 20,000 cast members over the next 20 years. And that means training!

When Disneyland opened in 1955, it quickly became apparent that they needed an in-house training program. Philosophies on customer service were the driving force behind the creation of Disney University.

In a workshop presented by Disney to the Society for Human Resource Management in Chicago in June 1996, I learned that their training begins with building pride. The first two days are spent at Disney Traditions class. Cast members learn the history, philosophy, and importance of quality guest service. Training continues on the job for two days to two weeks. Specific training is conducted in the field by human resource managers.

Decentralized skill-building classes are offered in addition to orientation. They've gotten away from training as a one-time event removed from where cast members work. Their long-term goal is university classrooms or satellite campuses throughout the Disney properties.

Of course, measuring the results of orientation and training is a challenge, but a necessary one. Training is measurable because they use a baseline survey to help identify the issues. They pre-measure performance. They measure again after training and over the next 12–18 months. In addition, they conduct cast member surveys to find out what keeps employees happy. It's viewed as important because all thoughts and actions impact guest satisfaction.

Disney is always looking for new ways to educate their managers to empower people. Leadership development training is built on a foundation of high expectations.

As a result of Disney University's success, there came a demand to know how they did it. They introduced the first Disney Professional Development Program in 1986. There are now four "Disney Approach" programs:

- ❖ The Disney Approach to People Management.

- ❖ The Disney Approach to Quality Service.

- ❖ The Disney Approach to Leadership—Focusing on Results.

- ❖ The Disney Approach to Orientation.

It seems their low turnover can be attributed to a combination of getting people in the right spot and to empowerment. For example, guests with Disney strollers had difficulty getting into the trains. People got frustrated. Finally, a cast member had an idea—when guests reach the train, simply have them leave the stroller behind and get another at the next stop. It worked—because the cast was listening to the guests and were empowered to make a change.

Walt Disney summed it up: "The growth and development of the Walt Disney Company is directly related to the growth and development of its human resources...our cast."

VALUE EMPLOYEES FROM DAY ONE

Orientation enables employees to get in sync with the organization. It helps people adapt to a particular situation by establishing and sorting out relationships within their new environment. Think of it as pointing an individual in the right direction.

Although employees are likely to have some prior knowledge about the organization and the job, they should still be provided with essential information. Orientation is a morale booster because it helps employees feel like part of the business. It's the first step in getting employees off to a good start.

In setting up a new-hire orientation program for my last employer, Bahlsen Inc., I recognized that new employees couldn't possibly learn everything about our company, its goals, and its philosophy in one sitting. I extended orientation meetings over a period of time. I had a well-integrated program that was developed and carried out by a cooperative and enthusiastic staff. It made all the difference in the world.

Aside from sharing goals and philosophies, new employees received information on conditions of employment, pay, benefits, and other areas that were not directly under the supervisor's direction. Factory workers, office personnel, and managers were all left with a lasting impression— I hoped it was good.

I also know when new hires start with an organization, they have a reserve of goodwill towards the new employer. That reservoir can easily be tapped dry within the first few days if the orientation fails to satisfy the needs of the individual. Confusion and enthusiasm are two dominant emotions during the new employee's first day at work. The person who started work this morning is as close to a "model employee" as you'll ever get. The orientation process keeps morale alive and well. It's the manager's responsibility to see to it that enthusiasm prevails.

Research shows that a negative perception of your company during the first 60–90 days of employment can lead new personnel to look for another job within the year—and that costs money.

One manufacturing company found that the disruptions in work flow created when a staff member leaves and the cost of getting employees on and off the payroll boosted the price of turnover to 150% of an employee's salary. Researchers concluded that if the company invested 50% of those costs in activities designed to reduce turnover, the company could recover its entire investment within a year.

Most U.S. employers now invest considerable time and money in the orientation process. According to *Training Magazine*, 85% of companies with more than 100 employees offer formal orientation programs.

LEADERSHIP 2000

In an interview with Cindy Neal, vice president of quality and training for ExecuTrain, the worldwide leader in computer training, she shared some ideas for consistency in training beyond new-hire orientation. "Our focus is on the quality of instruction and materials presented to our clients. Quality needs to permeate the entire organization."

With that in mind, ExecuTrain has launched a program called "Leadership 2000," which is based on the Malcolm Baldrige National Quality Award criteria. Many people, working on different pieces, helped design the program, which focuses on five key areas:

- ❖ Leadership.
- ❖ People.
- ❖ Customer focus.
- ❖ Process management.
- ❖ Results integration.

"When people don't have a sense of direction, morale is lower. We consider this training to be a 'living' program because it will go on," added Neal. She explained further. "By infusing these components into our network of ExecuTrain locations, we feel it will help us achieve common direction and purpose so that we may become our vision of ExecuTrain of tomorrow."

The privately-held company, founded in 1984, has 180 locations worldwide and 1,400 instructors exclusive to ExecuTrain. They believe that training their employees is a crucial part of their success. Their training materials are a key part of the business and a foundation for each class as well. Consistency in delivery is critical—another reason training is important. "We hire great people, provide excellent training and empower them to do their jobs," said Neal.

ENVIRONMENT MAKES THE DIFFERENCE

I've been a member of Australian Body Works health club in Atlanta for over four years. They really have it together, and to find out why, I spoke with several people including owner, Tony deLeede. "Training is paramount to launching and keeping good people. We do a good job in that area. The environment is super important. You can train people and encourage them to use the tools, but if they're not happy, all the training in the world won't make a difference," said deLeede.

In speaking with John Carsillo, general manager for one of the 15 clubs, I got his perspective on why they are successful in maintaining high morale in a traditionally high turnover industry. "Tony offers an environment that's friendly and upbeat. He likes everyone to have fun, but he also provides plenty of training and follow up to be sure employees understand their role in the company," said Carsillo.

They have a formalized training program for new front desk personnel and quarterly training thereafter. Salespeople start with a two-day workshop conducted by an outside consultant. They also receive follow-up training. "We don't offer any more training than our competitors, but the environment here makes a big difference," explained Carsillo.

Mary McGury, assistant director of aerobic instruction, shares similar feelings about the company. McGury, who's been with ABW for six years, started as a member and later became an instructor. She raves about the consistent and safe teaching that deLeede insists upon. "We teach classes that are safe and beneficial, ones that will enable members to exercise for the rest of their lives—not just exercise today with risky moves that could cause injury," explained McGury. "Instructors receive ongoing training so that they are current with the latest steps and techniques. There are over 200 part-time instructors, and that's a lot of people to keep up with; however, the environment in which we work keeps us excited about being a part of the ABW team," said McGury.

DON'T VIEW TRAINING AS AN EXPENSE

The Mirage Resorts in Las Vegas are well-known for their selection and training programs. Vice president of human resources, Arte Nathan, staffed the Mirage Hotel and then assisted in staffing Mirage Resorts' third Las Vegas enterprise, Treasure Island.

Nathan had a lot to share as a keynote speaker at the 1995 Society for Human Resource Management conference in Atlanta. He told the audience that new employees received extensive training. Nathan knows the value of training and sees it as an investment rather than an expense. Before the Mirage opened, he interviewed over 200 companies in a variety of industries. Most of them regretted not having done more training prior to opening.

Their commitment to training is evident in the hotel's turnover rate. They are far below the industry average, not only for the nation, but also in Las Vegas, where competition for good employees is fierce. Their hotels are also consistently full. They attribute their success to selecting and then training good people. They're respected for their competitive advantage—their employees.

CONSIDER APPRENTICESHIPS

As a final thought to the benefits of education and training, consider the concept of apprenticeships. It's been around for many years. However, some companies do better than others in making it work. One such organization is Siemens Energy & Automation, Inc., a German company that has encouraged its U.S. operations to take full advantage of all there is to gain from its school-to-work program. In addition to the students who become apprentices and get a head start on their careers, the company's regular full-time adult employees have benefited immensely from the experience.

In speaking with Travis Hembree, training coordinator in Alpharetta, GA, he proudly shared the reasons behind their success.

"We offer apprenticeships to high school students beginning with 10th graders. We pay the full cost of their education within the career path we have defined with no strings at-tached. We do not expect the students to necessarily come to work for us upon graduation, nor are we expected to offer everyone a job. We do hire many talented people who come out of the program, but there's another benefit to the com-pany in addition to the benefit to the students," said Hembree.

Under their program, the people on the floor do the training. Their employees are eager to participate; they help keep the students on the right track.

In an interview with Joanne Capinski, quality assurance manager, she had this to say about how the apprenticeship program has impacted morale. "The students have given us a fresh and younger perspective. I have them work in various functions in the lab, and they enjoy the work." Capinski admits that she feels proud when students talk about how much they have learned and like working in the QA department. "We feel good from a company perspective and also from a personal perspective because we are making a difference in their lives," added Capinski. One young man shared with his QA mentors that he plans go into the area of quality management for a career. That made everyone he interfaces with feel good about themselves and what they've been able to contribute to the success of an aspiring individual.

Sammy Wallace, production supervisor, offered similar feedback. "Our teams enjoy working with the students because they're interested in the electrical/electronic business. They're eager to learn and work on projects. We all benefit from the energy and enthusiasm the young students bring to the workplace."

Siemens' training programs span job responsibilities from shop floor to executive suite. Employees can receive training for their current assignments, as well as retraining to prepare them for future ones. Their apprenticeship programs in conjunction with the schools ensure a trained work force well into the future.

SUMMARY

Now that you've hired winners, it's imperative that you get them off to a winning start. It's often said that people "are what they eat." Businesses, in many respects, are what they employ. Peter Drucker said, "Executives spend more time on managing people and making people decisions than on anything else, and they should. No other decisions are so long-lasting in their consequences or so difficult to make. And yet, by and large, executives make poor promotion and staffing decisions. By all accounts, their batting average is no better than .333. At most, one-third of such decisions turn out right, one-third are initially effective, and one-third are outright failures." If Drucker's viewpoint is even close to reality, managers are spending a lot of time, effort, and money selecting and keeping unhappy people. Could some of the hassle be avoided by providing new hires with the support they need to get a good start? If you make a good hiring decision, but fail to provide orientation to the job along with follow up training, you may have the reason for many of your problems.

Orientation and training is one of the most neglected yet critical steps in helping new employees. Your orientation should be well-integrated and carried out enthusiastically, with cooperation from everyone who interfaces with the new employee. The human resources department generally is responsible for coordinating orientation activities—providing information on conditions of employment, pay and benefits, and processing paperwork. Managers have the most important role. They must allow time on the employee's first day of work for establishing a cordial relationship that will facilitate communication and learning. Many managers mistakenly believe that new employees have the basic knowledge about the job and organization to get started on their own.

Orientation and subsequent training allows employees to get in sync with the company. It helps people adapt to a particular situation—think of it as pointing employees in the right direction. There are two important elements to consider: (1) the goals of the business, and (2) the employees' roles with respect to the goals.

Those who plan orientation programs often expect new employees to immediately assimilate all types of facts and details about the organization. While there are many things that new employees should know, much of the information can be extended over a period of time and in a series of meetings.

Use a checklist to avoid overlooking items that are important to employees. It will help you pay more attention to new employees at a time when personal attentiveness is critical to building a long-term relationship.

Since an organization must meet ever-changing conditions, its policies, procedures, and job responsibilities, along with goals, will change. Unless employees are kept up-to-date on changes, they may become confused and discouraged. Therefore, you will need to continually reorient and retrain your personnel to meet the needs of the business.

Future training may include the following:

- ❖ On-the-job training.
- ❖ Work sample exercises.
- ❖ Videos and audio tapes.
- ❖ Classroom instruction.
- ❖ Reading.
- ❖ Observation learning.
- ❖ Simulations.
- ❖ Experimentation learning.
- ❖ Conference or discussion.
- ❖ Programmed instruction.
- ❖ Computer-assisted instruction.
- ❖ Education-employer cooperative training.
- ❖ Apprenticeship training.

Information is a big motivator—it can have a major impact on morale in your organization, either good or bad.

CHECKLIST FOR

ORIENTATION & TRAINING

√ Have you made sure the new employee has an office or work location and the appropriate equipment and supplies?

√ Are you prepared to greet the new worker and pronounce his or her name correctly when making introductions?

√ How will you follow up through the days and weeks to be sure the employee is feeling comfortable?

√ Are you prepared to explain job duties and expectations?

√ How much time will you set aside for questions?

√ What will you do to support the socialization of the new employee?

√ What training objectives do you want the employee to meet during the first 6 months on the job? Second 6 months?

√ Do you have money in the budget for training? If so, how much?

√ How could your organization benefit from an on-the-job training program?

√ How comfortable are you with adult learning methods and techniques?

√ What types of training methods are best for the kinds of people you employ?

√ Do you prefer individual or group training? There are advantages and disadvantages to both.

Additional Reading

Barbazette, Jean. *Successful New-Employee Orientation—Assess, Plan, Conduct & Evaluate Your Programs.* New York, NY: Pfeiffer & Company, 1994.

Barlow, Janelle and Claus Moller. *A Complaint is a Gift—Using Customer Feedback as a Strategic Tool.* San Francisco, CA: Berrett-Koehler Publishers, Inc., 1995.

Chang, Richard Y. *On-The-Job Orientation and Training.* Irvine, CA: Richard Chang Associates, Inc., 1994.

Delgado, Figueroa J. *Training for Non-Trainers—A Practical Guide.* New York, NY: HRD Press, 1994.

Edward, Marshall. *Transforming the Way We Work—The Power of the Collaborative Workplace.* New York, NY: AMACOM, 1995.

Jacobs, Ronald L. and Michael J. Jones. *Structured On-the-Job Training—Unleasing Employee Expertise in the Workplace.* San Francisco, CA: Berrett-Koehler Publishers, Inc., 1995.

Jerris, Linda. *Effective Employee Orientation: A Worksmart Guide.* New York, NY: AMACOM, 1993.

Kirkpatrick, Donald J. *How to Train and Develop Supervisors.* New York, NY: AMACOM, 1993.

Marquardt, Michael J. *Building the Learning Organization.* New York, NY: McGraw Hill, 1996.

Masi, Dale. *Developing Employee Assistance & Counseling Programs.* New York, NY: AMACOM, 1992.

Mitchell, Garry. *The Trainer's Handbook,* 2nd ed. New York, NY: AMACOM, 1992.

Nilson, Carolyn. *How to Manage Training—A Guide to Administration, Design, and Delivery.* AMACOM, 1991.

Rothwell, William J. *Beyond Training & Development.* New York, NY: AMACOM, 1996.

Rubino, John A. *Communicating Compensation Programs—An Approach to Providing Information to Employees.* New York, NY: American Compensation Association, 1992.

Stern, Nancy and Maggi Payment. *101 Stupid Things Trainers Do to Sabotage Success.* Irvine, CA: Richard Chang Associates, Inc., 1995.

Swanson, Richard A. *Analysis for Improving Performance—Tools for Diagnosing Organizations & Documenting Workplace Expertise.* San Francisco, CA: Berrett-Koehler Publishers, Inc., 1994.

Tracey, William R. *Designing Training and Development Systems.* New York, NY: AMACOM, 1992.

Tracey, William R.. *Training Employees with Disabilities*. New York, NY: AMACOM, 1994.

Vella, Jane. *Learning to Listen, Learning to Teach: The Power of Dialogue in Educating Adults*. San Francisco, CA: Jossey-Bass, Inc., Publishers, 1994.

Vella, Jane. *Training through Dialogue*. San Francisco, CA: Jossey-Bass Inc., Publishers, 1995.

APPENDIX

(Sample Behavior-Based Questions)

1. Give me two examples of things you've done in previous jobs that demonstrate your willingness to work hard.

2. Building rapport is sometimes a very challenging thing to do. Give an example of a time when you were able to build rapport with someone at work.

3. In what ways have your previous jobs prepared you to take on greater responsibilities?

4. The word "honesty" means different things to different people. Tell me what this word means to you by giving me an example of a time when you were concerned about something dishonest that happened at work.

5. In your last job, what problems did you identify that had previously been overlooked?

6. Describe a time when you encountered obstacles in your last job while you were in pursuit of a goal. What happened?

7. Tell me about a time when you used good judgment in solving a problem.

8. How have you used authority to influence another person?

9. What did you do in your last job that made you more effective?

10. What suggestions did you make in your last job to increase profits, improve morale, cut costs, increase output?

11. Give me an example of a time when you helped a staff member accept change and make the necessary adjustments to move forward.

12. Tell me about a time when you and your previous boss disagreed but you still found a way to get your point across.

13. Tell me about a time when your last supervisor asked you to do a job that was not part of your job description.

14. Give me an example of a time when you had to deal with an unexpected event on the job.

15. Tell me about a technical problem you were recently called upon to solve.

16. Which of your ideas and actions helped you move up in your present/prior organization?

17. Describe a time when you were under pressure to make an immediate decision.

18. Tell me about a specific time when you had to influence someone.

19. What risks did you take in your last or present job?

20. Tell me about a project that you were responsible for initiating.

21. In your last job, how was your approach to the work different than in jobs you held before?

22. Tell me about a time when your ability to listen helped you communicate better.

23. What did you do to make your last job more interesting?

24. What three things have you done on your last job that have given you the most satisfaction? Why?

25. Tell me about your efforts to "sell" a new idea to your boss.

26. Tell me about a suggestion you made on the job to improve the way things worked. What was the result?

27. Describe a time when you were especially successful in being tactful.

28. Tell me about a time when you reached out for additional responsibility.

29. What have you done in your last job that makes you feel proud?

30. Can you give me an example of how you have been creative?

31. Tell me about a time when you used competition as a means of encouraging others do their best.

32. How did you handle your biggest career disappointment?

33. Give me an example of a time when you recognized others in order to encourage them.

34. Tell me about a project you really got excited about.

35. What have you done that shows initiative?

36. Select an event that happened at work during the last three years, and tell me why it was an example of your motivation.

37. Tell me about a time when you surpassed all job expectations by going the "extra mile."

38. Tell me about a time when your positive attitude caused others to be motivated.

39. Give me an example of a time when you were given an unpleasant task. How did you react?

40. In what ways have you improved your productivity?

41. Describe two specific contributions you made to your last organization.

42. Give me an example of a time when you sacrificed what you personally wanted to happen in order to get the job done.

43. Give me an example of a project which you were completely responsible for initiating.

44. Tell me about the most complex information you have had to read and understand.

45. Tell me about a time when you were successful in challenging others' ideas. What does this say about your ability to be assertive?

46. Give me a specific example of a time when you showed high energy in order to create positive motivation in others.

47. Select a job you have had and describe the paperwork you were required to complete. What specific things did you do to ensure your accuracy?

48. Tell me about a time when you were highly motivated.

49. Give me an example of a time when you used a systematic process to define your goals.

50. Communication and leadership go hand in hand. Tell me about a time when your communication skills helped you be a better leader.

GLOSSARY

ADA—Americans With Disabilities Act.

Apprenticeship—a program of classroom study combined with practical on-the-job experience.

Behavior-based questions—those which ask candidates to describe a specific past event that is used to rate a skill.

Benchmark—a point of reference from which measurements of any sort may be made.

Body language—facial expressions, gestures, eye contact, and body movement which expresses feelings.

Celebrity-hosted events—Occasions where a well-known person or celebrity appears at company-sponsored event to gain attention for the organization.

Change—variation affecting something or someone essentially or superficially.

Diversify—engaging in varied operations and activities.

Downsizing—reduction in work force.

EAP—Employee Assistance Program.

Executive privilege—special perks or benefits usually reserved for executives but awarded to other levels of employees.

Exit interview—interview conducted after terminating an employee.

Expectations—specific requirements for acceptable job performance.

Friendly bravery—confident and enthusiastic greeting when meeting strangers.

Golden eggs—problems that provide opportunity for innovation.

Grapevine—gossip.

Hidden paychecks—benefits beyond the obvious that keep employees excited about working for the organization.

Inplacement—finding new and/or challenging opportunities in an effort to help surviving employees replan their futures, especially after layoffs.

Internal candidates—employees who already work for your organization.

Interview evaluation form—guide for evaluating the candidate's interview performance in relation to the essential functions of the job.

Mental barometer—how you feel about life at any given time.

Mentor—trusted counselor or guide.

Merit pay—compensation based on tenure.

Morale—a state of individual psychological well-being based on such factors as a sense of purpose and confidence in the future.

Olympic Performance Events (OPEs)—highly motivational periodic events.

Pay for performance—compensation based on skills and abilities.

Performance appraisals—evaluation of employees' work.

Personal Mission Statement—individual life goals and commitment to accomplishment.

Potential—capable of developing into actuality.

Pygmalion—someone who stimulates confidence and high expectations in others.

R&R Fund—money set aside for rest and relaxation.

Recruitment sources—resources for locating potential employees.

References—a statement of the qualifications of a person seeking employment or appointment given by someone familiar with them.

Reinvest—allocating a portion of the resources saved through a cost-reduction action back to the work environment and remaining employees.

Retention—number of people working for an organization as compared to turnover.

Rolestorming—a combination of roleplaying and brainstorming.

Sabbatical leave—time off with pay to relax and rejuvenate.

Self-fulfilling prophecy—believing something enough to make it happen or come true.

Small talk—inconsequential discussion or chatter.

Team interviewing—an interview in which more than one employee is involved with interviewing candidates. Interviews can be done by a panel or sequentially, one-on-one.

Turnover—number of people within a period who leave employment with an organization or are dropped from the work force.

Unsolicited resumes—resumes received without advertising.

Vision—projection into the future.

Work ethic—a set of moral principles or values governing individual or group behavior.

Workplace violence—behavior which may include harassment, threats, assault, suicide, or homicide.

INDEX

A

Aaron, Henry 67
ABB Power T & D Company 158
Abramis, David J. 139
Accustaff 62
Ace Products 148, 149
Adams, Greg 65
A.G. Sanderson, Inc. 190
Allison, David 73, 74
Alton, Bob 62
Alumni associations 4
Alyeska Pipeline Service Company 43
Amazing Grace 46
American Association of Women 143
American Compensation Association
    177
American Family Insurance 92
American Management Association 90
American Media Incorporated 90
American Software 34
Americans with Disabilities Act (ADA)
    23, 204, 205
  information file 205
  information line 205
Angel's advocate 41
Anorexic 227
Antilistening behavior 105
Antimanagement 195
  behavior 195
Apple Computers 153

B

Apprenticeship 239, 240
Argumentative type 200
AT&T 86, 232
Atlanta Chapter of American Society
    for Training and Development
    (ASTD) 231
Atlas Van Lines 151
Auditions 10
Australian Body Works 238
Auto Service and Tire Super Mart 9

Babcock, Arnie 129
Backbones 193
Backstabbers 214
Badger Meter 95
Bahlsen Inc. 236
Barnes, Scott 158
Basadur, Min 172
Bates, Lynn 46
B/E Aerospace, Galley Products
    Division 122
Bednarczyk, Jim 92
Behavior-based questions 5, 8, 16, 247,
    248, 249, 250
Bell South Advertising and Publishing
    10
Berner, Robert 133
Bernstein, Ellen 34
Berry, William 13

Black, Jennifer 47
Blanchard, Ken 167
Blank, Eddie 73
Blumsack, Joel 175
Body language 84, 106,
Boston Globe, The 50
Bottom line 21, 132, 153, 213
    impact 26, 156
    results 21, 172
Boyer, Blair 33
Bracey, Hyler 94
Brainstorm 199
    session 153
Brainstorming 104, 105
Branches of the military 4
Branchises 63
Brand, Moses 49
Brickle, Sue 181
Bridges, William 115
Brininstool, Bill 178
Brown, Ron 3
Buckaneers 194
Buffalo Bills 70, 167
Bulimic 227
Bunker Hill Consulting Group 102
Burkhardt, Joan 85
Business Advantage, Inc. 90
Business image 18
Button, Tim 198
Byers, Jeff 95

C

Canon 11
Capinski, Joanne 240
Carr, Bob 157
Carsillo, John 238
Cartwright, Jon 190
C.C. Hayes 223
Celebrity-hosted events 4
Center for Research in Applied
    Creativity 172
Center for Values Research xv
C.H. Coakley & Co./Mayflower 131,
    132, 133
Chaet, Bob 97

Champion, Tom 181
Chang, Saun 21
Change reaction 122
Chapman, Elwood N. 51
Chart Your Course International 155
Checked-in 90, 91
Chrysler Corporation 206
Cinema billboards 4
City of Chula Vista 156
Cline, June 100
Coakley, Kathleen 131, 133
Coastal Human Resources 90
Coca-Cola Company 163
Columbia University 60
Comer, Gary 133
Complainers 214
CompUSA, Inc. 229
Conceptual Systems 90
Conover, Donald 232
Cooney, Mike 5
Cornell University Medical College 37
Corporate Comedy 182
Corporate culture 21
Corrao, Jo Ann 141
Cost Management Services 168
Court Jesters Club 100
Covey, Stephen 37, 38
Creative attitude 41
Crisp Catalogue, The 90
Criticism without causing defensiveness
    89
Crocker National Bank 115
Crofts, Jim 117
Curtis, Dave 128

D

Daniel, Barbara 53
Davis, Brenda 149
Dean Witter Reynolds Inc. 141
Defensible hiring decisions 26
Delaware North Companies, Incorpo-
    rated 120
deLeede, Tony 238
Demetriou, Tom 22
Deming, Dr. W. Edwards 140

Denford, Lynn E. 234
De Pree, Max 164
Devil's advocate 41
DeVry Institute of Technology-Atlanta
    33
Dial Page 117
Direct mail 4
Disney
    Approach to Leadership-Focusing on
        Results 235
    Approach to Orientation 235
    Approach to People Management
        235
    Approach to Quality Service 235
    Professional Development Program
        235
    University 234
    Walt 170
    World 170
Disneyland 234
Doolittle, Eliza 59
Door hangers 4
Doran, Al 36
Dorchester-Waylyn Baptist Church 54
Drake Beam Morin, Inc. 9
Dries, Mrs. 32
Drucker, Peter 15, 240
DuCharme, Beverly 181
Due diligence 23
Duggan, Jane, M.D. 40
Duke University's Sanford Institute of
    Public Policy 164

E

Eastman Kodak Company 96
Eating disorders 228
Eckerd College 96
Einstein, Kurt 96
Elmer's Glue™ Principle, The xv
Emory University System of Health
    Care 40
Employee Appreciation Day 143
Employee Assistance Program (EAP)
    197, 198, 206
Entrepreneurial Energizer, The 41

Ernst & Young L.L.P. 222
Espirit de corps 88
Excel Temporary Services 62
Excellence in Training Corporation 90
Executive Adventure, Inc. 157
ExecuTrain 237
Exit interviews 210, 211, 212, 213,
    216
    form 211, 212, 213
Ex-offender programs 4
External candidates 17

F

Facial expressions 84
Fel-Pro 144
Firestone 9
5 Key Result Areas of a CEO, The 174
Flowers, Marianne 16
Flowers, Vincent S. xv
Flynn, Gillian 226
Ford Motor Company 52
Foreman, Dennis 181
Fork, Edith 119
Former employees 4
Forsyth, Patricia 40
Four-stage process 127
Franchises 63
Fratto, Fred 13
Frenner, Don 51
Frieder, Bill 180
Friendly Bravery 173
Frito-Lay 172

G

G. Leblanc Corporation 204
G. Neil Companies 25
Gag Nite 146
Garber, Janet 37
Garner's Inc. 129
Gates, Bill 170
GE Power Systems 36
General Motors 19
Geodesy, Inc. 21, 22
Gerhart, Ann 31
Ginty, John 50

Glaxo Wellcome Inc. 69
Global Payment Systems 35
Goizueta Business School of Emory
    University 71
Golden Eggs 172
Goody Products, Inc. 13
Gordon Flesch 11
Goss, John 156
Gossips 196, 214
Grapevine 119, 127
Greene, Kurt 36
Grimme, Don 36
Gut feelings 6, 7, 24, 122

H

Hackett, Jim 102
Hair Concepts 170
Hallett, Jeffrey J. 54
Hallmark Cards, Inc. 154
Hamburger University 226
Hanley Bell Associates 233
Hardening of the attitudes 42
Harper, Sherri 24
Harrell, Keith 32
Harvard University 60, 143
Hastings, Becky 49
Hatfield, John 102
Hawes, Ron 145
Hayes-Budd, Carol 223
H.C. Brill, Inc. 107, 181
Heil Co., The 178
Heisler, Joe 233
Helping spirit 88
Hembree, Travis 239
Henski, Greg 202, 203
Hiatt, Mary Ellen 165
Hickory Tech Corporation 62
Hidden paychecks 147, 148
Hierarchy of Needs xviii
Ho, Claire 147
Hockaday, Irvine 154
Hoeksema, Timothy E. 91
Holiday Inn Worldwide 224, 225
Hooker, General 89
Horizon Media, Inc. 85
Hoyle, John 76

HRMS York University 36
Hughes, Charles L. xv
Huseman, Richard 102
Huser, Larry 122
Hypocrites 214

I

IBC Engineering Services, Inc. 119
Idiot episodes 100
Ingram, Jim 69
Ingwersen, Terry 10
Inplacement 115
Internal candidates 17, 20, 21
Internet 4, 226
Interview
    etiquette 18
    evaluation form 24, 27, 28
    stress 16
    team 16, 17
Intuition 24
Investing 130

J

Jackson, Linda 105
James, William 31, 184
Janus, Kathryn 71
Jawbones 193
J.D. Brand Corporation 193
Jenkins, Robb 62
Jepson, H. Lincoln 77
Jewish Family Services of Rochester,
    New York 207
JM Family Enterprises, Inc. 126
Joan E. Rush & Associates 93
Job 4
    fairs 4
    hotlines 4
    lead organizations 4
    posting 20
    requirements 20
Johnson, Jimmy 80
Jose, Jim 43
Justice, Jeff 182

K

Kaiser, Anne 66
Kaplan, Phil 152

Kawasaki, Guy 22
Keen, Arlene V. 54
Kelleher, Herb 142
Kelly, Jill 120
Kemp, Jack 70
Kennedy, Rod 37
Keough, Donald R. 163
Kettering, Charles F. 183
Kick the habit 51, 52
K-Mart 19
Knucklebones 193
Koehler, Kurt 126
Koenigsberg, Bill 85
KPMG Peat Marwick 66
Kudo bars 47

L

Laabs, Jennifer 36
LaCroix, John 52
Laissez-faire 32
Land, Edward 41
Lands' End 133
Lao-Tzu 135
Lashley, LeRoy 9
Layoffs/closings 4
La-Z-Boy 183
Leader of the band 156
Leadership 2000 237
Levi Strauss & Co. 145
Lewis, Jackie 78
Lincoln, Abraham 87, 89
Lincoln, Joe 21
Lindquist, Richard 204
Livingston, J. Sterling 60, 80
Loeb, Francis 150
Loeb AG 151
Logan, Cindy 227
Lottery tickets 153
Luciano, Bob 208
Luciano Packaging Technologies, Inc. 208
Lucid, Dr. Shannon 170

M

Macintosh 10
Magnetic leader 169

Magnetic signs 4
Malcolm Baldrige National Quality Award 231, 237
Management Review, The 148
Marks, Sue 173
Maslow, Abraham xviii
McCall, Mel 229
McCann, Mark 146
McDonald's Corporation 226
McGhee, Mike 167
McGury, Mary 238
McKay, Harvey 69
McMaster University 172
Melohn, Tom 59
Mendelson, Michele 207
Mental barometer 38
Mentor 229, 233
    program 233
    system 220
Mentored 233
Mentoring 220
Mentors 228, 233, 234
Mercer, Michael 7
Merit pay 176
Merton, Robert 60
Mescarhenas, Maurice 174
Metropolitan Property and Casualty Insurance Company 228
Meyer, Louis B. 22
Miami Dolphins 80, 167
Microtraining Plus 10
Midwest Express Airlines, Inc. 91
Mihalik, Bruce 192
Minnesota Women's Fund 143
Minuteman Press 78
Mirage Hotels 239
Mirro Company 180
Mirror Test 19, 20
Mission
    impossible 85, 86
    possible 85, 86
    statements 221
Morale
    boosters 235
    busters 50, 214, 187
Moran, Kelly 11

Motivation
  extrinsic 139
  intrinsic 139
Motorola 36, 231
  philosophy 232
  Training and Education Center 231
  University 231
Ms. Foundation for Women 143
MTS Systems Corporation-Sensors
  Division 24
Muscles 181
Mynatt, Clyde 12

N

Nantz, Ron 86
Nathan, Arte 239
National Data Corporation 225
Neal, Cindy 237
Negative employee 201
Negligent hiring 22
Negotiation 201, 202
Newcomers 4
Newell 180
New Jersey Machine Inc. 77
Nichols, Nick 169
Nightengale, Earl 33, 40, 49
Nonverbal communication 106, 107
  cues 106
  signals 106
Northwestern Mutual Life Insurance
  Company 207

O

Oberg, Bob 146
Occidental College 70
O'Conner, Cloris 194
Odiorne, George 96
OHMEDA Pharmaceuticals-Products
  Division 146
Olympic Performance Events 155, 156
Omni Hotels 38
On-campus interviews 4
Open houses 4
Orientation 17, 219
  process 221
  program 220

P

Peachtree Software 74
Peal, Dr. Norman Vincent 38
Pence, Glenn 193
People factories 231
Peoplis, Nancy 64
Performance appraisal 103
  appraisals 102, 103
Personal
  Growth Leave program 152
  mission statement 43
Pharmacia & Upjohn Company 64
Picasso 163
Pick 'N Save grocery stores 143
Pizza Hut 99
Planned Parenthood of Atlanta 40
Platt, Hal 34
Play dead 195
Posters 4
Post-interview consensus 17
Poyner Spruill L.L.P. 22
Pre-employment questionnaire 19
Presentations at community events 4
President Baking Company 5
President Clinton 3
Price Waterhouse L.L.P. 223
Procter & Gamble 47
Professional associations 4
ProMax & Associates, Inc. 169
ProStaff 173, 174
Protected class 23
Pygmalion 59, 60–62, 64, 66, 73–79

Q

Quad/Graphics, Inc. 147
Quadracci, Harry V. 147
Quality Bucks 97
Quantro, Inc. 192
Quarter Century Club 154

R

R&R fund 141
Radar screen 71
Radio advertisement 4
Ranking system 17
Rawlings 98

Reasonable accommodation 204
   test 205
Recruitment policy 20
References 5, 6, 22, 24
Referral cards 4
Reinvesting 130, 131
Remuda 227
Renfro, Samantha 71
Resources & Solutions of JEL Enter-
   prises, Inc. 105
Resume
   application file 4
   databases 4
Richardson, Ted 168
Rittenhouse, Robin 78
Robert Bowden, Inc. 146
Rode, Jean 35
Rogers, Chief Petty Officer 70
Rogers, Reverend John 70
Rolestorming 104, 105
Roper Starch Worldwide poll 144
Rosenthal, Robert 61
Rotten apple principle 40
Roundy's 143
Ruiz, Candus 11
Rush, Joan E. 93
Russo, Ben 222
Russo, Sue 222
Ruth, Babe 67

S

Sabbatical 152, 153
Sanders, Elsie 145
Sanderson, Harry 181
San Diego Police Officers Association
   167
Sandwich technique 88
Santo-Tomas, Olga 90
Sarah's Place 222
Saturn 19
Schaffell, Andrea 177
Schaffer, Robert 155
Schlinkert, Tom 9
Schneider, Michael 38
Scholarships 4
Scopa, Marian 107

Sea World 16, 17
Self-fulfilling prophecy 60, 68, 69
Selwyn, Padi 41
Selwyn Associates 41
Senior organizations 4
Serenity Prayer 36, 46
Shaw, George Bernard 59
Shingler, John 224
Shock 127
Shula, Don 167
Siemens Energy & Automation, Inc.
   239
Siemens Medical Systems, Inc. 73
Sievers, Sam 20
Sievers Electrical 20
Silent types 187
Silgan Plastics, Inc. 175
Skyline South 75
Smart, Bradford D. 1
Smith, Gregory P. 155
Smith, Michael 133
Smith, Terry 153
Smith Barney, Inc. 152
Smith James Group 22
SmithKline Beecham 205
Snellen, John 75
Snipers 214
Society for Human Resource Manage-
   ment 22, 43, 234, 239
Soupata, Lea 232
South Baldwin Hospital 14
Southern Home Furnishings Associa-
   tion 165
Southwest Airlines 142, 143
Spielberg, Steven 170
Squeaky wheels 193
Standard operating procedure 18
Steamrollers 214
Sterling Institute 60
Stewart, Bonnie 74
Stick-in-the muds 187
Storehouse, Inc. 12
Stybel, Laurence 209
Sweeney, Jim 60
Sweeney's Miracle 60
Sweet tart award 47

T

1212 Club 151, 152
Take Our Daughters to Work Day 143, 144
Tank, Kathleen 64
Telemarketing 4
Television advertisement 4
Think it over 86, 87
Thiraveja, Donna 225
Tietjens, Jim 98
Toastmasters 92
Trade magazines 4
Treasure Island 239
Tulane University 60
Turner Entertainment Group 177
Turn-offs xv
Turn-on-plus xv
Turn-ons xv

U

United Parcel Service 232
University of Chicago Industrial Research Center 140
Unsolicited resumes 4
US Personnel 117
U.S. Department of Labor 26, 37
U.S. Labor Department's Office of the American Workplace 222
U.S. Postal Service 51

V

Video Arts 90
Vogel, Rhona 195
Vogel Consulting Group 195
Volcanos 214
Volunteer Leave program 152
Vuja de´ 223

W

Wallace, Sammy 240
Walter, Pat 151
Ward, Brenda 181
Warm body philosophy 20
Waterman, Robert H., Jr. 114
Way Kidd & Associates, Inc. 76
Weight Watchers 151
Wells Fargo Bank 115, 152
Wesley Woods Geriatric Hospital 40
Western Electric Hawthorne plant 99
Whiners 187
Whitley, Joe L. 219
Widmer, Steve 11
Wiggenhorn, Bill 231
WIIFM 109
Wilkerson, William 193
Williams, Mike 149
Winfrey, Oprah 170
Win/Win Performance Appraisals 189
Wishbones 193
WITI-TV 64
Wolf, Laura 170
Wood, Randy 12
Wood, Sharon 90, 91
Workforce 2000 26
Workplace violence 206

Y

Yarbrough, Caroline 205
Yell and tell technique 10
Yergens, Linda 143

Z

Zadall Systems Group, Inc. 46
Zest factors 155
Zorn, Steve 39